Nature Painting
in Watercolor

Learn to paint florals, ferns, trees, and more in colorful, contemporary watercolor

KRISTINE A. LOMBARDI

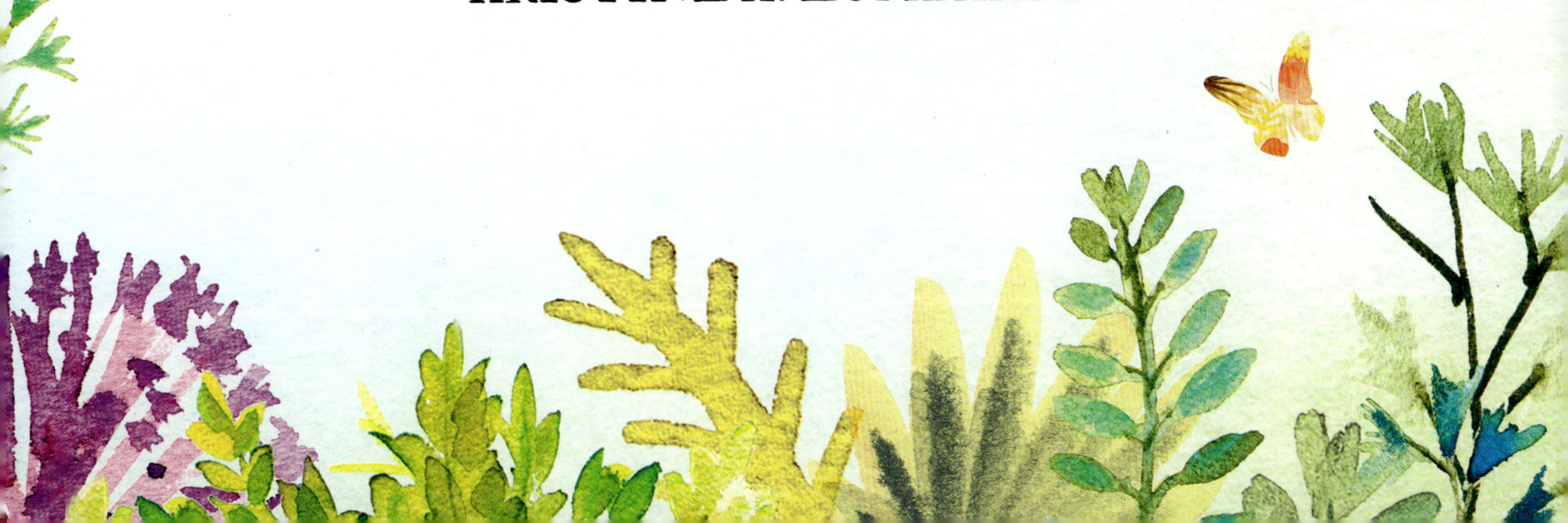

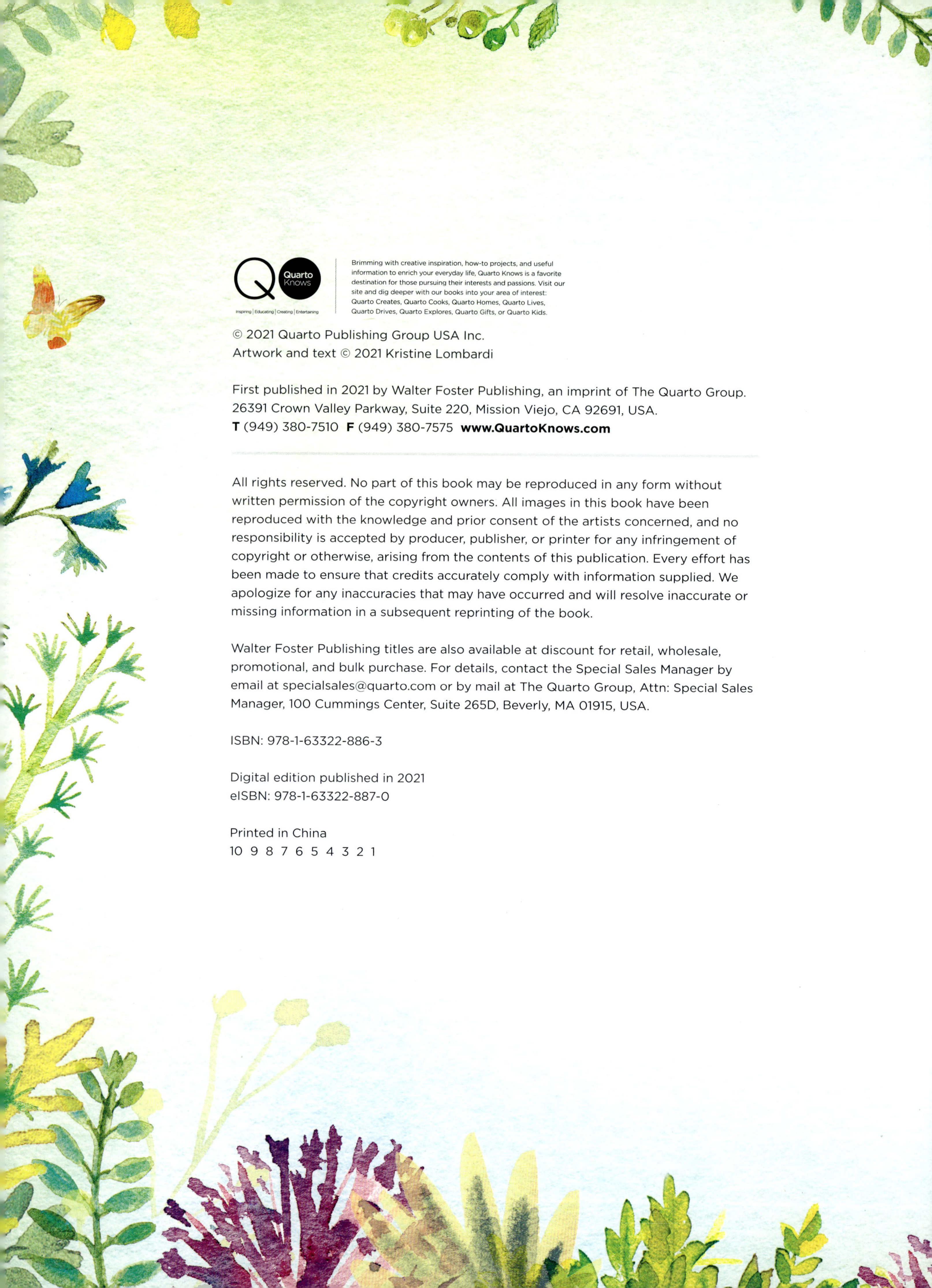

Brimming with creative inspiration, how-to projects, and useful information to enrich your everyday life, Quarto Knows is a favorite destination for those pursuing their interests and passions. Visit our site and dig deeper with our books into your area of interest: Quarto Creates, Quarto Cooks, Quarto Homes, Quarto Lives, Quarto Drives, Quarto Explores, Quarto Gifts, or Quarto Kids.

First published in 2021 by Walter Foster Publishing, an imprint of The Quarto Group.
26391 Crown Valley Parkway, Suite 220, Mission Viejo, CA 92691, USA.
T (949) 380-7510 **F** (949) 380-7575 **www.QuartoKnows.com**

ISBN: 978-1-63322-886-3

Digital edition published in 2021
eISBN: 978-1-63322-887-0

Printed in China
10 9 8 7 6 5 4 3 2 1

TABLE OF CONTENTS

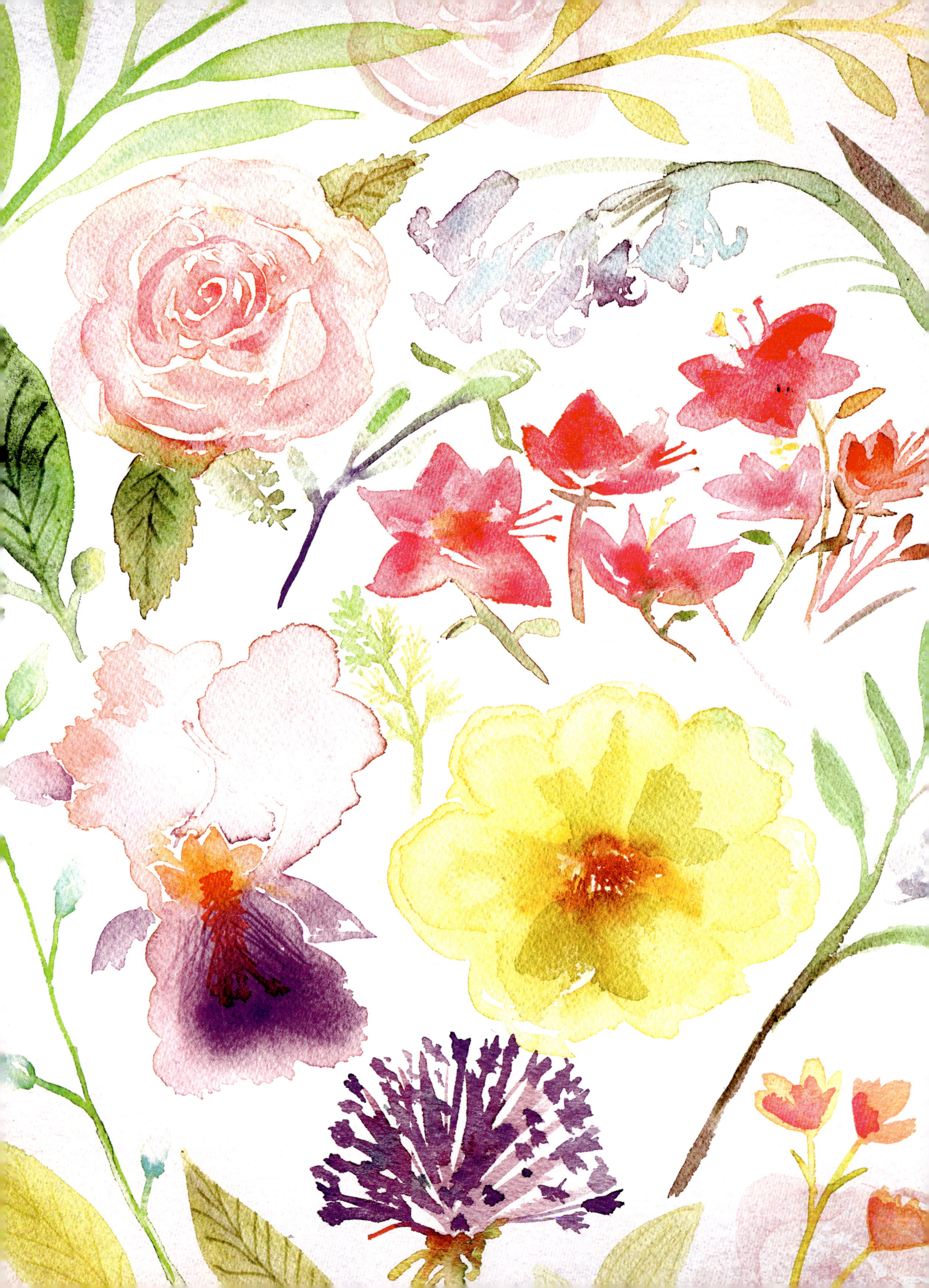

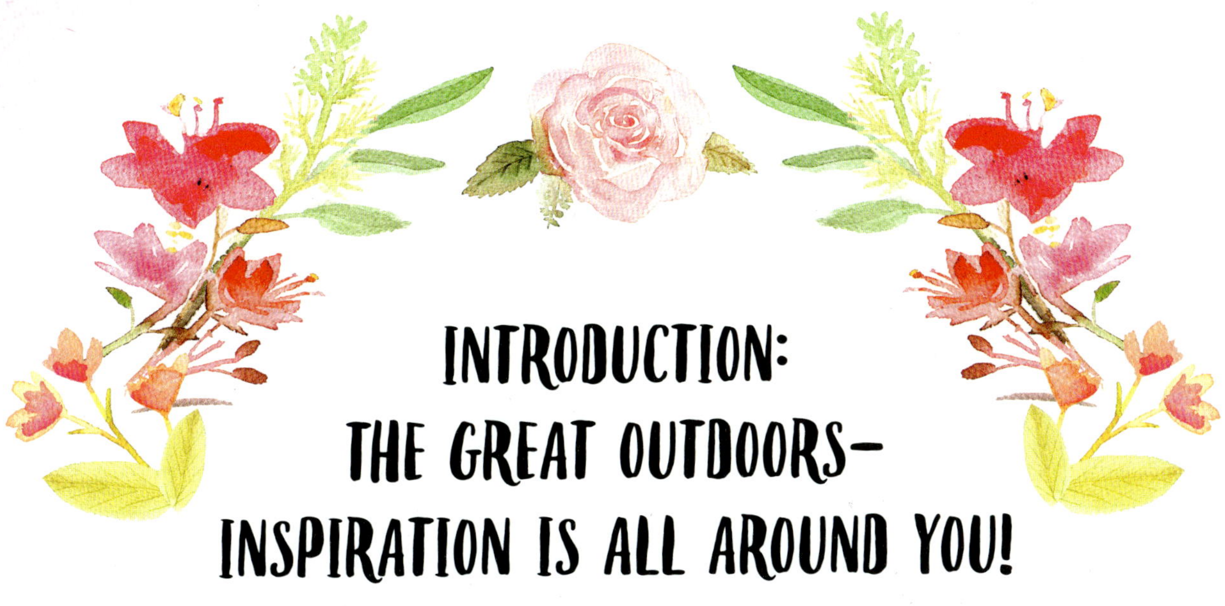

INTRODUCTION: THE GREAT OUTDOORS— INSPIRATION IS ALL AROUND YOU!

I became a nature enthusiast once I began taking long walks outdoors. Several years ago, I mentioned to my physician how stressed out I was feeling (due to my work schedule, social commitments, and so on), and she immediately suggested that I begin walking.

I must admit that I secretly rolled my eyes a bit. We live in very stressful times, where everyone is inundated with busy schedules, the news, and constant alerts from our phones, so I was skeptical that something as simple as walking could alleviate all of this. My doctor explained that taking long walks in nature can be both peaceful and meditative. She advised me to focus on what was right in front of me versus staying in my head. She mentioned trees, clouds, and the different seasons. "You're an artist," she said, smiling, "so you should enjoy this even more!"

I began the next day.

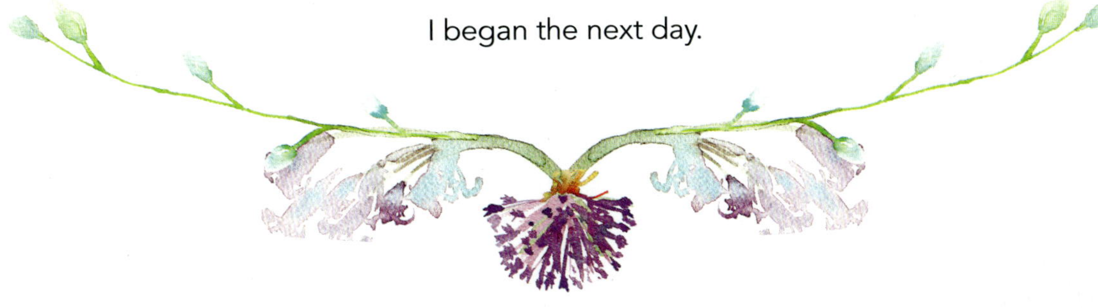

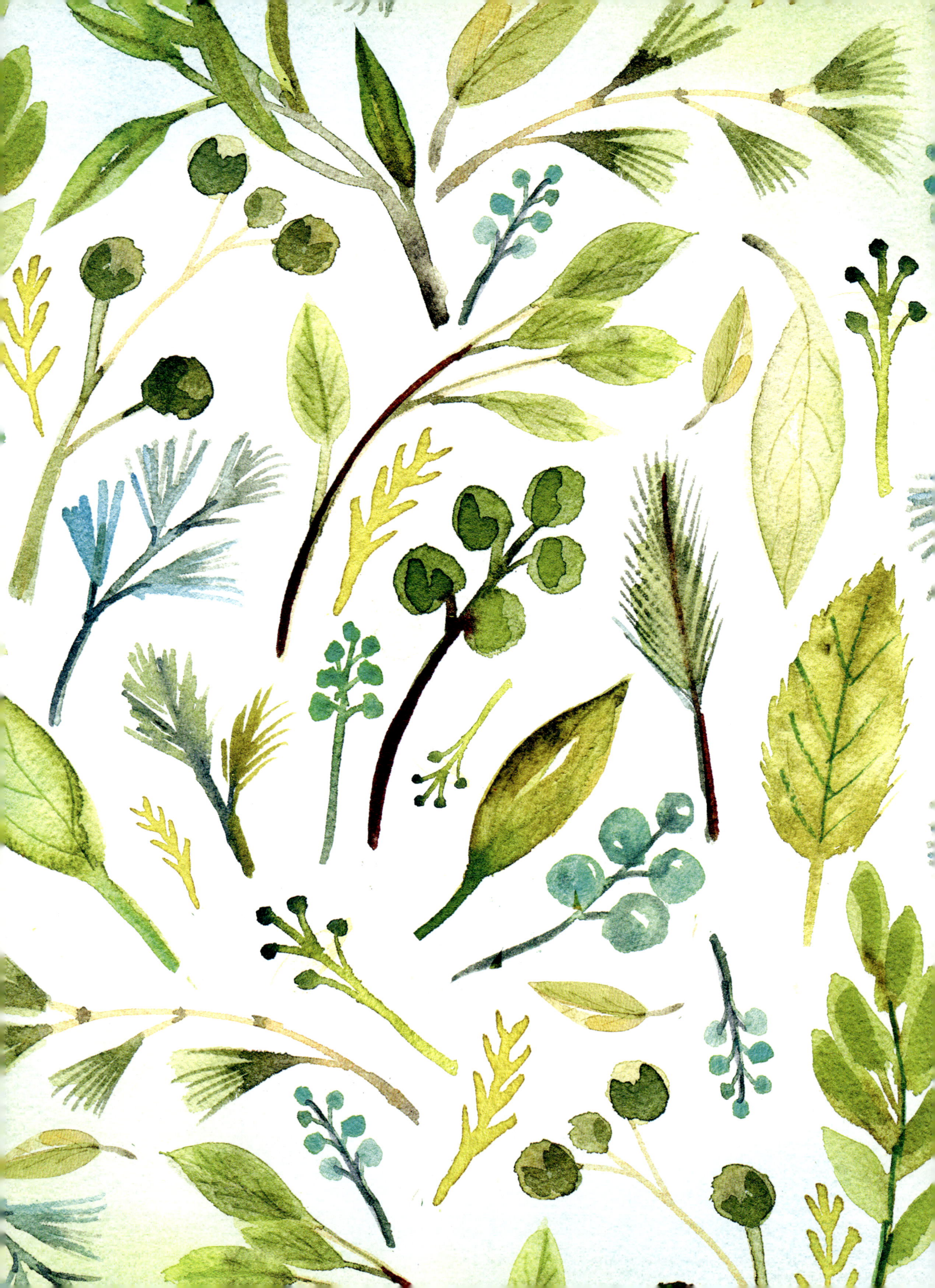

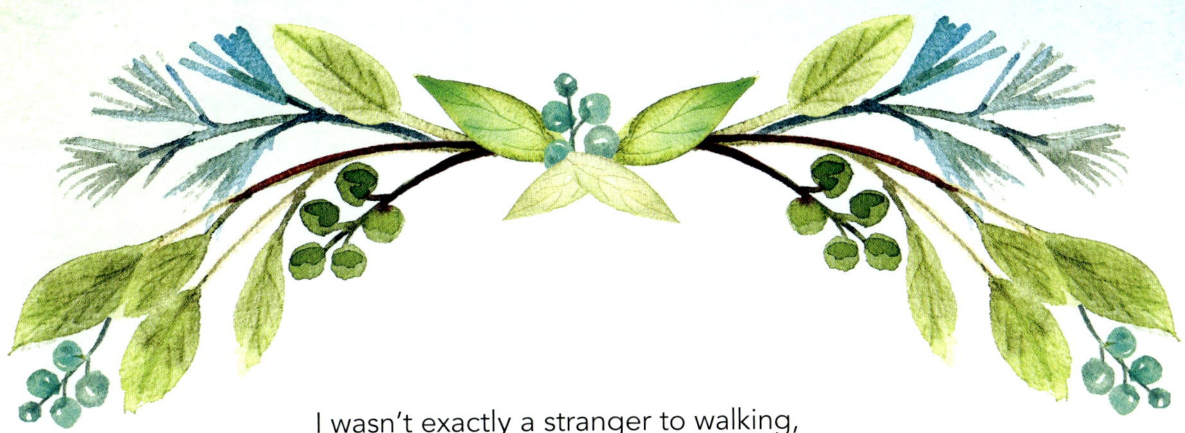

I wasn't exactly a stranger to walking, but my intent changed. Prior to that day, I had walked either for cardio or as a fast-paced way to get from one part of New York City to another, always running to make the bus or train. But at my doctor's advice, I embarked on these walks a bit differently. It wasn't easy at first to "get out of my head," but I made a concerted effort to acknowledge the beauty that was all around me and let go of modern-day concerns for a while.

Soon I found myself snapping photos of amazing 100-year-old trees, spring flowers, and cottonlike clouds in the sky. I was less in my head and more in the moment, whether marveling at the intricate colors of an autumn leaf, the crusty bark of an old oak tree, or the way the bare trees' bluish shadows fell across the winter snow. It didn't take long to make these walks a habit. I was hooked.

I tend to head straight out my front door and walk through the quieter streets in my town, but at times I drive to one of the parks or reservations in the area. Both provide so much inspiration—and in different ways.

No matter where you live, whether the climate is tropical, arid, humid, oceanic, or cool, you likely have a great spot to observe nature, and you will find yourself feeling more peaceful. There really is beauty everywhere you look! I am constantly seeking it, and I hope you do too.

-Kristine

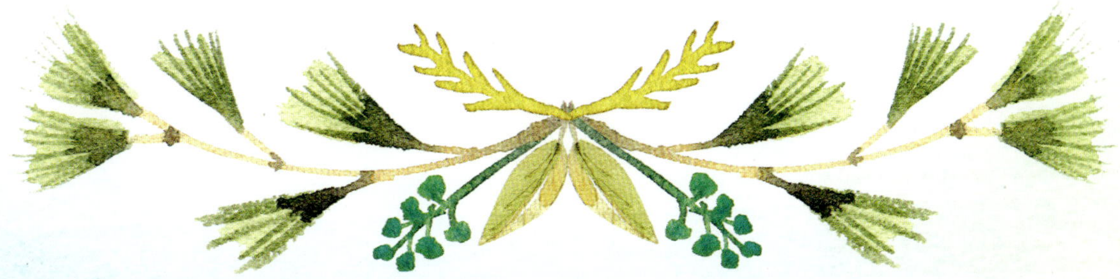

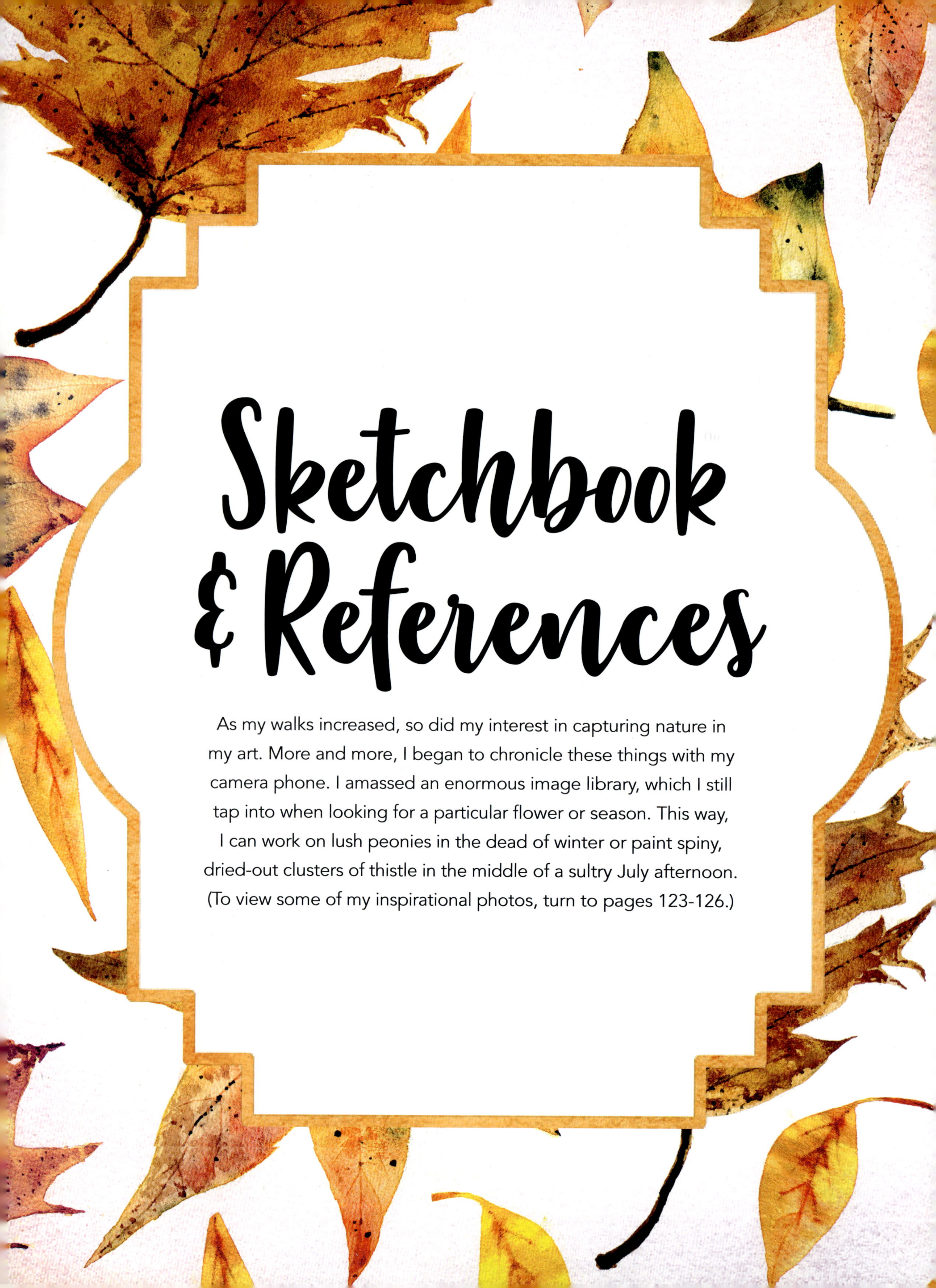

Sketchbook & References

As my walks increased, so did my interest in capturing nature in my art. More and more, I began to chronicle these things with my camera phone. I amassed an enormous image library, which I still tap into when looking for a particular flower or season. This way, I can work on lush peonies in the dead of winter or paint spiny, dried-out clusters of thistle in the middle of a sultry July afternoon. (To view some of my inspirational photos, turn to pages 123-126.)

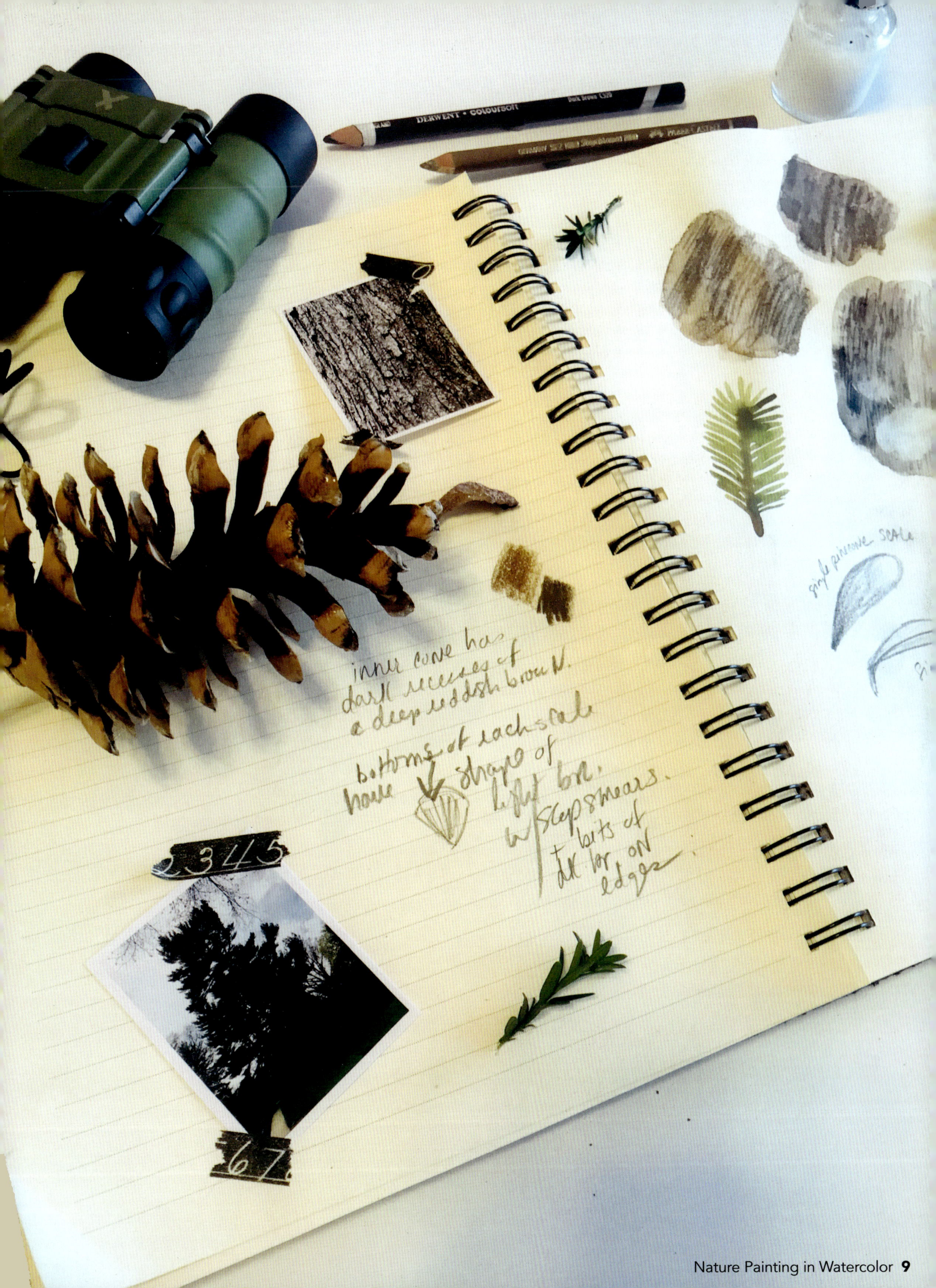
DERWENT • coloursoft
inner cone has
dark recesses of
a deep reddish brown.
bottoms of each scale
have shape of
light brn.
bits of
dk brn on
edges
single pinecone scale
345
67

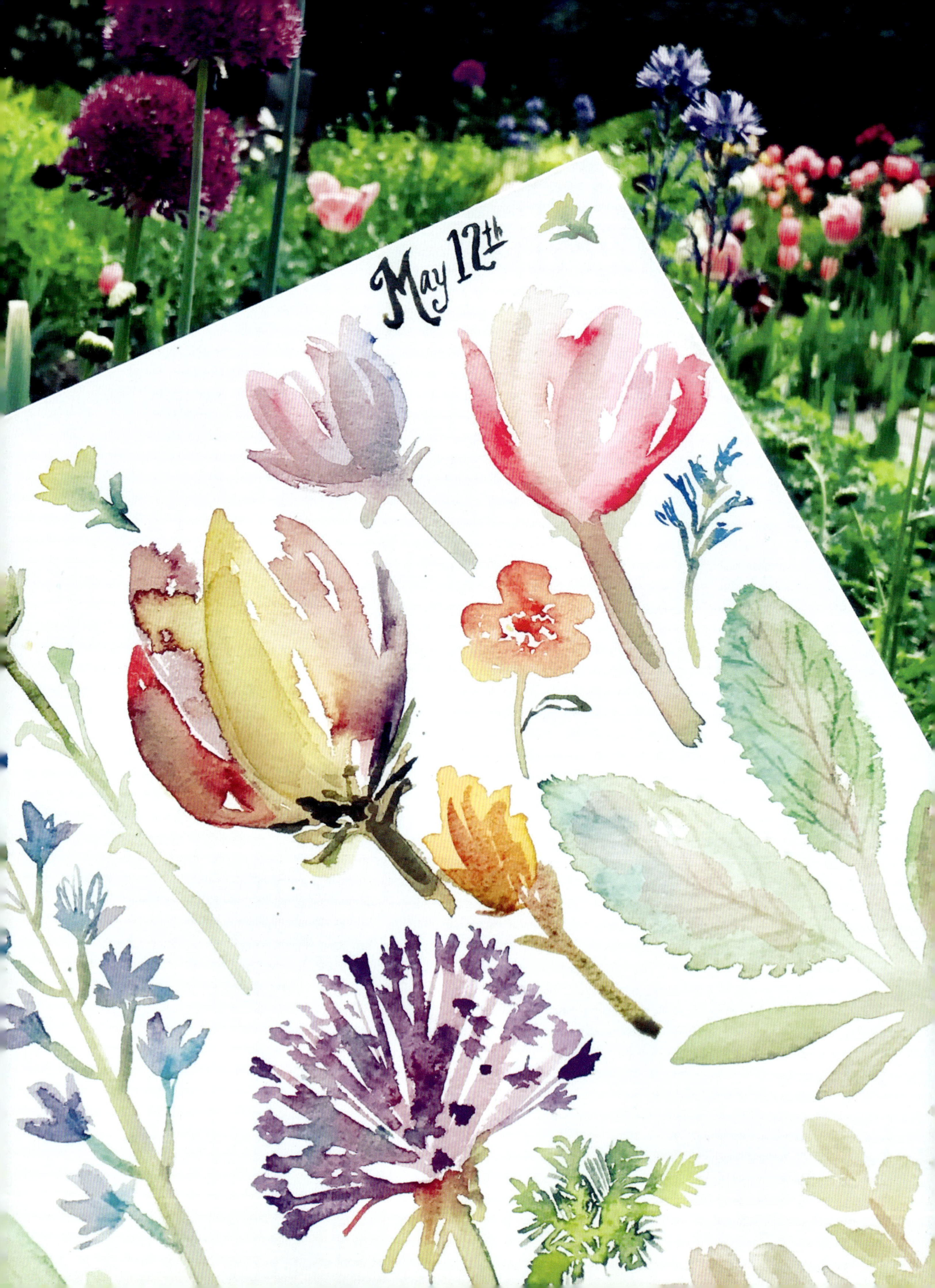
May 12th

I often look low when I am out—getting very close to the ground—and study the tiny blooms that grow. Nearly invisible from a standing position, these bits are just as detailed as the larger blooms that command our attention. Sitting beneath our feet are complex ground cover plants, mushrooms, and earthy mulch. If you are lucky, you might see the tiny shell of a snail or a fallen feather from a robin or jay. You just need to look!

I have found myself outside on the coldest days feeling so grateful to spot a deer darting through the woods, a hawk gliding across the pink sky, or a red fox trotting across the snow. Winter is a stunner if you embrace it. It is incredibly quiet and peaceful, and I am always amazed by its beauty. Here in the Northeast, so many of us complain about how long this season lasts, but if you get outside and look around, you won't suffer the same cabin fever as those who remain inside for months on end.

In addition to documenting my finds with a camera, I collect samples of nature—leaves, pods, acorns, pine cones, bits of bone, shells from the beach, and so on—and tuck them into my pockets. I then lug these back to my studio and create little studies in my sketchbook. If I don't have time to do so immediately, I add them to a giant glass jar.

Sketchbooks are a great way to dive in. Sometimes just knowing that they are for your eyes only takes the pressure off creating.

We can all feel trepidation when starting a painting, but using a sketchbook is quite freeing. Over the years, my students have questioned why their sketchbooks are so much closer to their vision than the finished paintings that they create. I firmly believe this is due to the fact that our sketchbooks are a place to play and observe what we take from the world around us, without the nagging sense that the art must be perfect.

My sketchbooks are filled with cross outs, failed attempts, quick washes with watercolor, pencil drawings, smudges, taped leaves, printed-out photos, notes, smears, and more! Don't make them too precious or you risk setting yourself up to avoid just diving in. Make your sketchbook your friend, and experiment with wild abandon!

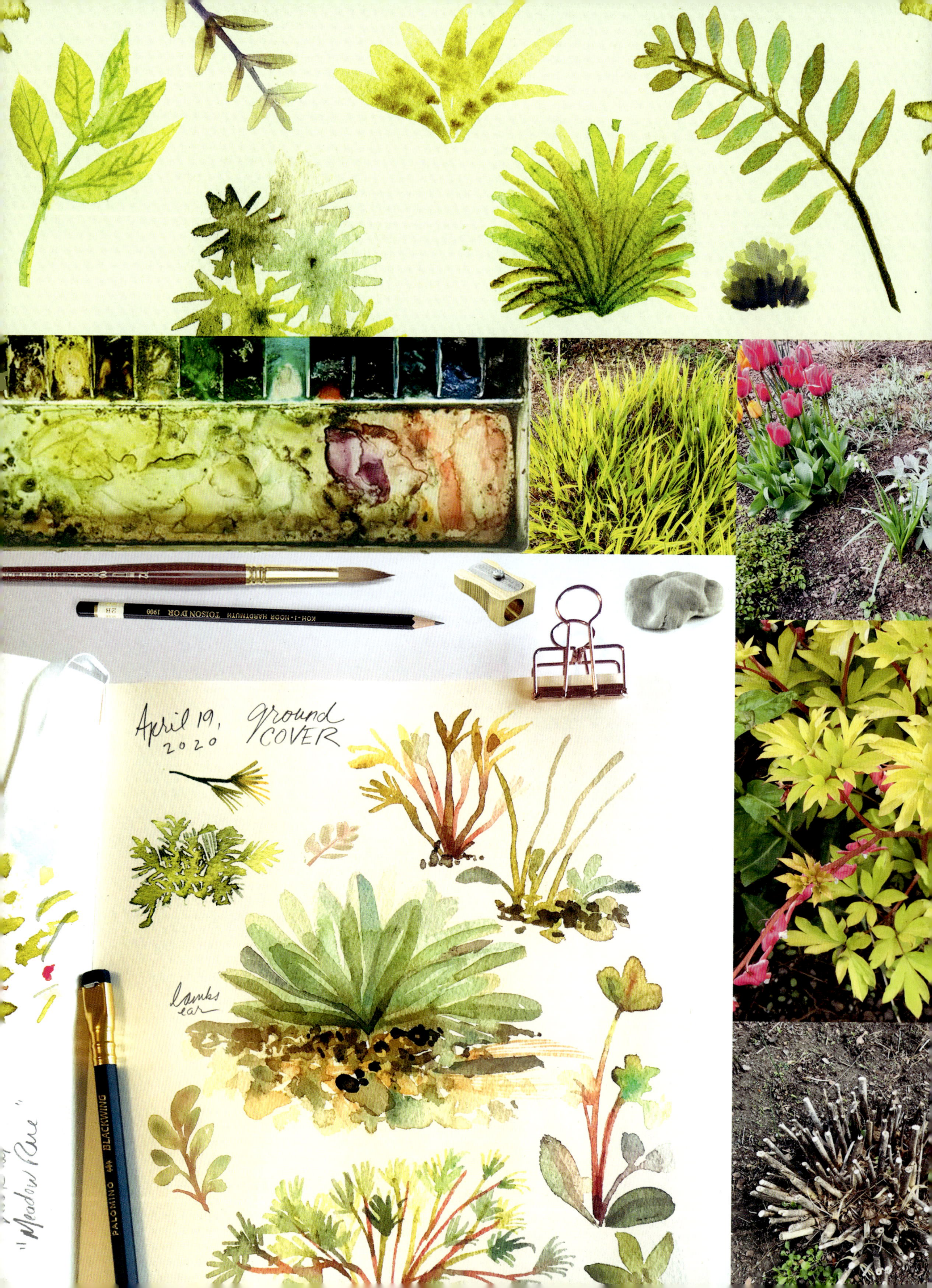

April 19, 2020
ground COVER
lambs ear
"Meadow Rue"
KOH-I-NOOR HARDTMUTH TOISON D'OR 1900
PALOMINO BLACKWING

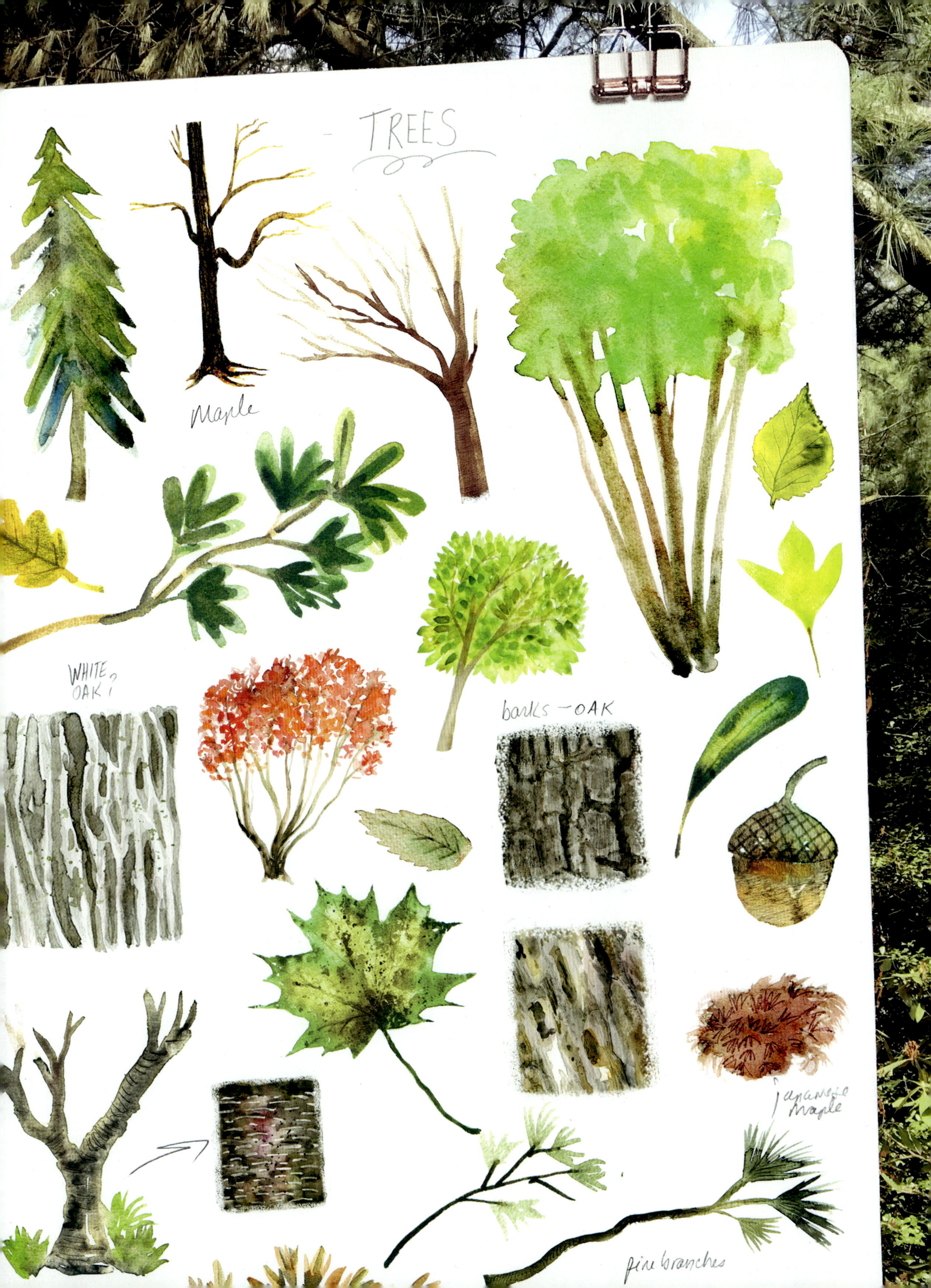
TREES
maple
WHITE OAK?
barks - OAK
Japanese maple
pine branches

TOOLS & MATERIALS

BRUSHES

There are tons—and I mean tons—of artist brushes out there. But don't be fooled: You can do a lot with very few brushes. And while I like to mix it up and add new brushes to my collection, I find myself returning again and again to the same six brushes. With that in mind, I will give you a list of those brushes so that you too can keep it simple.

Invest in quality versus quantity when buying brushes.

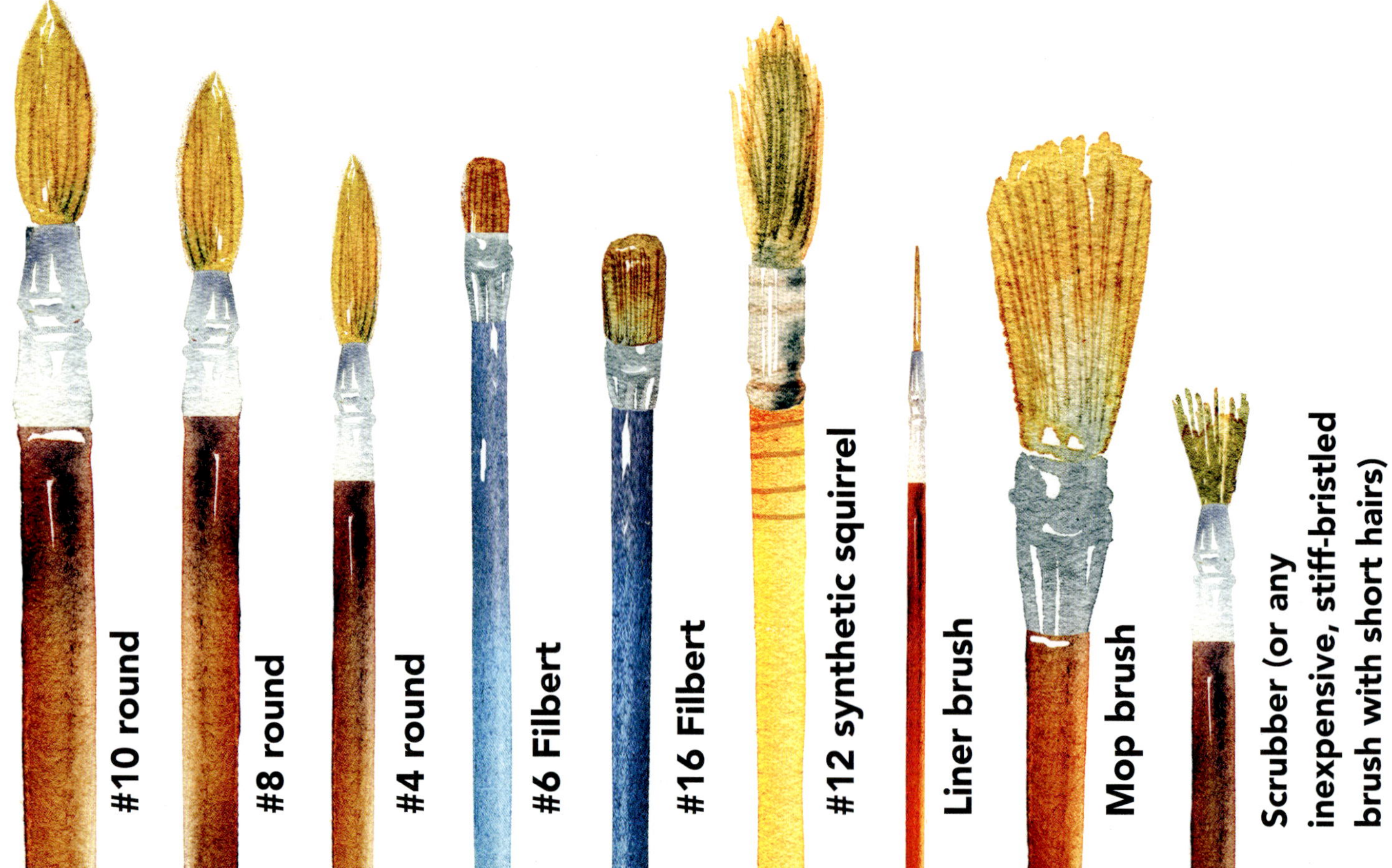

THESE BRUSHES WILL SUFFICE TO PAINT THE PROJECTS IN THIS BOOK:

- The **liner brush** allows you to paint small details.
- The **round brushes** will prove helpful for various blooms, foliage, and shrubs.
- The **Filbert** has a rounded rectangular shape that's great for broader subjects, such as barks and stones.
- I use the **mop brush** to lay in background colors for skies, tree trunks, and other large objects. You can soak up a lot of water and pigment with mop brushes, so they come in handy.
- Last is the **scrubber brush**, which can be used for rubbing a painting to gently remove the pigment. Create a highlight by moistening the brush and agitating the surface, then wiping with a paper towel.

PAPER

With watercolor, there are three basic paper choices: rough, hot-pressed, and cold-pressed. **Rough paper** has a coarse surface that works well for a looser technique. **Hot-pressed paper** features a smooth surface, allowing for more detailed work. **Cold-pressed paper** is in between rough and hot-pressed, as it does have some coarseness, which allows for texture in your work. This is my preferred paper and I purchase it in 140-lb. pads or blocks. I really love its versatility and carry it with me for working *en plein air*.

OTHER MATERIALS

Other supplies to consider are toothpicks and skewers for scoring lines into wet watercolor. I use these just as much as brushes! You should also add a kneaded eraser, masking fluid, a water spritzer, a squeeze bottle, and blotting implements, such as cotton swabs (perfect for small areas!), paper towels, and napkins.

If you should come across any of those disposable hand towels found in fancy restaurants, grab a few! They are the most absorbent and typically free of lint. I love to keep one by my palette to blot my brushes in between steps. And a side note: These towels look so pretty by the time they are filled with blots, you could almost frame them and call them "abstracts."

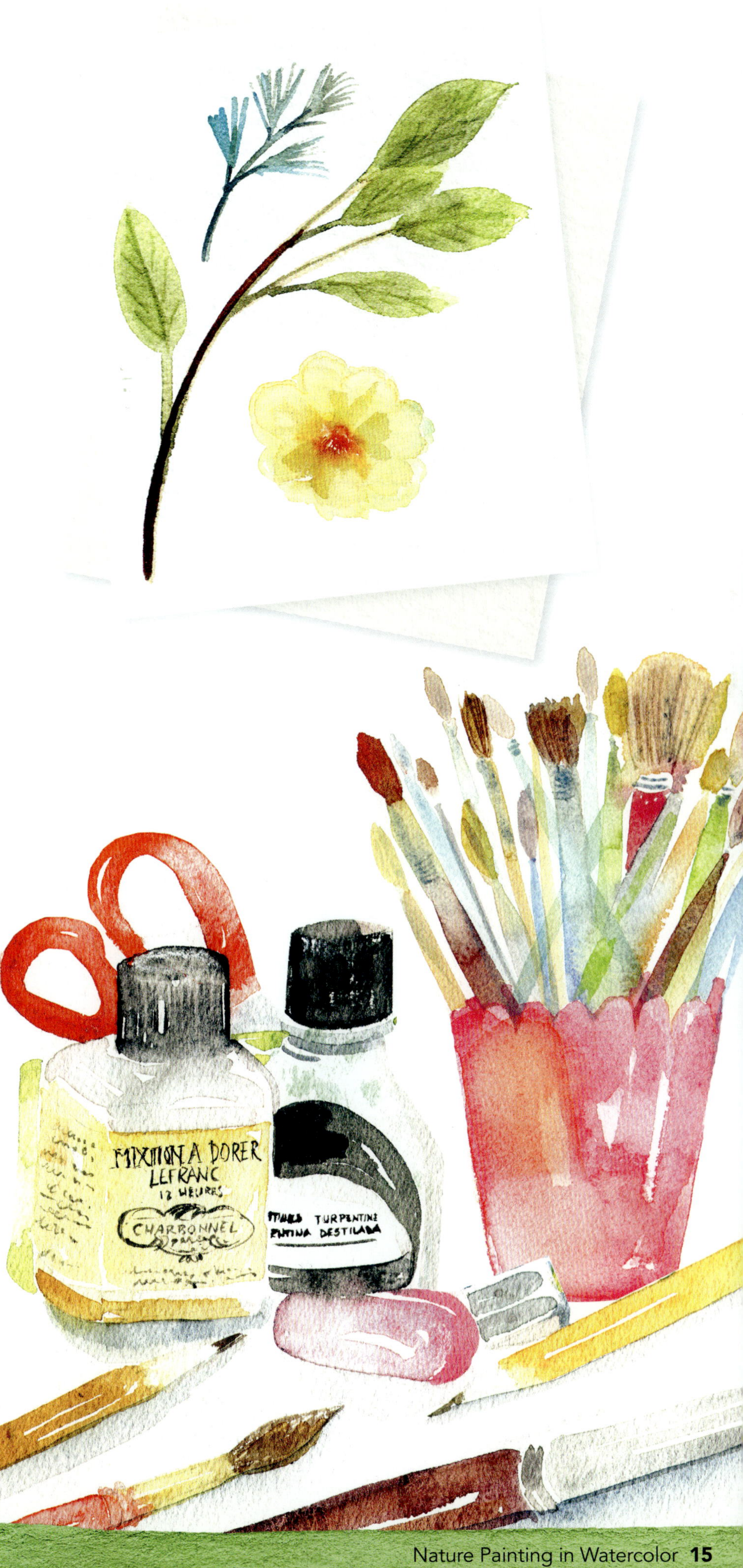

PAINT

When it comes to choosing watercolor paints, there are basically two choices: pans or tubes. Pan paints are small cakes of color that dry during the manufacturing process. Tube paints are filled with wet pigment. Dry pans are activated by water, while wet tubes are ready for use and can be thinned with water.

All paints are comprised of two main ingredients: pigment and binders. Less-expensive student-grade paints tend to have more "fillers" (binder ingredients—typically gum arabic) and less pigment, while professional paints often have a more concentrated amount of pigment with fewer fillers. There is a big difference between student- and professional-grade paints in both tubes and pans, so if you become serious about watercolors, buy the best you can afford.

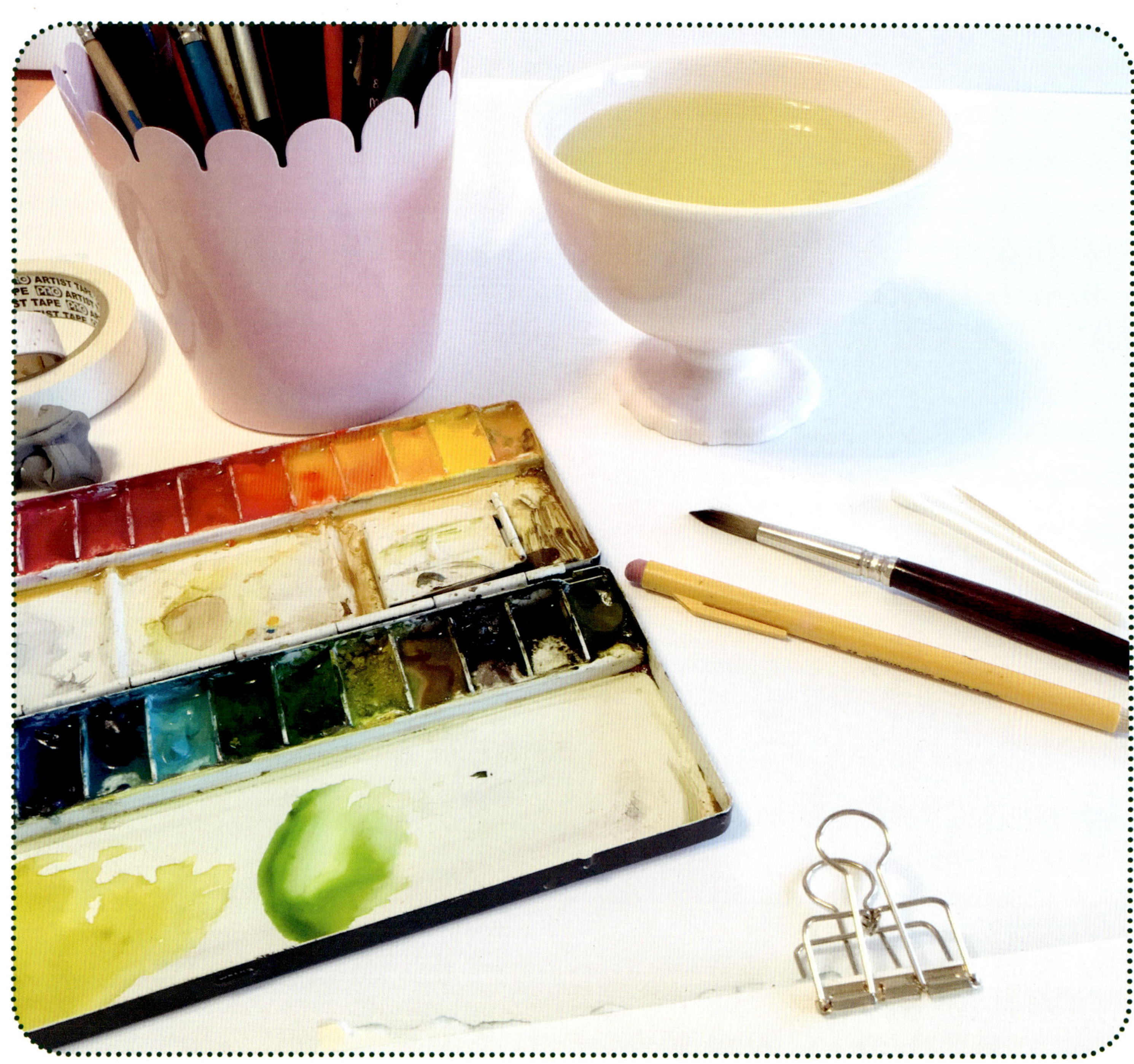

TIPS & TRICKS

Hands down, I find that tube paints make the best choice for my needs. I love the vibrancy of their color and also find them economical, with a single tube lasting a long time. I love to set up my own palette with colors from tubes.

Here's where it might be a little confusing, though. I am essentially creating my own pans once I fill the wells of my palette and allow the paints to dry. Dried tube pigments are easily activated by water. This gives me the option to take my smaller tin palette outside to paint without wet colors running in the tin.

- After painting outside, make sure the pans aren't too wet before heading back inside with them. It's best to place your tin flat down inside a bag so that wet colors won't run. I find that the sun usually dries out my tin. You can always make a few sketches while you allow the palette to dry a bit, or take a deep breath and study your surroundings.
- Tubes are often easier on brushes than pans since you don't have to "scrub" with your brush to pick up a cake color. I keep a small squeeze bottle nearby and run a stream of water over all of the wells to activate my colors. If I am just painting greenery outside, I will restrict the number of wells I activate to keep things tidier.
- When working in my studio, I often use a larger plastic palette with deep wells so that I can add lots of water for washes and larger areas. I squeeze a small dab of pigment into the back corners of the wells and then dip and drag my brush toward the center of the palette to control how much I use.
- You never want to fill the wells too much, even in a travel tin. It helps to give the paints some breathing room so that you have watery, less-opaque pigment and can use the edge of the tin to drag off excess.
- I love both of my palettes and how I can create variations on them as I wish. For example, I use only colors of nature when painting *en plein air*. But in studio, I may have some wild-card colors for more decorative work. I don't think I would ever be satisfied with a premade watercolor pan or tube kit. I love to customize in general, so why would my palettes be any different?

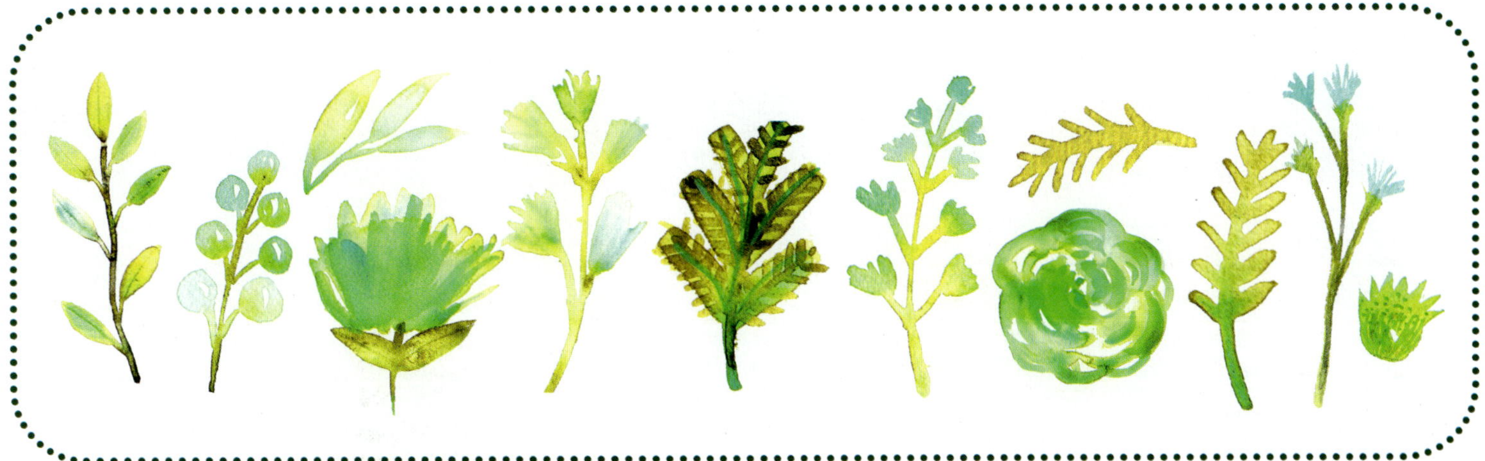

PAINTING TECHNIQUES

There's a plethora of basic techniques for the application and manipulation of watercolor. For painting nature, I tend to employ the following practices most often.

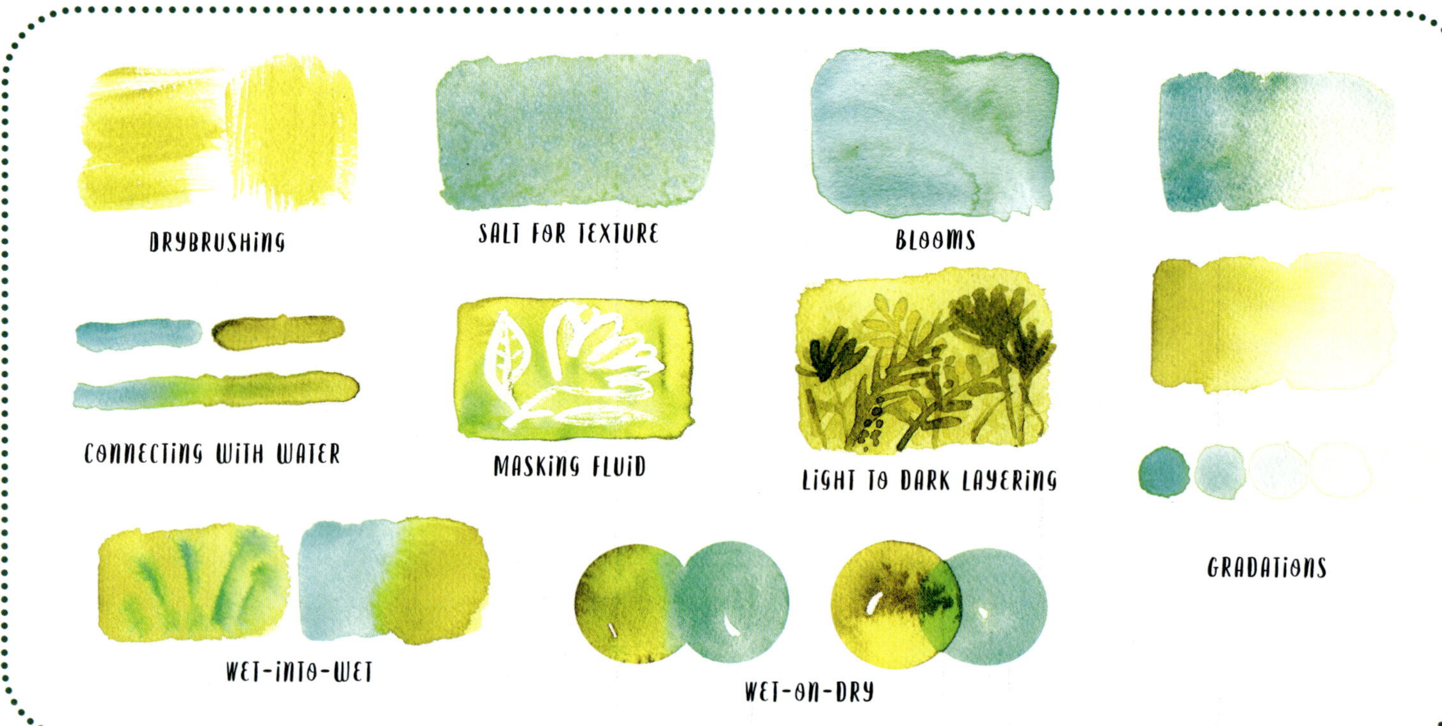

WET-INTO-WET

Adding watercolor paint onto wet paper is a fun way to merge colors that will blend into each other with the water that they share. This technique is great for creating softer lines as opposed to hard ones.

I like to paint wet-into-wet when working on flower petals, leaves, and large areas like tree trunks or rocks. While the initial wash of paint is wet, I tap into it with different colors that then blend themselves.

A perfect example of this is a simple rock. Start with a wash of pale to medium gray, and while it's still wet, tap in darker hues like blues and blacks to give the rock a mottled appearance. The darker colors become subtler as the pigment moves about and then dries.

Autumn leaves are another wonderful subject for this technique. When you study an autumn leaf up close, you see an almost infinite number of colors in one small area. Painting wet-into-wet will help you capture these colors.

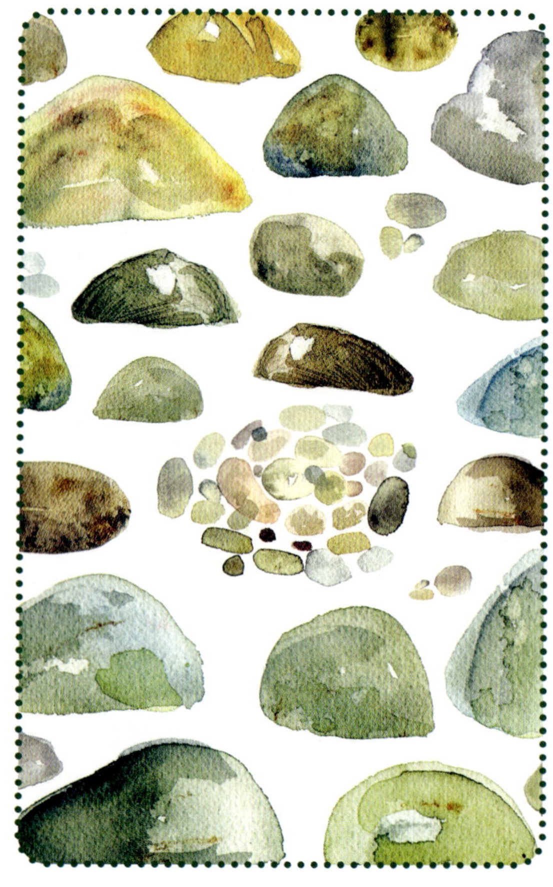

WET-ON-DRY

As the name implies, with this technique, you paint one color, let it dry, and then go over it with a second color. Rather than blending, the second color will sit transparently on top of the first.

I use this technique to add details when I'm almost finished painting a subject—for example, using a liner brush to add delicate lines to a flower. You can use this technique to add small areas in the center, like pistils or stamens, or small, recessed areas that require stippling and darker hues.

GRADATIONS

Apply a single color with a brush, and then dip the brush into the top of your water container as you apply the next coat. Repeat until the brush runs almost clear.

I use this method for large areas, like the sky, or flowers with pigment that is deepest in one area and then fades near the end of the petal. This technique also offers a strategic way to handle certain stems. Some are darker where they connect to the flower, so you can start the gradient from the top down, stopping well before the water runs clear.

CONNECTING WITH COLOR

Apply one band of color in a straight line; then add a second color in a similar manner, with space between the two lines. Now apply clear water to your brush and draw a line between the two bands of color. You will see the two pigments move in toward the middle.

I like to use this technique when creating individual flower petals. Sometimes I will flood an area with a pigment on one side and another pigment on the other and "connect" the two by tapping clear water in between. You will see the water moving about, and it can be gently coaxed along with your brush too.

MASKING FLUID

This technique comes in handy when approaching any subject matter that is arduous to paint around. For example, consider the white dots of an *Amanita* (fairy-tale) mushroom. It would be difficult to create complex washes while reserving the white of the mushroom cap, so I use masking fluid to save those small dotted areas. (For complete instructions on painting the *Amanita* mushroom, see pages 40-41.)

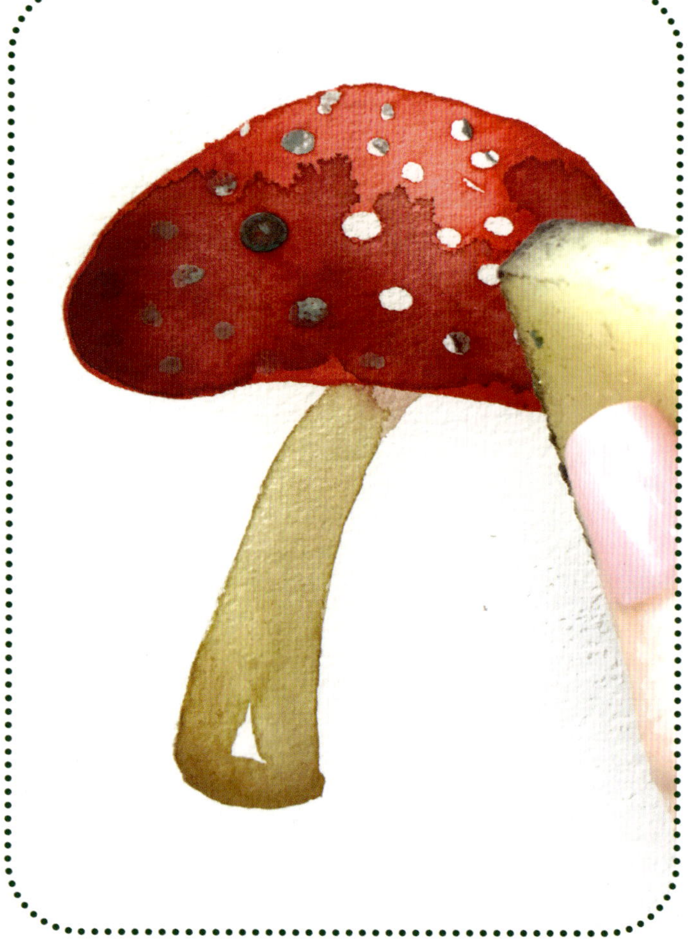

To use commercial masking fluid, tap simple shapes or lines on the paper and let them dry thoroughly. You will find that the fluid remains tacky to the touch when dry, but you want to make sure that no masking fluid comes off on your finger. Once dry, wash over the area with the colors and techniques of your choice. The paint will go right over the areas you've masked. Let everything dry thoroughly, and then remove the masking fluid with a rubber cement square. You can also remove it with your fingers, but make sure they are clean and completely dry to prevent smearing the paint.

Reserve an inexpensive brush for masking. If you clean your masking brush with soapy water immediately after use, you should be able to remove most of the fluid residue, but the brush cannot be used again for painting.

I like to use masking fluid with a blue tinge to make it easier to see.

BLOOMS

Blooms, also known as "blossoms," occur when you apply a wash of color or clear water one to two minutes after the first wash. The color will form an unusual edge and add stunning visual interest to a watercolor painting. This technique is often unpredictable and can be difficult at first. I find that these blossoms usually occur when I am not expecting them, which is why I call them "happy accidents."

LIGHT TO DARK LAYERING

I like to follow this approach when painting objects in a group setting. For example, if I'm painting a small scene of ground cover in a meadow, I begin with the objects that are far away before advancing to those that are closer. Light objects recede, and darker ones come to the foreground. This simple technique can be used when the objective is to create depth.

Start with a wash, and let it dry. Add a pale layer of subject matter—in this case, grasses, ferns, and so on. Let the paint dry. Paint the next layer a bit darker so that it stands out from the initial pale layer. Continue until the darkest layer is the very last in your painting.

SALT

Although the use of salt can be a bit gimmicky, if used sparingly, it's a wonderful way to add texture to a subject. I like it for capturing natural elements, like beach sand, and coarser objects, such as stone pavers. Simply sprinkle some salt into a still-wet wash, and leave it alone. You can have fun experimenting with different salts; coarser ones will make a more dramatic mark than fine table salt. Once dry, just sweep the salt off your painting. You will see that the granules absorb the water and pigment.

DRYBRUSHING

Dip your brush in water and blot until you've removed most of the moisture. Dip the brush into the pigment of your choice and scrape the brush along the paper. The paper provides the texture. This technique is great for painting bark and fine lines into flower petals.

CREDIT CARDS

Use the side of an expired credit card to create interesting textures in a watercolor painting. I like to snip mine into thirds and use them in smaller areas. This technique is particularly fun for creating the dry, peeling bark of a tree like the white birch. Just dip the side of the card into medium gray-black pigment and gently scrape downward in small, alternating areas. Be light-handed, and don't forget to use the corners of the card to make tinier marks.

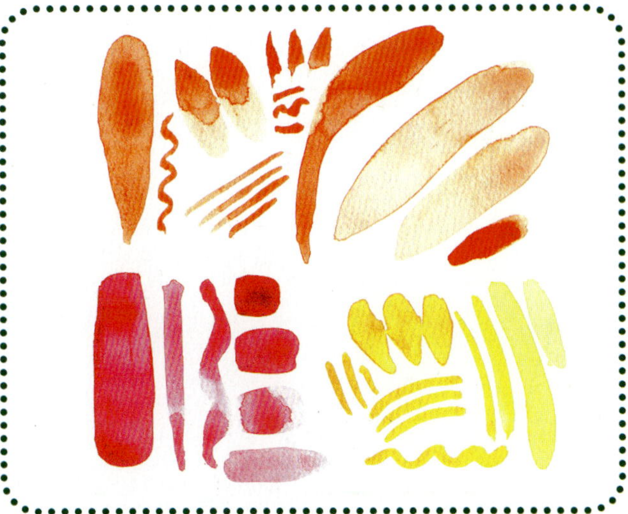

Utilize the broad side and tip of your brush to paint a subject. It's amazing how much work can be done with just one brush! In this sketch, I've made the marks in the top row with a #10 round brush, the marks at the bottom left with a #16 Filbert, and the marks in the bottom right with a liner brush. Experiment with mark-making—it's a lot of fun!

NATURE'S PALETTE: COLOR THEORY

ESSENTIAL COLORS

- Lemon yellow
- Cadmium yellow
- Windsor orange
- Cadmium red
- Sanguine red
- Scarlet lake
- Opera rose
- Raw umber
- Sepia
- Prussian blue
- Cobalt blue
- Light turquoise
- Violet
- Perylene green
- Olive green
- Green gold
- Sap green
- Neutral tint

There are many books dedicated to the subject of color theory and the process of setting up a palette. It's a very personal process, as each artist uses the colors that resonate most with that person's own subject matter and style.

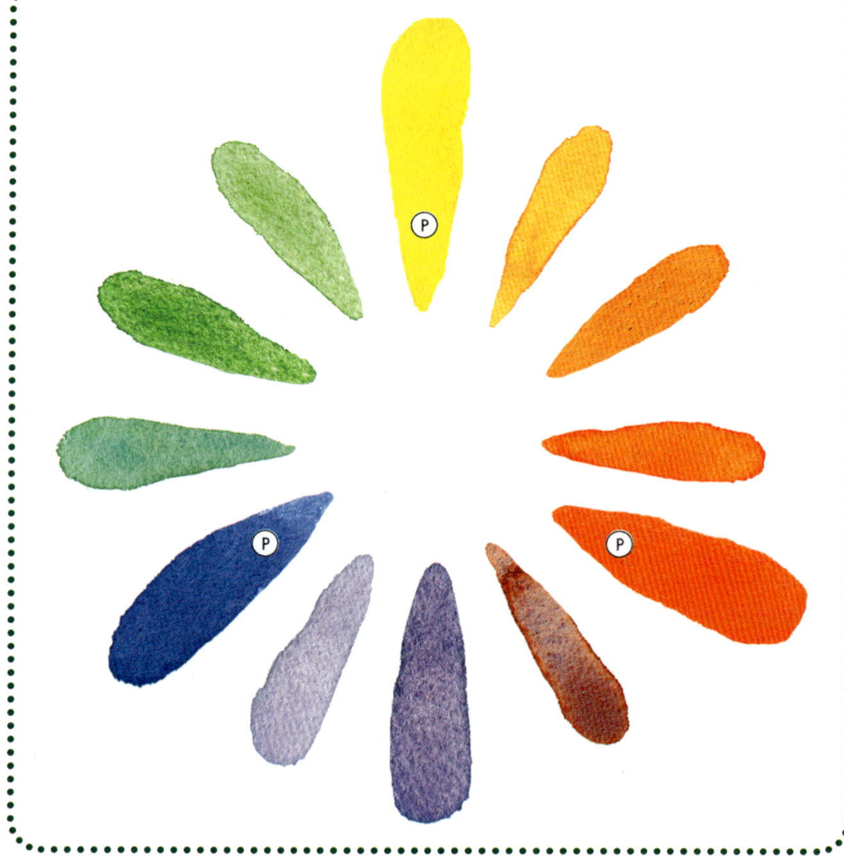

There are many ways to go about organizing your palette. I advise keeping warm and cool colors together, with a special section for neutrals, like warm gray, neutral tint, ivory, black, and so on. Most other decisions are up to you!

The primary colors—red, yellow, and blue—are the most basic and pure colors, from which you can mix their complementary colors—orange, green, and violet. Tertiary colors are created by mixing a secondary color (complementary) with one of its primary components (for example, orange with red or green with blue).

You can create the most amazing colors by experimenting with different amounts of the colors described above. By mixing more or less of a primary with a secondary color, you can achieve completely different results.

Analogous colors are the colors that sit next to each other on the color wheel. They work in harmony with each other—for example, red, orange, and red-orange.

SOME BASIC COLOR TERMS

Hue: A pure color on the color wheel, such as red, blue, or green.

Saturation: A measure of the purity of a color.

Tone: The relative lightness or darkness of a color.

Value: A range of tones that spans from pure white to pure black.

Tint: Adding white to a color to create a high value.

Shade: Adding black to a color to create a low value.

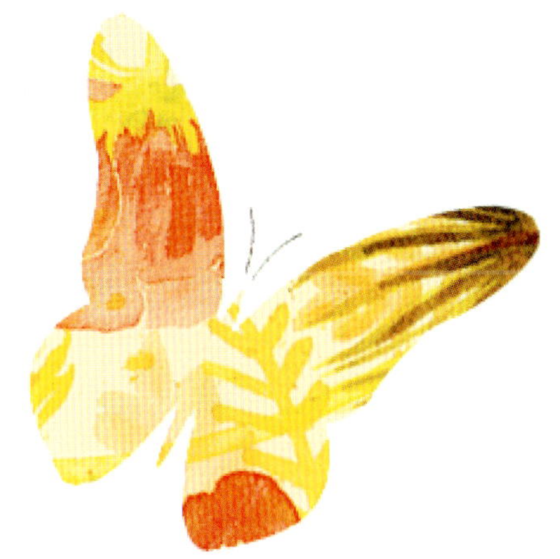

COLOR PALETTES

When painting nature, I tend to alternate between two palettes: earthy (greens, browns, and neutrals) and brights (reds, pinks, oranges, yellows, and violets). I find that having two separate tins with these color groupings makes it very easy to access my colors while painting outdoors.

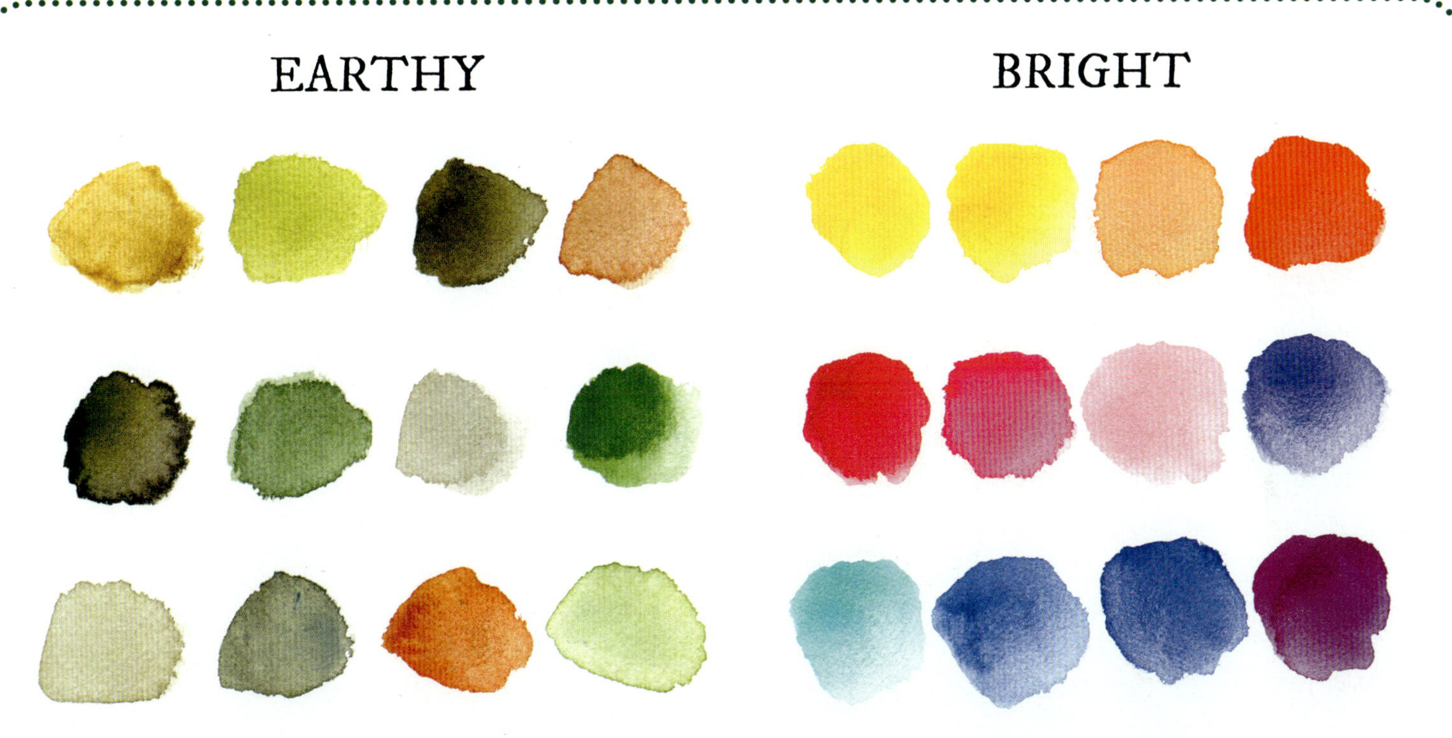

Complementary colors are always a joy to incorporate when painting nature. Consider the red berries on a dark green holly branch or the delicious combination of yellow and violet present on *Coleus* leaves. Even if your subject matter lacks these combinations of complementary colors, you can still use them to your advantage. For example, if you are painting an orange tiger lily, you could place it against a beautiful blue sky. For a flower with a yellow main color, add violet to the sky. Using complementary colors will always make a subject pop!

No matter which colors you choose for your palette, I hope you will consider mixing your own. There is something so satisfying about creating your own custom colors. They are truly unique, rich, and a wonderful way to capture the unique colors of what you are painting.

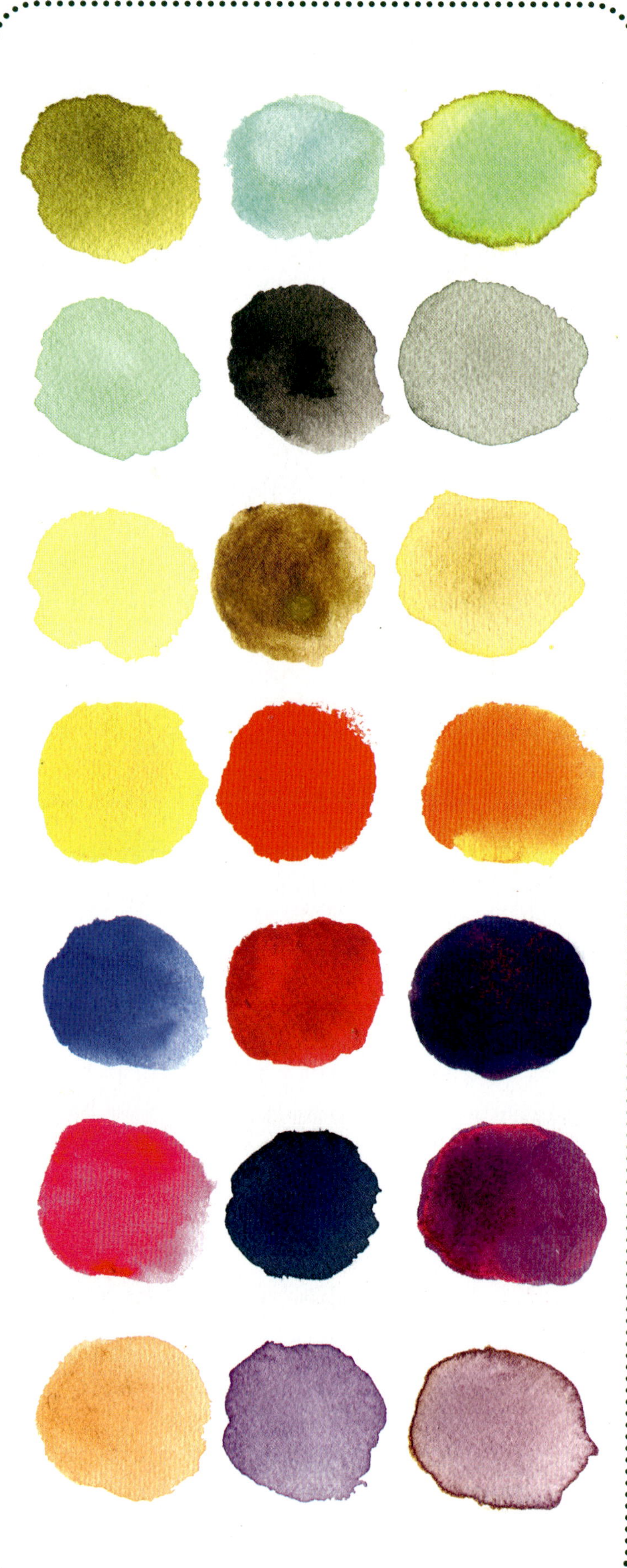

For the earthy colors I use in painting nature, I tend to mix nearly every color to my liking. I rarely use paint straight out of the tube. It's rare to have just the perfect color sitting there in your palette, so why not experiment? Instead of flat black from a tube, try combining raw umber and Prussian blue. Mixing your own pigments gives the color so much more uniqueness and depth. See how adding one color to another can transform the hue in your tin.

HOW ABOUT...?

- Adding a bit of turquoise to a green-gold? *(This is one of my all-time favorites!)*
- Adding a touch of sepia to viridian green?
- Adding some raw umber to lemon yellow?
- Adding scarlet lake to cadmium yellow?
- Adding a bit of sanguine red to cobalt blue?
- Adding some violet to Windsor orange?
- Adding rose dore to Prussian blue?

What colors can *you* create? I encourage you to experiment as much as possible. Mixing can be magical! Whether I am painting the relatively neutral bark of a tree or a bold, colorful flower, I really try to look at the subject and study the unique colors within the obvious. For example, you may just see grays and browns on a tree's bark, but when you peer a bit closer, there are often lavenders, soft caramels, and pale greens as well. Even if you use a paint straight out of the tube, you can always tap in a bit of another color to give it more depth.

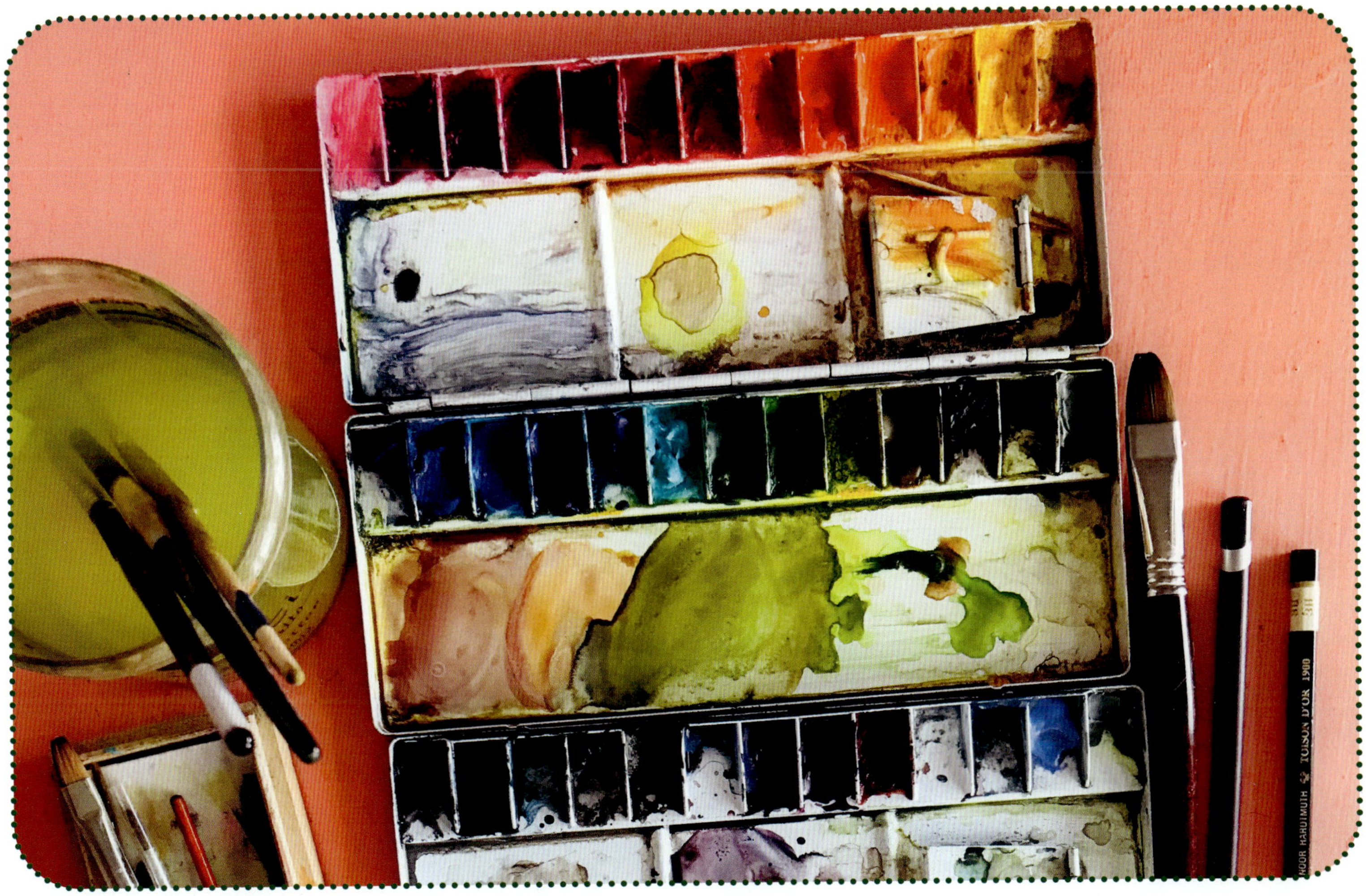

Dirty Water

It can sometimes be difficult to see a very light wash on white paper. To fix this problem, I use what I call "dirty water" to create the subtlest value. Dirty water is a highly diluted combination of colors from your palette. Depending on which colors dominate the palette, you may have dirty water that skews more blue, green, or red.

When I want a specific neutral, I like to make my own dirty water, which is a mixture of 2 parts black to 1 part yellow. The resulting paint is the very palest warm gray. This mixture allows you to see the wash on the paper, without competing with any of the other paint colors.

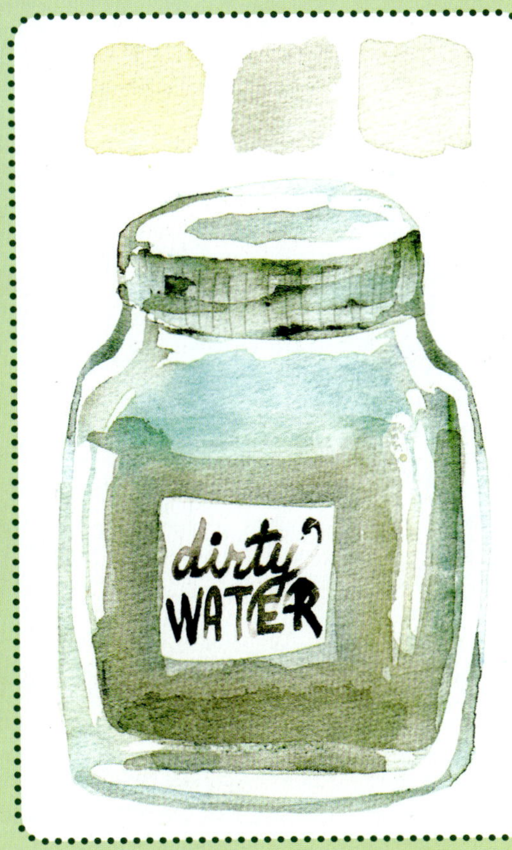

Ground Cover: Ferns, Mushrooms & Rocks

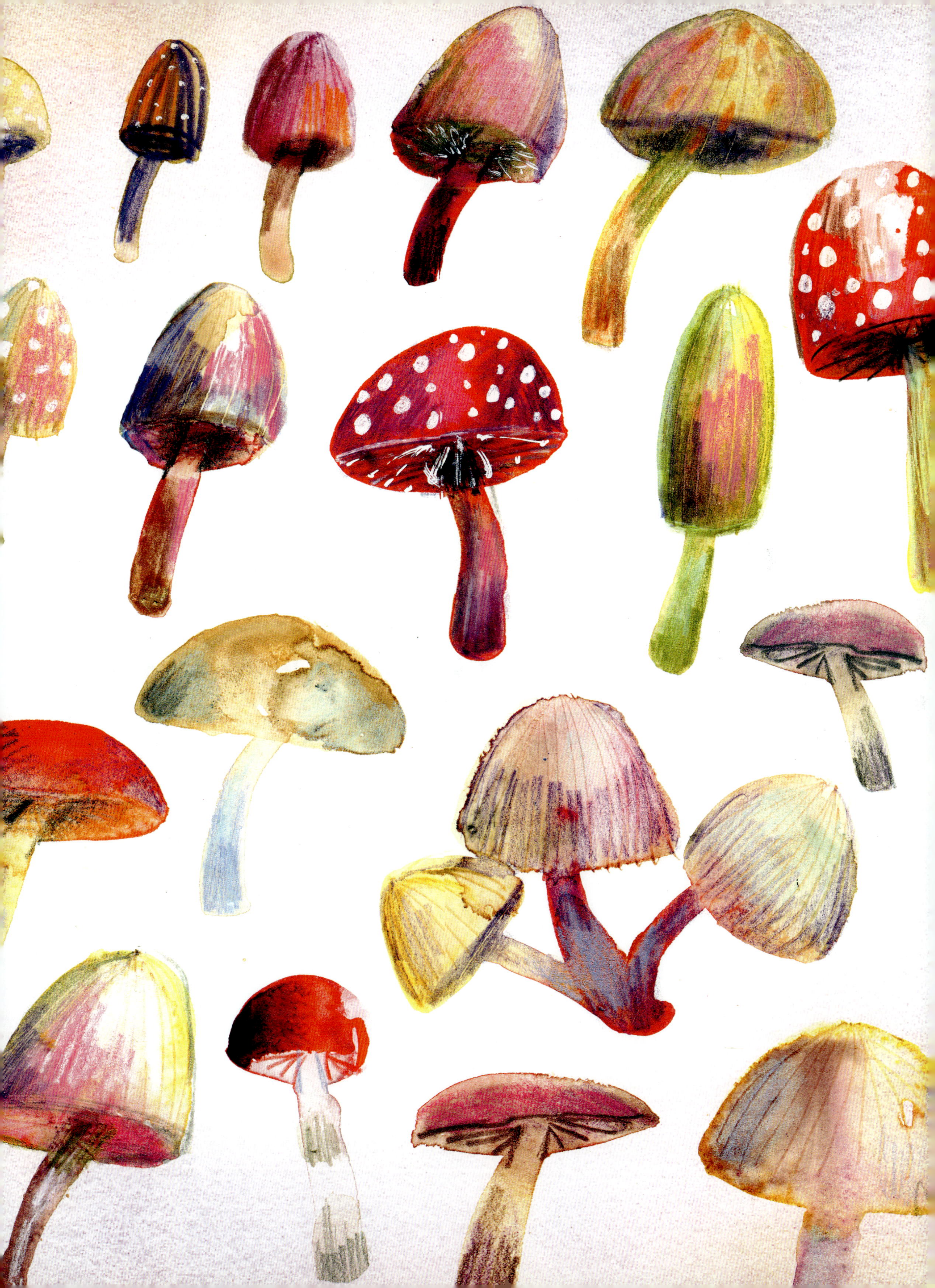

SIMPLE FERN

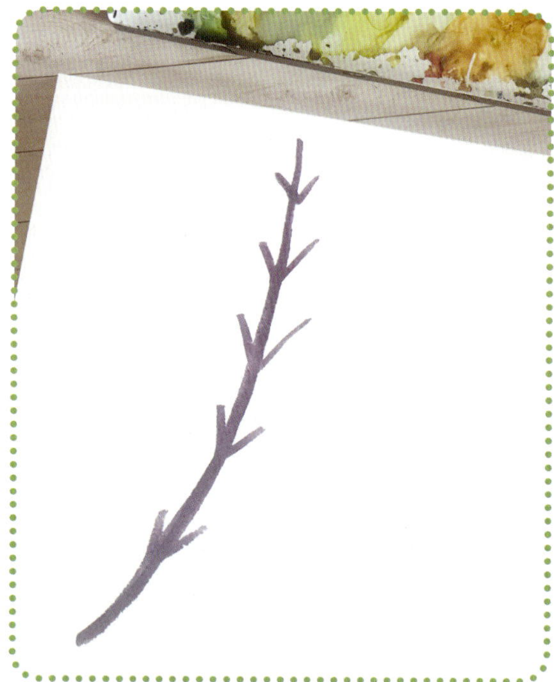

1 Using a #4 round brush and a violet hue, make a simple stem; then add smaller, offshoot stems that reach up.

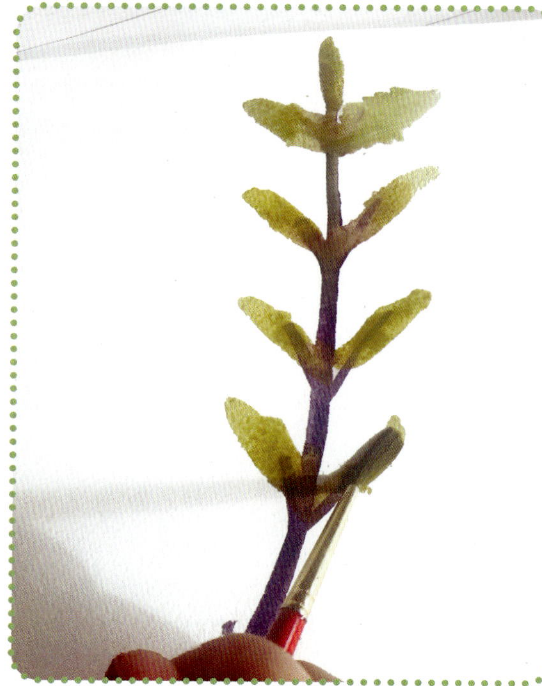

2 Now use green and the flat of a #8 brush to touch down the tip and bring it back toward the stems so that the wider part of the leaf is closer to the center. Don't be afraid to use a lot of water here; you want the colors to bleed into each other.

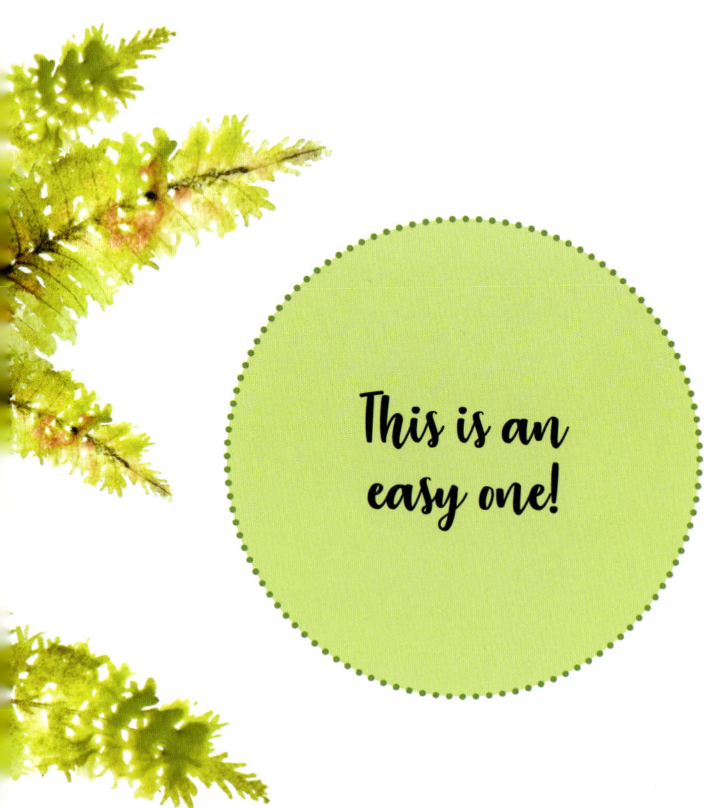

This is an easy one!

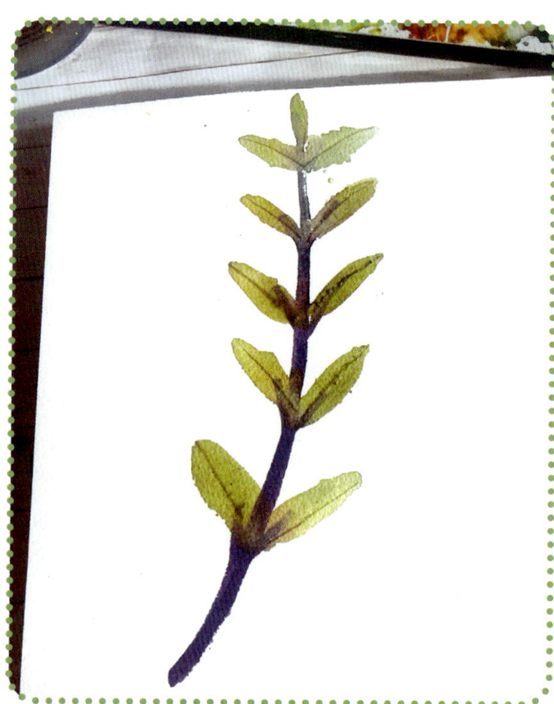

3 Use a toothpick to score center veins into each leaf. It's that simple!

SIMPLE GRASS

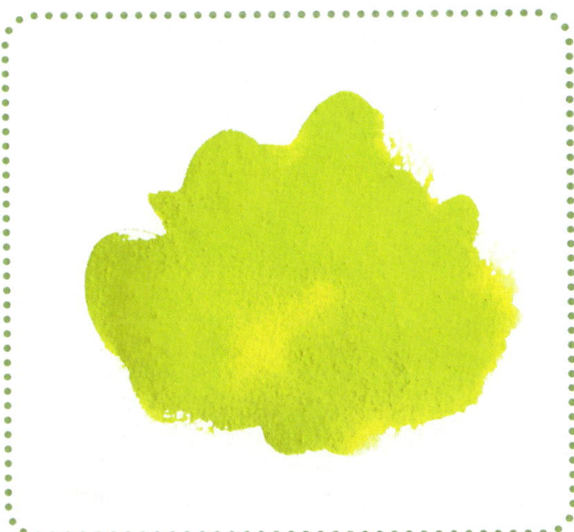

1 Load a #10 round brush with a generous amount of watery light-green paint; then create an oval-like shape with rounded, irregular edges.

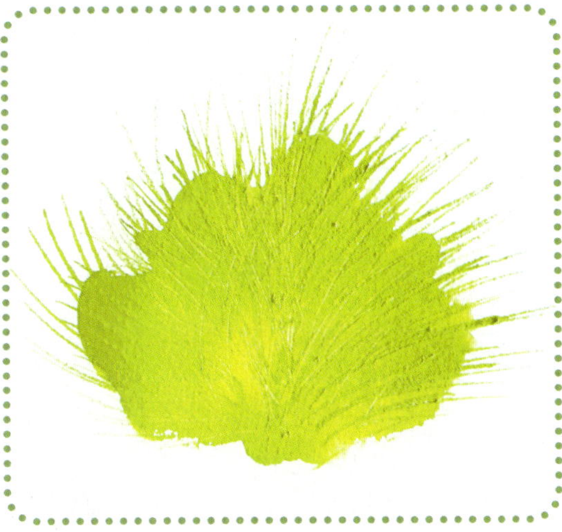

2 Score the shape with a toothpick, dragging it from the center outward to mirror how grass grows. Go crazy here—there are many blades of grass in a single bush!

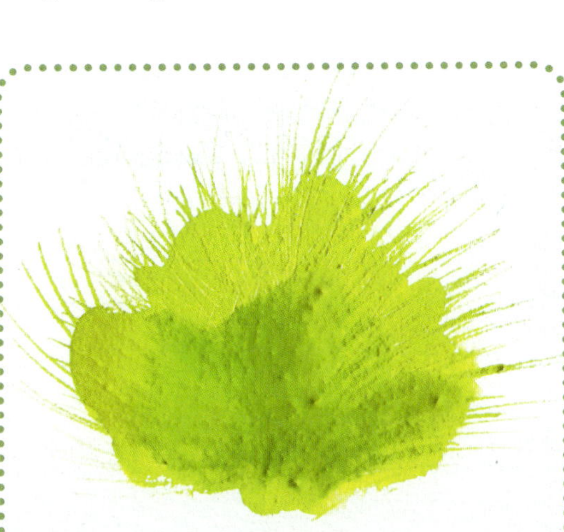

3 While the paint is still wet, dip the #10 brush into a deeper hue of green and tap into the center of the bush to give it more depth and dimension. Let this color move about and travel to the outer edges—you may want to coax it a bit!

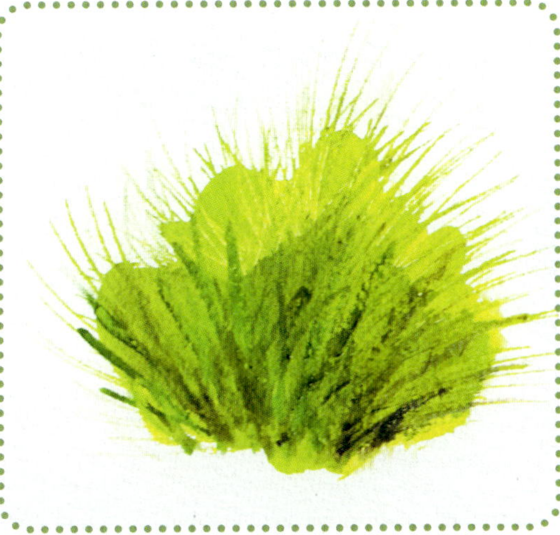

4 With that same deeper hue of green, add color to the bottom of the bush to give it some weight.

This is another easy project! You can use the techniques featured here to create so many grasses. Change them up using different color combinations.

PURPLE PAMPAS GRASS

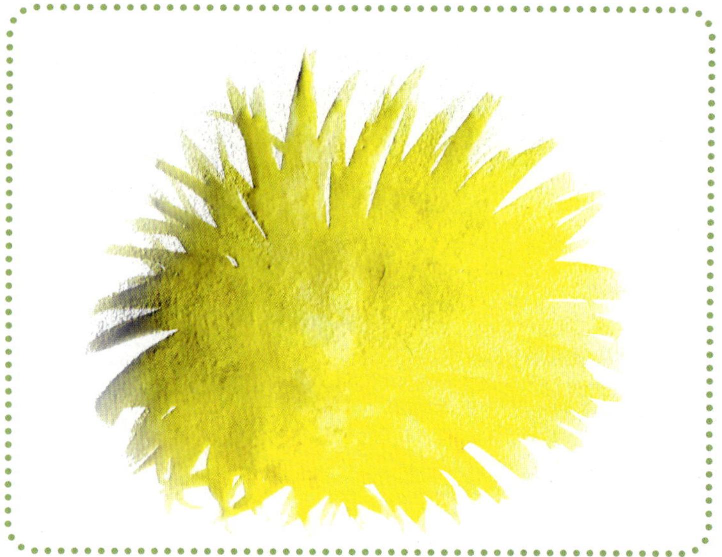

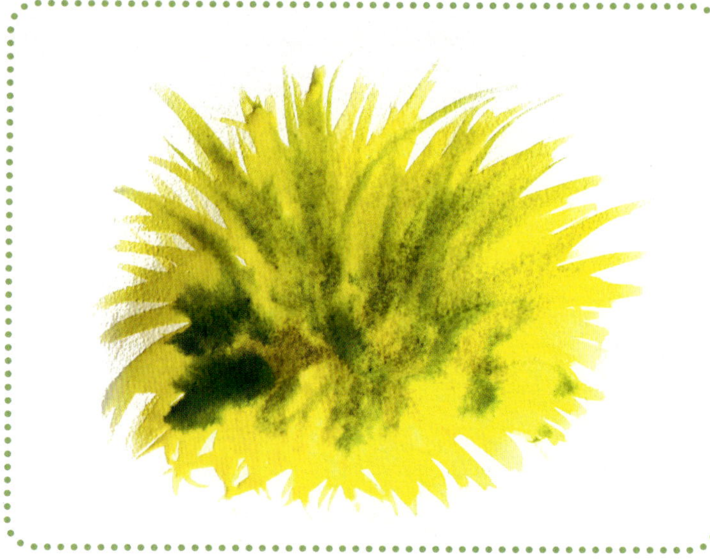

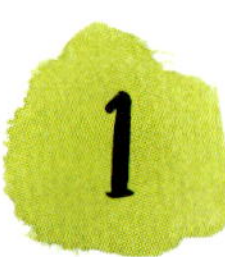

Using a #8 round brush and lots of water, make a simple oval. Then use the tip of your brush to draw the water out toward the edges of the oval and create smaller blades of grass. Remember to move in the direction of growth—upward and outward—and where the plant sits on the ground—downward.

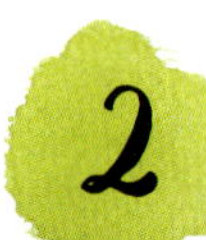

While this area is still wet, go back in with your #8 round brush and add a deeper shade of green. The center of the plant should remain darker than its outer edges; this gives it depth.

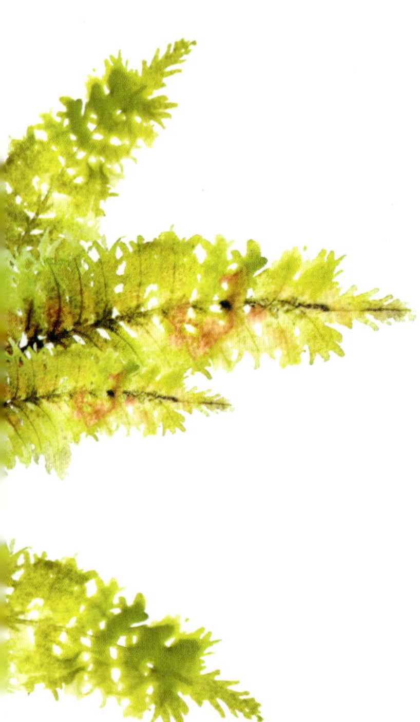

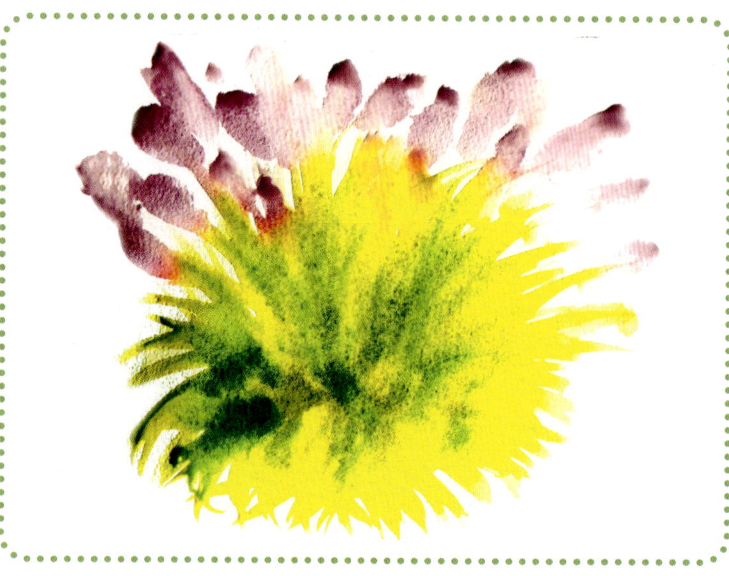

3

While the paint is still wet, dip your #8 brush into violet or another purple hue, and press down with the flat area of the brush to make vertical blooms. These will be fuzzier in the end; for now, you just want to achieve a conical shape.

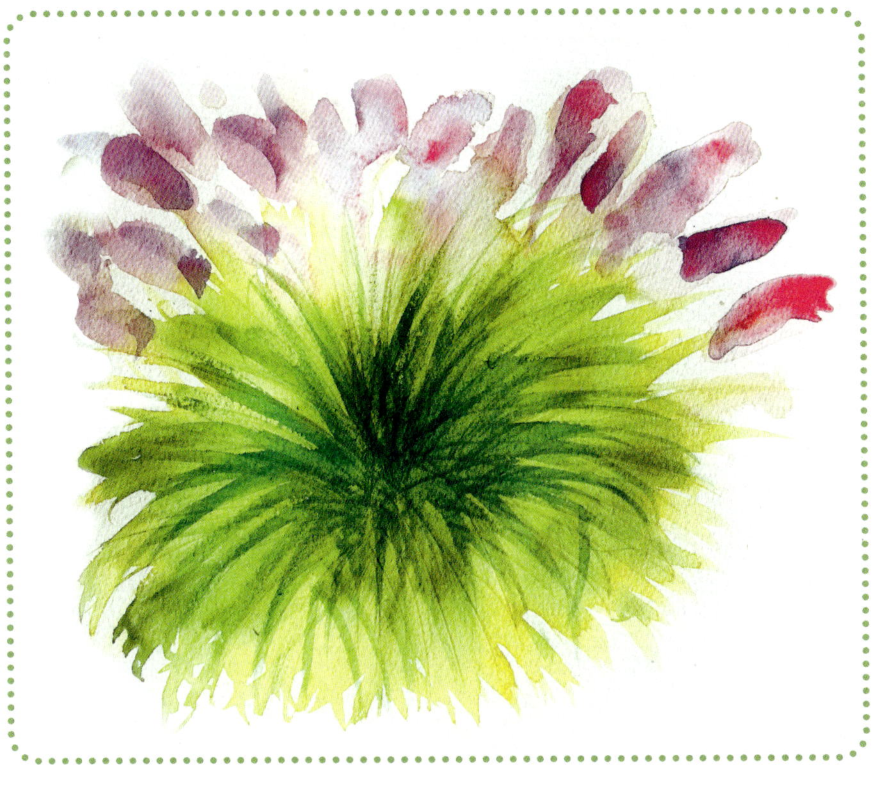

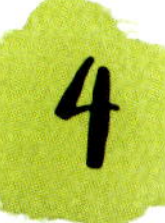

4 Tap another color, such as pink, into the blooms. This is also a good time to score the greenery, using the tip of your brush to add more wisps of green to indicate darker blades of grass.

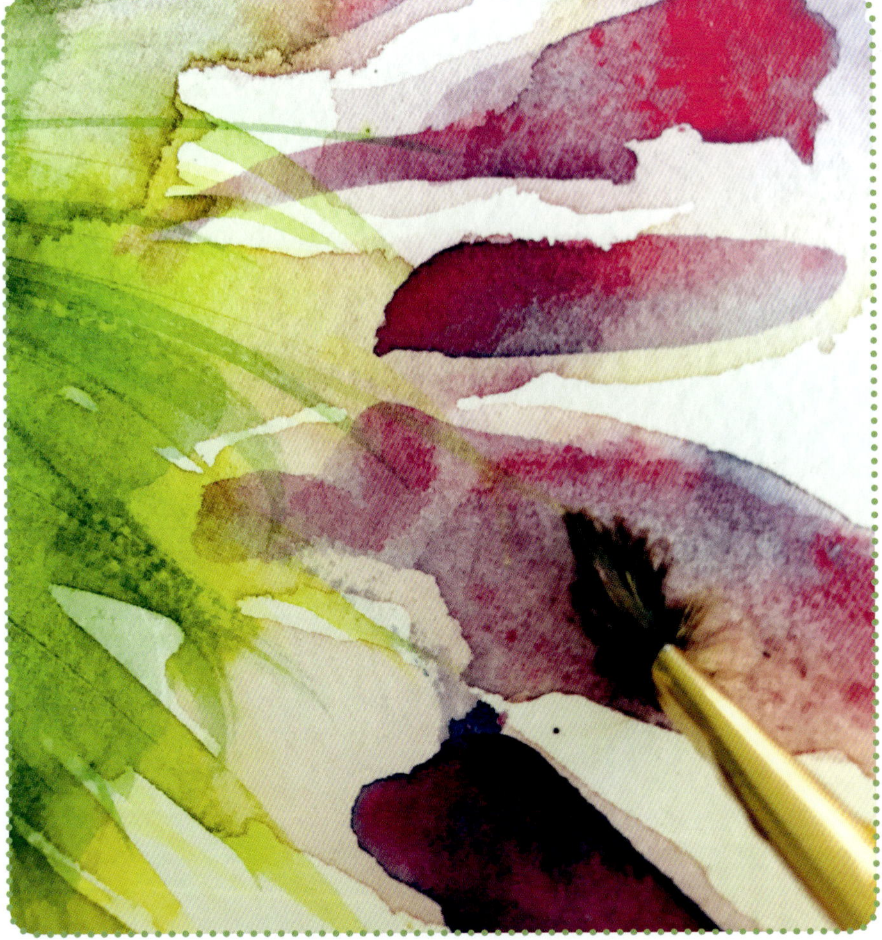

5 Once the paint is completely dry, use a stiff-bristled scrubber brush to remove some of the pigment in the centers of the blooms. This will give the blooms a conical shape by creating a highlight in the center. Working subtly but strategically, dip the scrubber brush into the paint to agitate it. Go back and forth several times and you should see pigment coming up.

Now take a twisted bit of paper towel and wipe away the water in the plant. This area should now be paler than the areas around it.

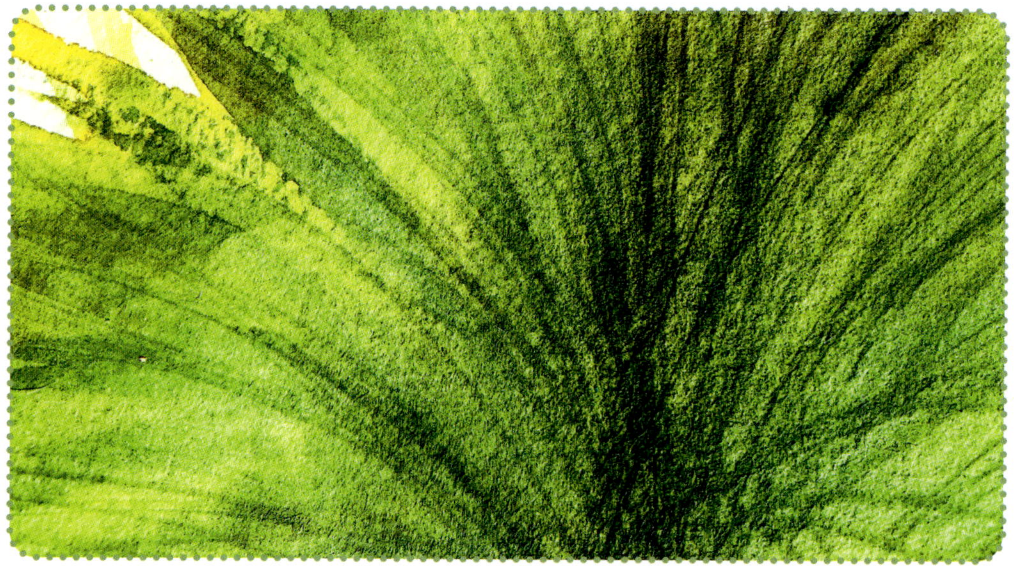

Score the greenery some more, dragging your toothpick up into the blooms. If the center needs darkening, add a bit more color.

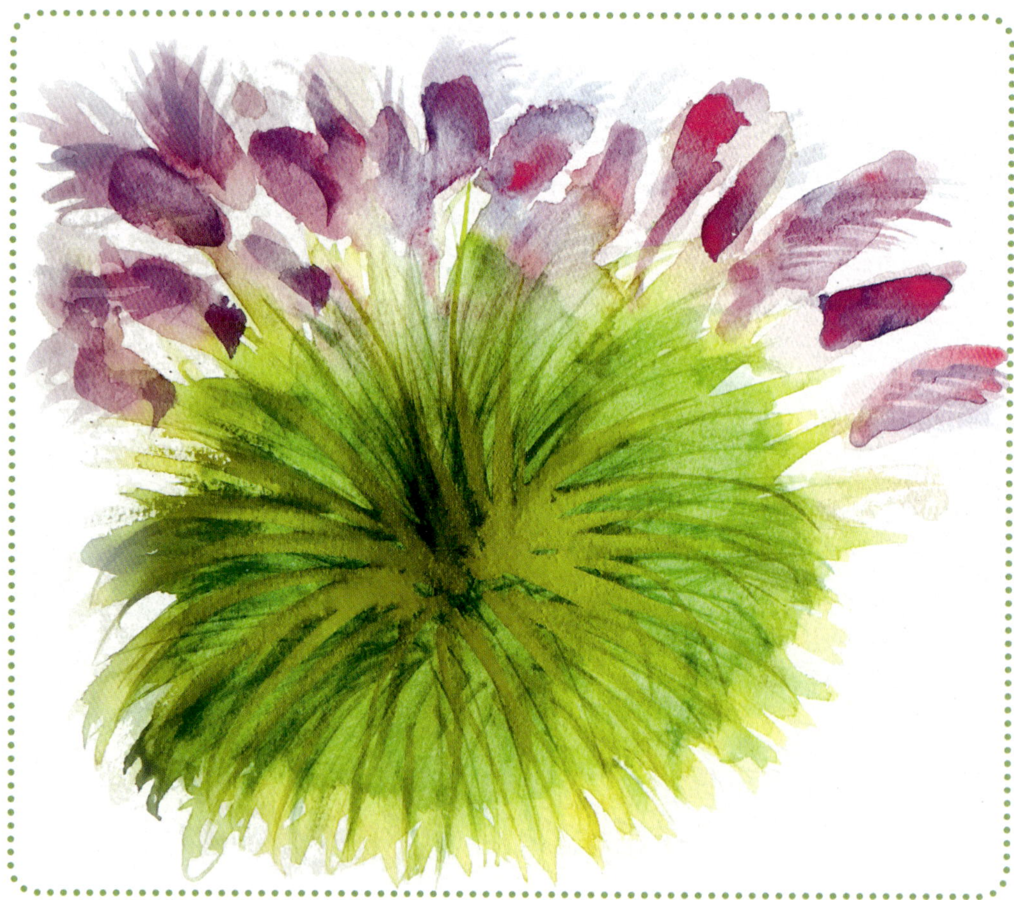

Dip a liner brush into a paler shade of lilac or purple and make fine lines on the blooms. Pampas have soft, featherlike blooms with lots of fine hairs; be sure to go in the direction that they face. The blooms on the outer edges that hang toward the ground will have hairs that face down. The hairs of the upright blooms will be on the right or left side.

WOOD FERN

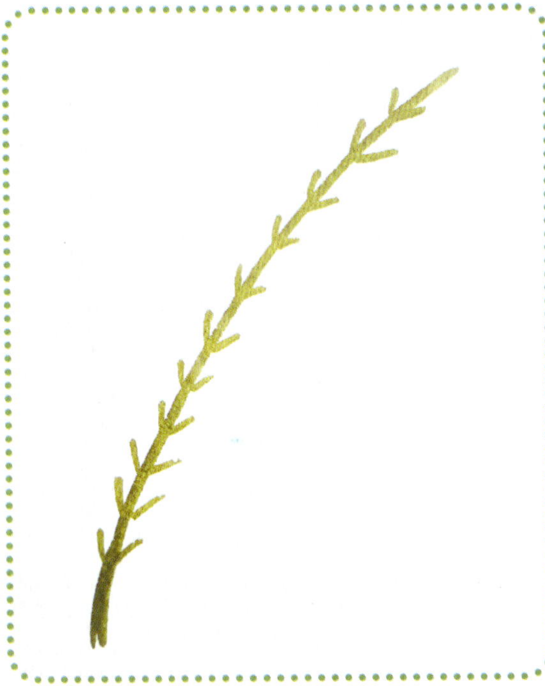

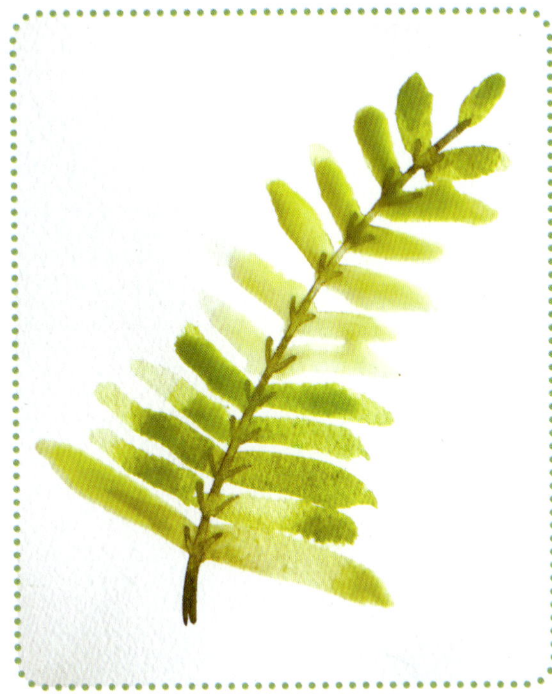

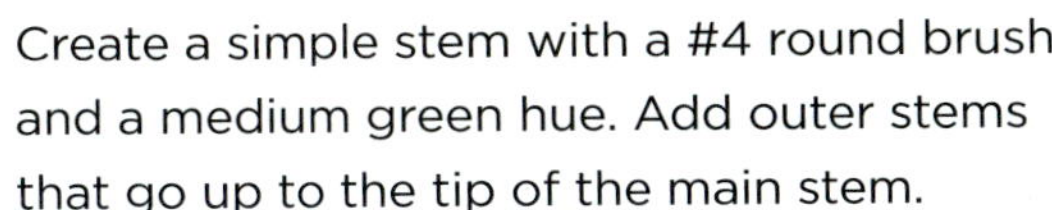

1 Create a simple stem with a #4 round brush and a medium green hue. Add outer stems that go up to the tip of the main stem.

2 Use a #8 round brush to create simple leaves, touching the tip down and bringing the flat of the brush into the center. Let the two colors merge.

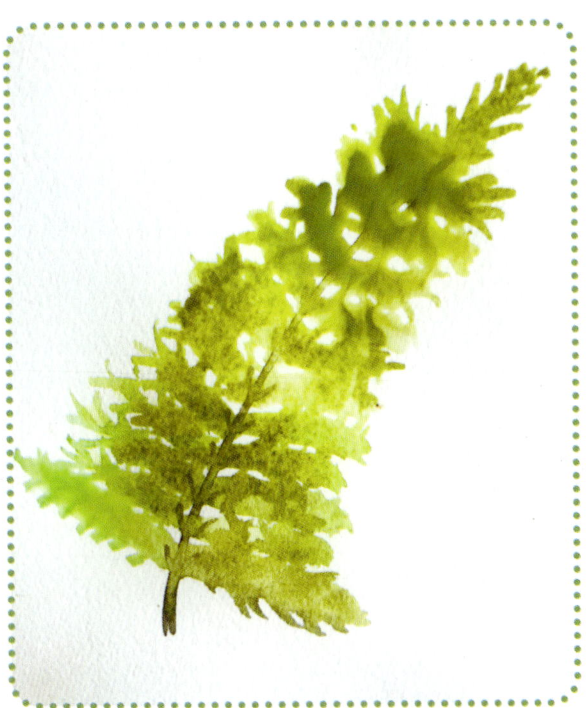

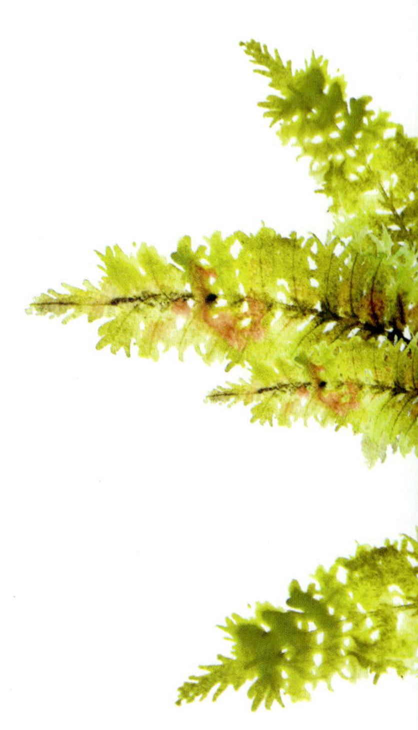

3 While these areas are still wet, grab the #4 round and make small notches on each leaf, moving the tip of the brush around so that each notch appears to grow outward. Do this all the way up the fern on each leaf.

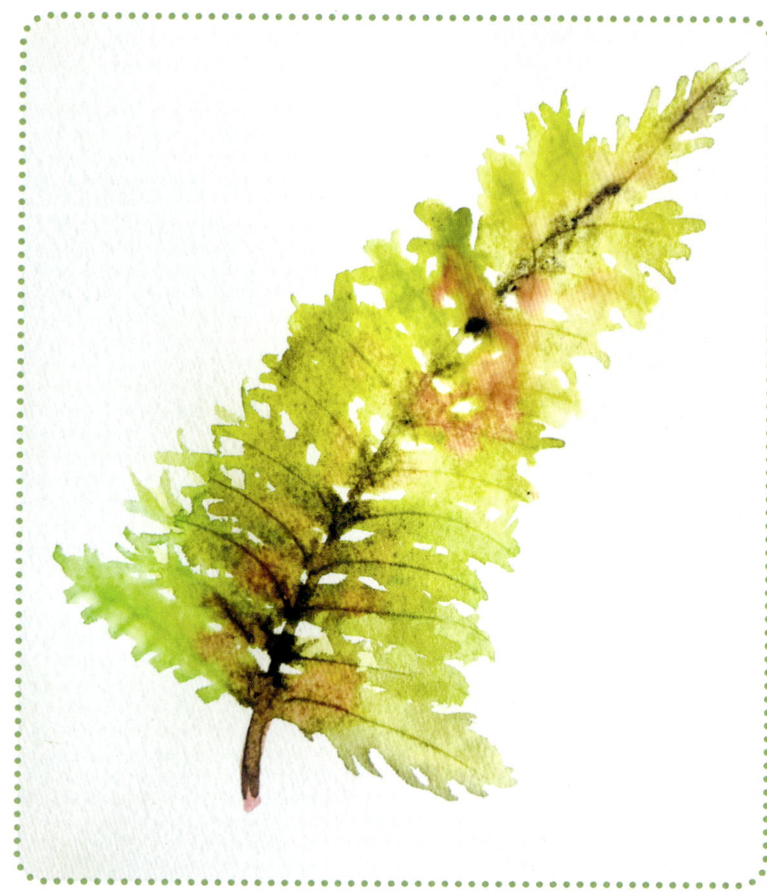

4

Dip your #8 round brush into some burnt umber or another shade of brown, and make a tapered stem by lightening your pressure on the brush as you move toward the tip of the stem.

5

While the brown paint is wet, tap some violet paint into the tip of your brush and add smaller branches to the main stem. Tap a little violet paint into the main stem too, letting the two colors flow into each other.

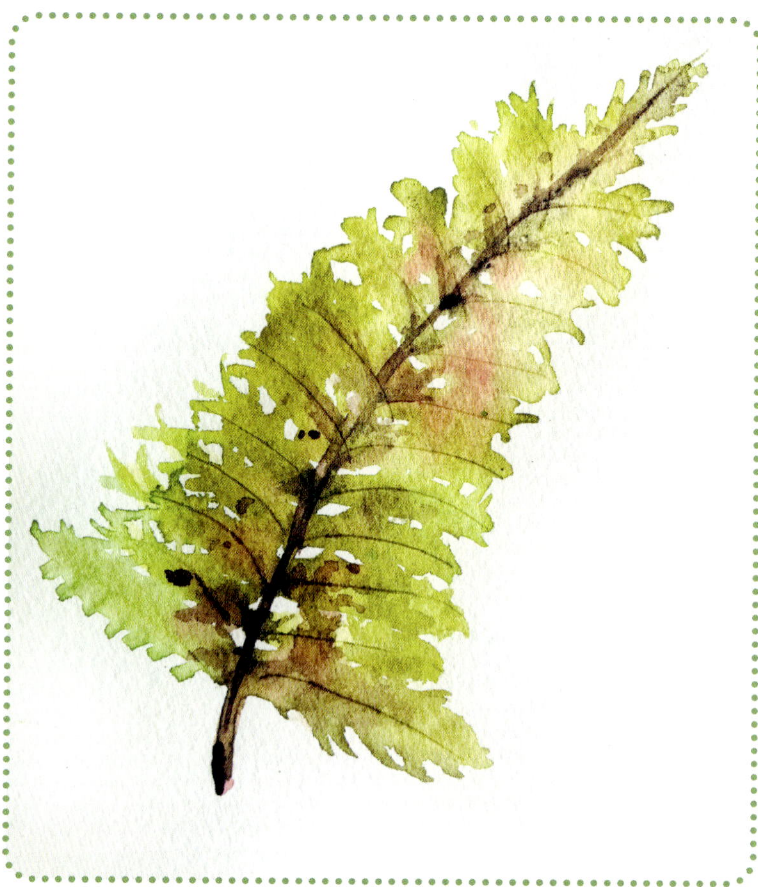

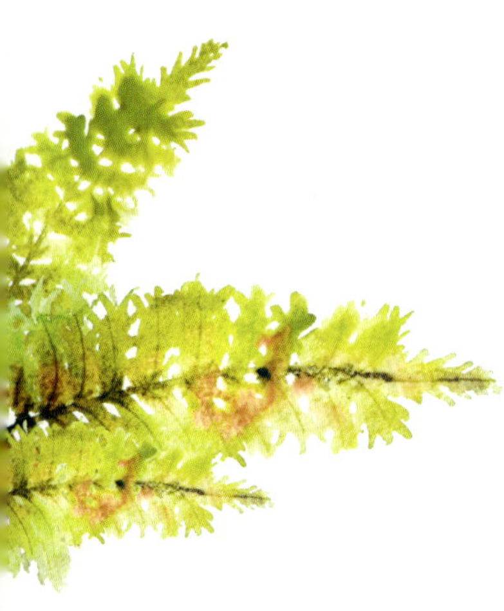

BASIC ROCK

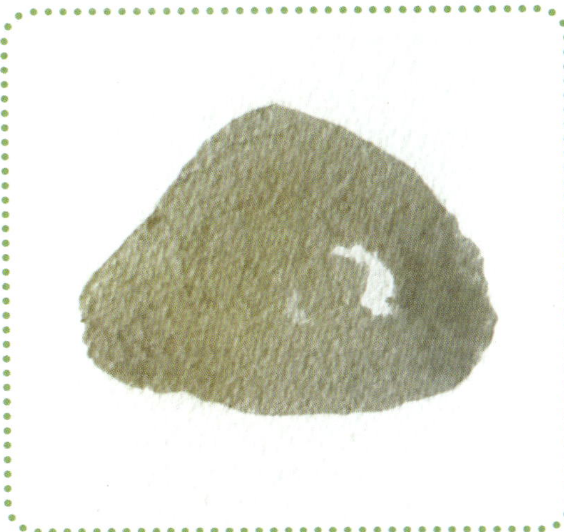

1

Using some dirty water (see page 25) or warm gray and a #10 round or Filbert brush, make a rounded triangular shape for the mass of the rock. Leave a small area of paper uncovered to create an eventual highlight.

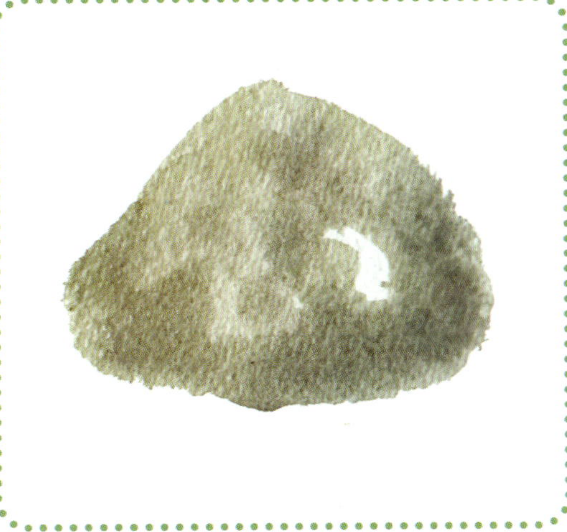

2

While the wash is wet, tap darker gray into different areas of the rock, applying the gray more heavily at the base of the rock. See how the pigment travels. Rocks have a mottled pattern, so have fun here!

Experiment with different hues if you like. If you look closely at a rock, you often see varying shades of reds, greens, and blues, even when the overall appearance is gray.

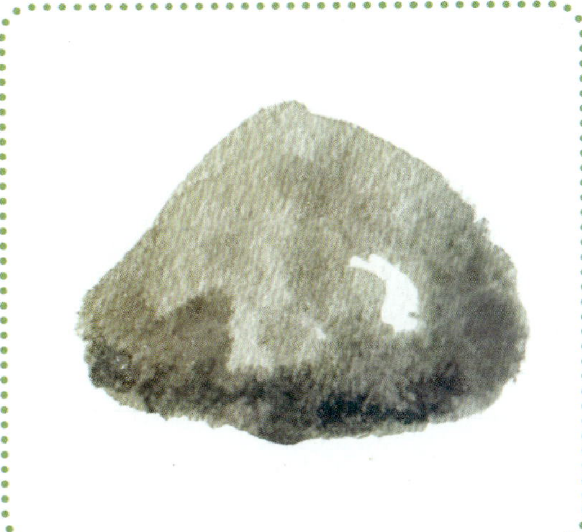

3

When the brush is partly dry, dip it into diluted black and add color to the base of the rock. Since the paper is now partly dry, you will see more pronounced contrast with the possibility of a blossom. Rocks offer a great opportunity to play with texture.

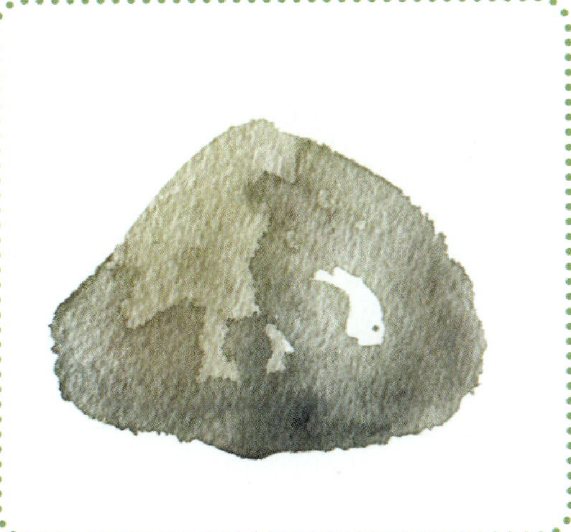

4

Sometimes, when the rock dries, the contrast looks less pronounced than with wet paint. If you like, you can go back in and add more contrast. But go lightly at first, as the paper is dry and the wash will not blend.

I'm happy with leaving my rock as it is. I like how it dried, especially with the way the paint danced about in the center area. The highlight is a nice touch!

BEACH ROCK

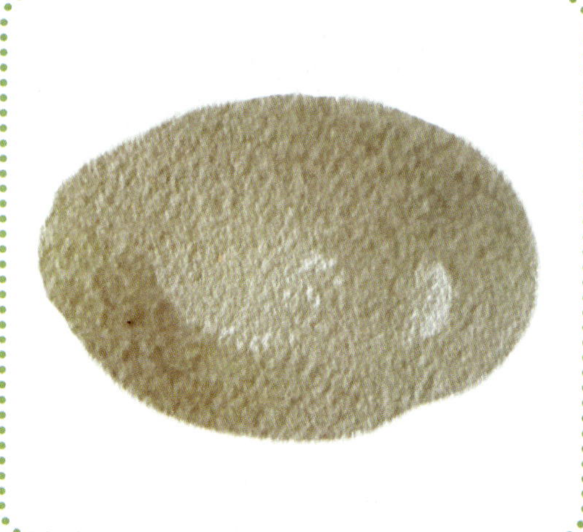

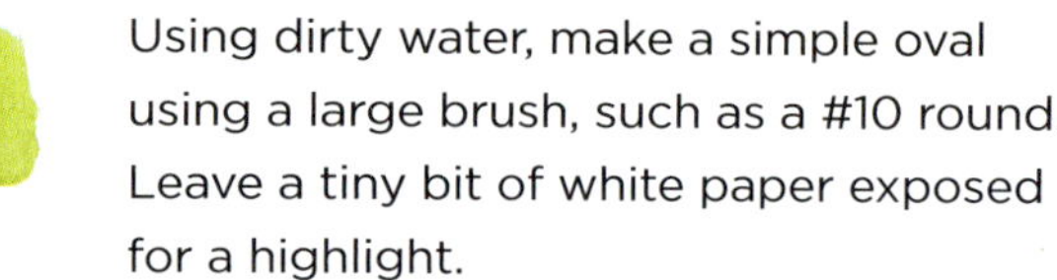

1 Using dirty water, make a simple oval using a large brush, such as a #10 round. Leave a tiny bit of white paper exposed for a highlight.

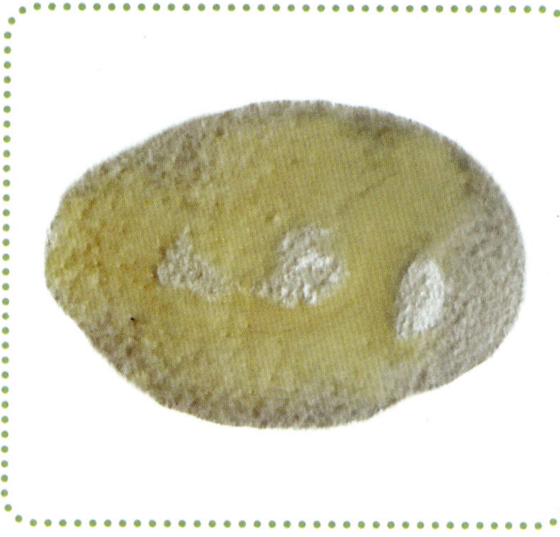

2 Now tap raw umber or another warm brown hue into the wet paint.

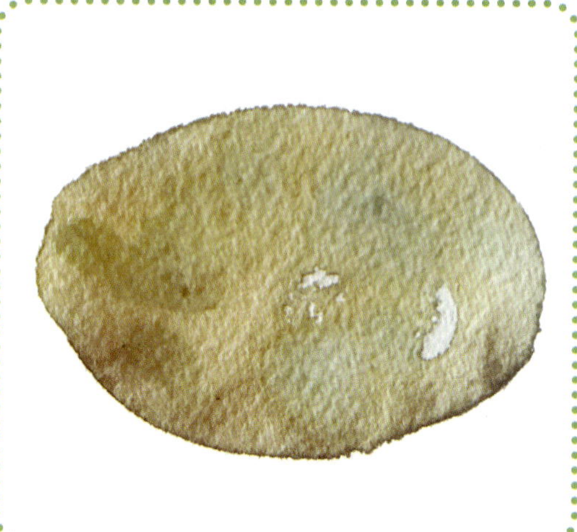

3 Keep tapping the tip of your brush into the wet paint using different colors like orange, mossy green, and blue. Allow these to dry before moving to the next step.

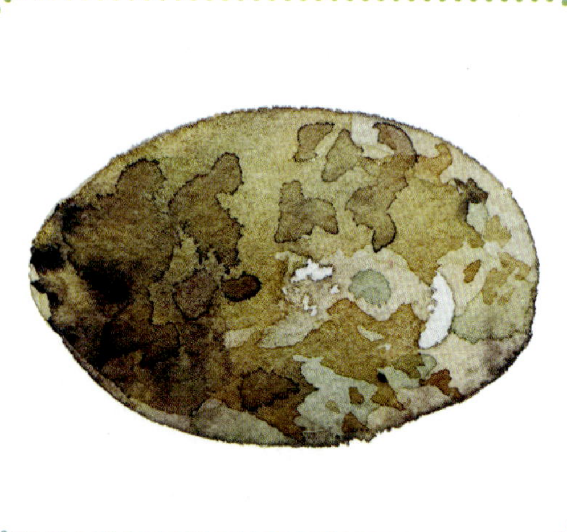

4 Now that the rock is dry, it's time to add some contrast. Dip your brush into sepia paint and begin dotting the surface. I love how this step really brings out the subtleties of the previous additions of color, and that little highlight gives the rock a great sense of dimension.

GNEISS ROCK

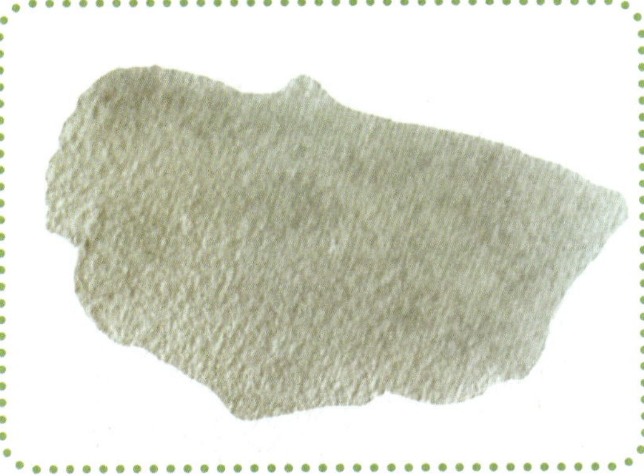

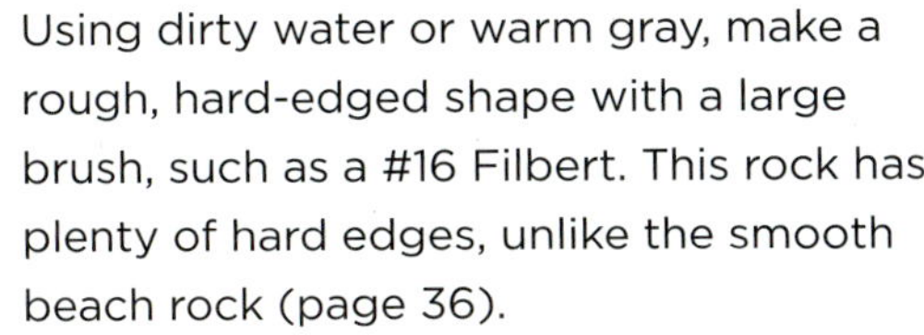

1 Using dirty water or warm gray, make a rough, hard-edged shape with a large brush, such as a #16 Filbert. This rock has plenty of hard edges, unlike the smooth beach rock (page 36).

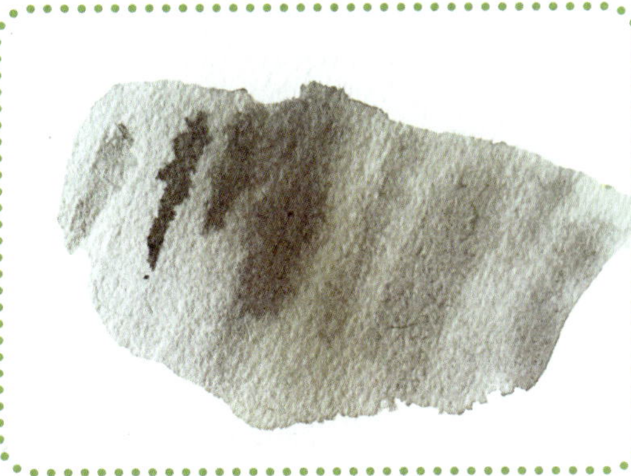

2 While the paint is still wet, add a black wash to the surface. Let the paint bleed and blend into the first wash.

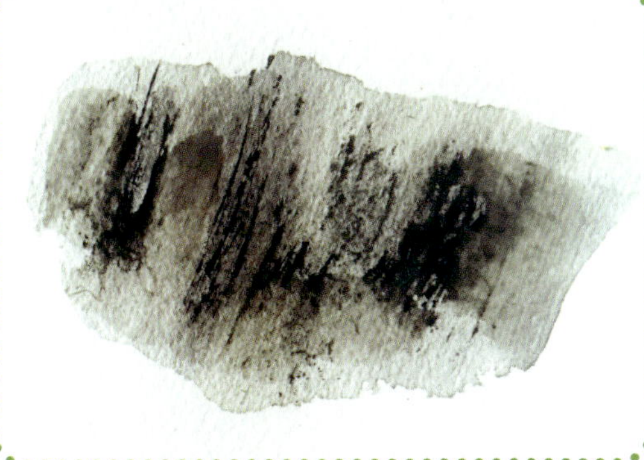

3 Let the paint dry completely; then, with a dry mop, squirrel, or round brush, lightly touch the brush into black paint right out of the pan. Test it on scrap paper first; otherwise, the paint can look a bit heavy-handed. You want the bristles to have some pigment on each hair so that you achieve separated detail without creating a giant blob. Scrape the brush over the rock and let the texture of the paper pick up the black. Gneiss rocks feature interesting striations.

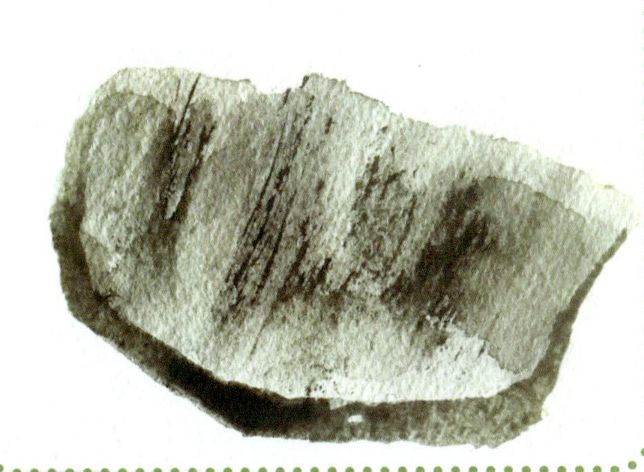

4 For your final touch, give the rock some dimension. Follow the contours of the rock's bottom side with a black wash, making sure the bottom of the rock has some hard angles. You may want to practice tapping more black into the midsection to give it more depth.

FAWN MUSHROOM

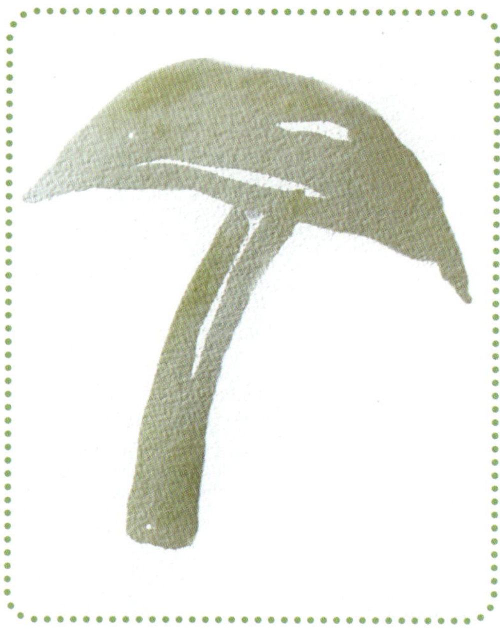

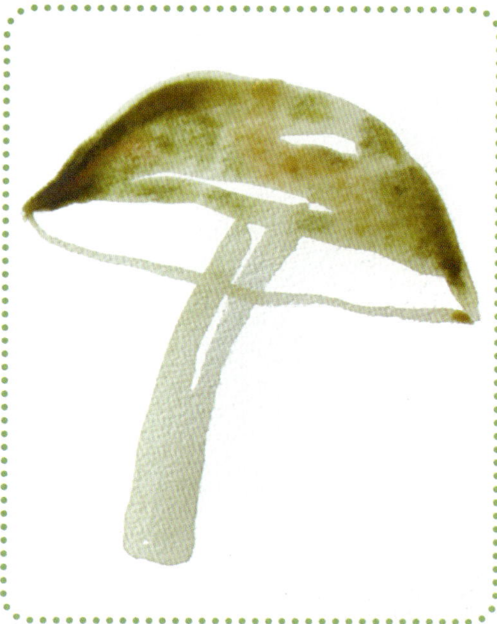

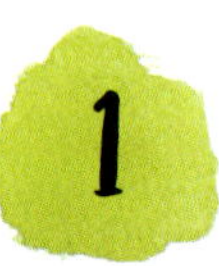

Using a #8 round brush and dirty water, make a simple cap and stem shape, leaving a small area of white paper on both the cap and the stem to act as highlights.

2

While the wash is still wet, tap assorted shades of browns and oranges into the mushroom cap. Let the colors move about to create a mottled pattern. Then, with the tip of your brush, finish the underside of the cap shape. Let the wet paint from the cap seep into the outer edges of the line. Let the paint dry.

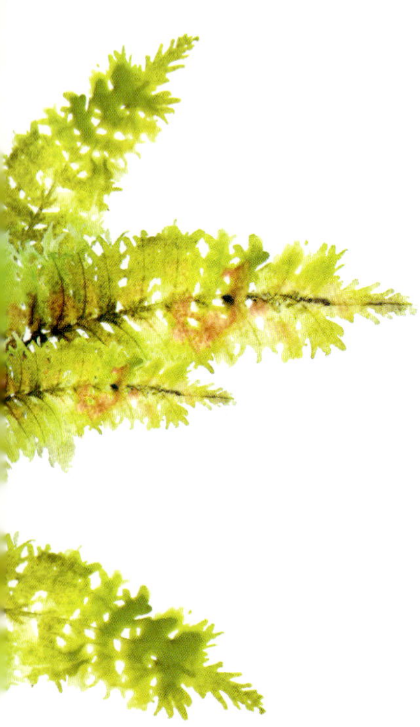

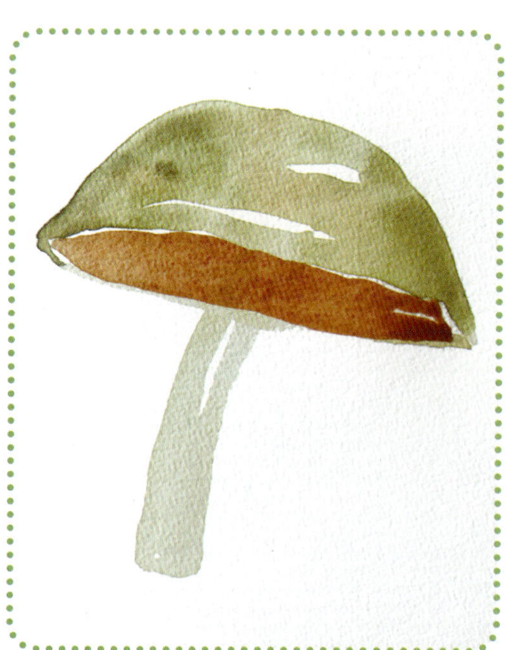

3

With warm brown mixed with orange (I've used raw umber mixed with Windsor orange), fill in the underside of the cap.

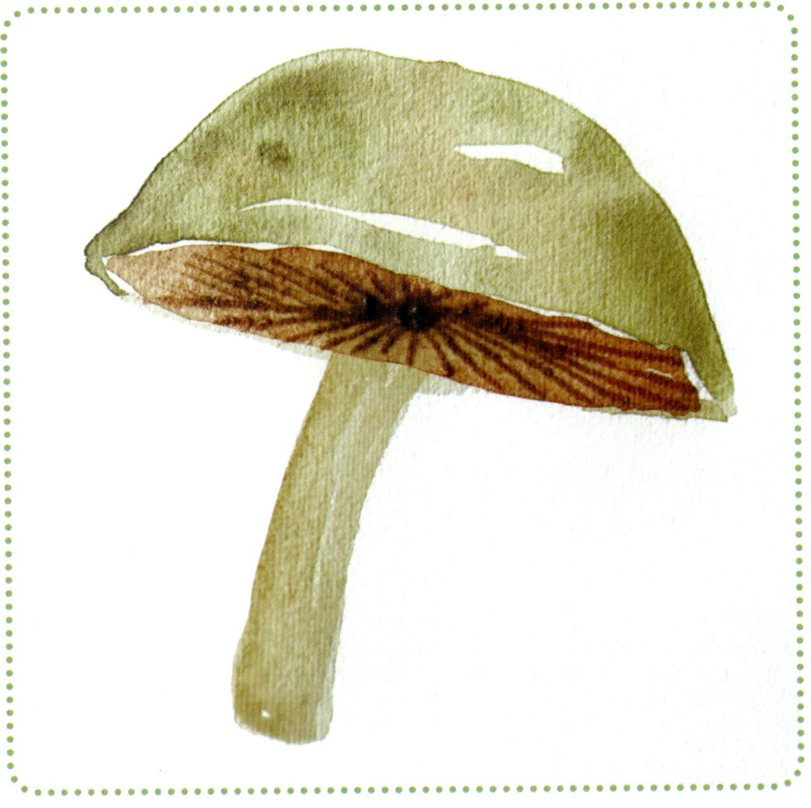

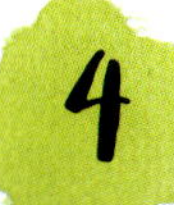

Use a toothpick to score the mushroom's gills. Start at the center and work outward in a starburst pattern. While the paint is still wet, tap your brush into sepia paint and give the center of the mushroom a flood of color to add depth.

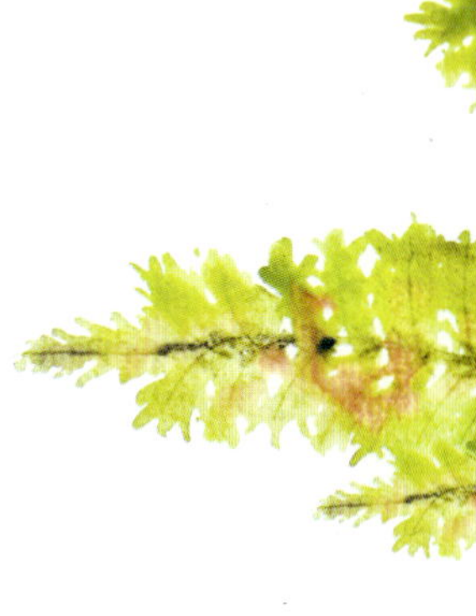

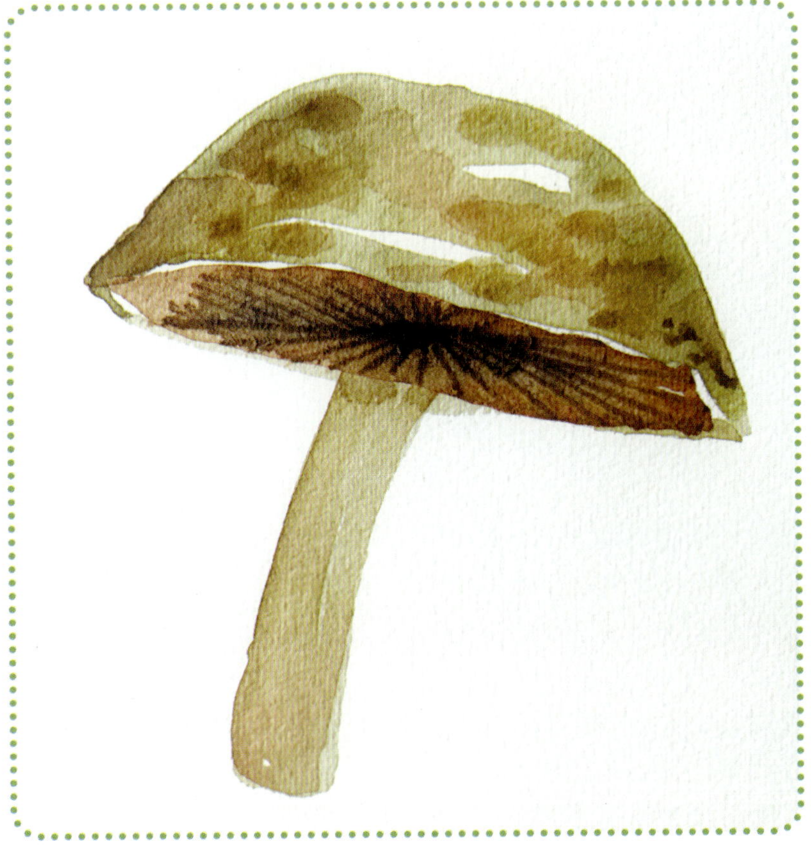

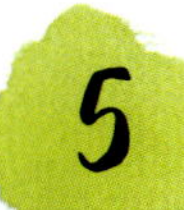

Going back to the cap, use the colors you've already mixed to create additional mottling so that you see more contrast with the already-dry layer. You can also add subtle shadows beneath the cap and base of the stem if you like.

AMANITA MUSHROOM

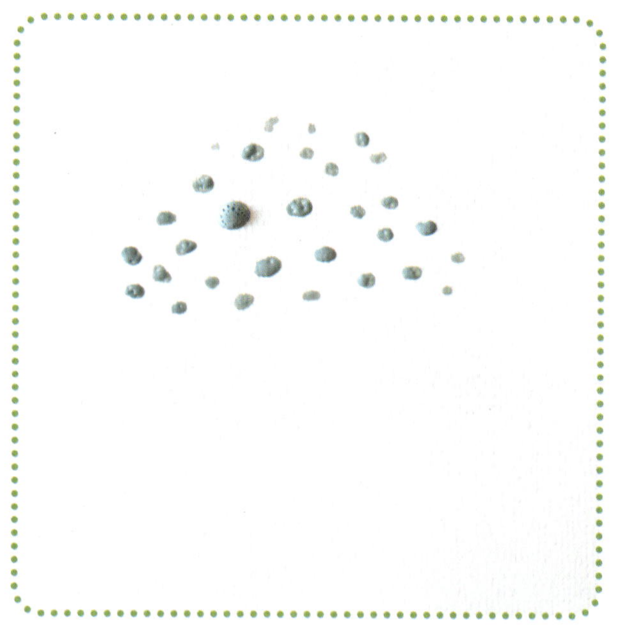

1 Use the bottom of a small brush and masking fluid to tap dots into a mushroom-cap shape. Form bigger dots in the center and smaller ones at the edges. Let the masking fluid dry thoroughly.

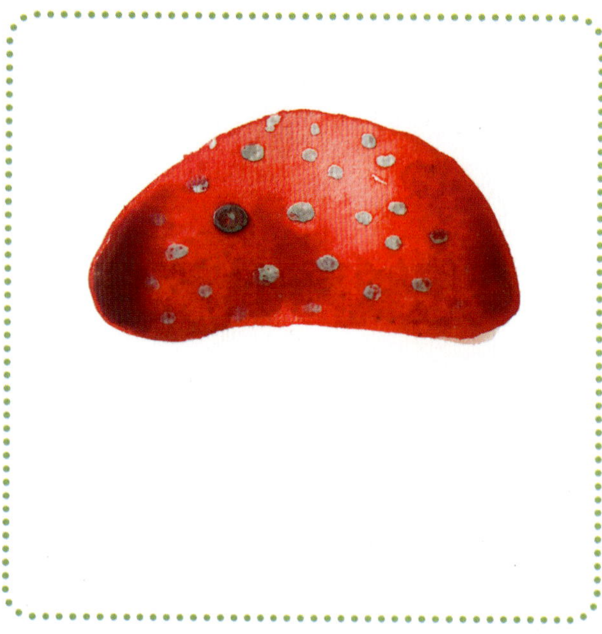

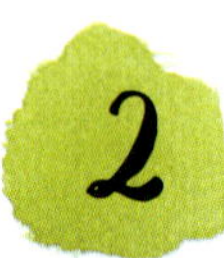

Load a #10 round brush with red paint and create a cap shape. Flood the shape with water and tap darker red into the corners of the cap.

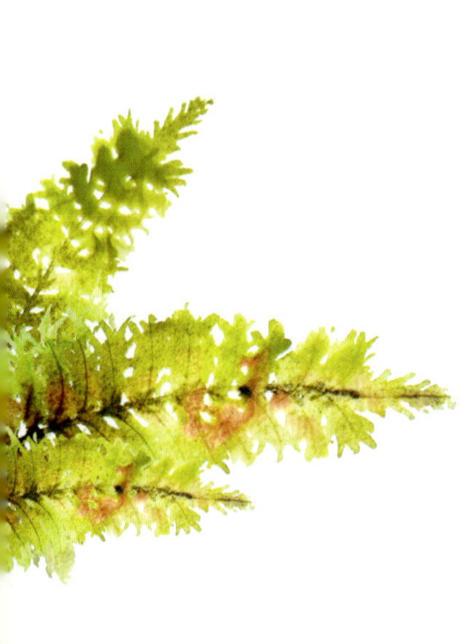

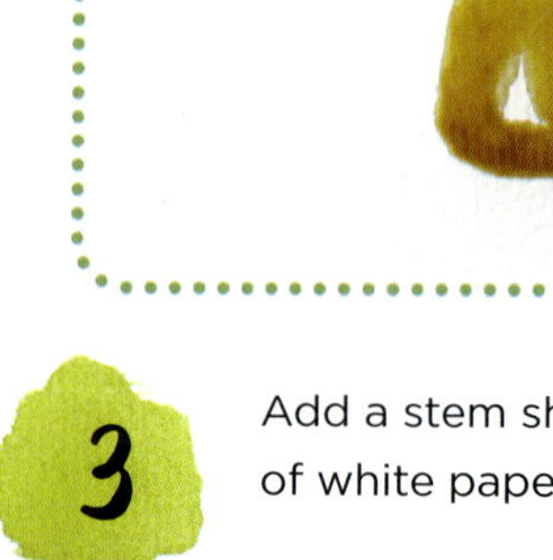

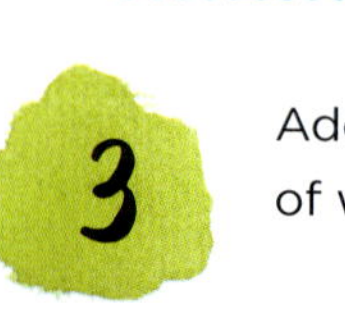

Add a stem shape, leaving a small patch of white paper for a highlight.

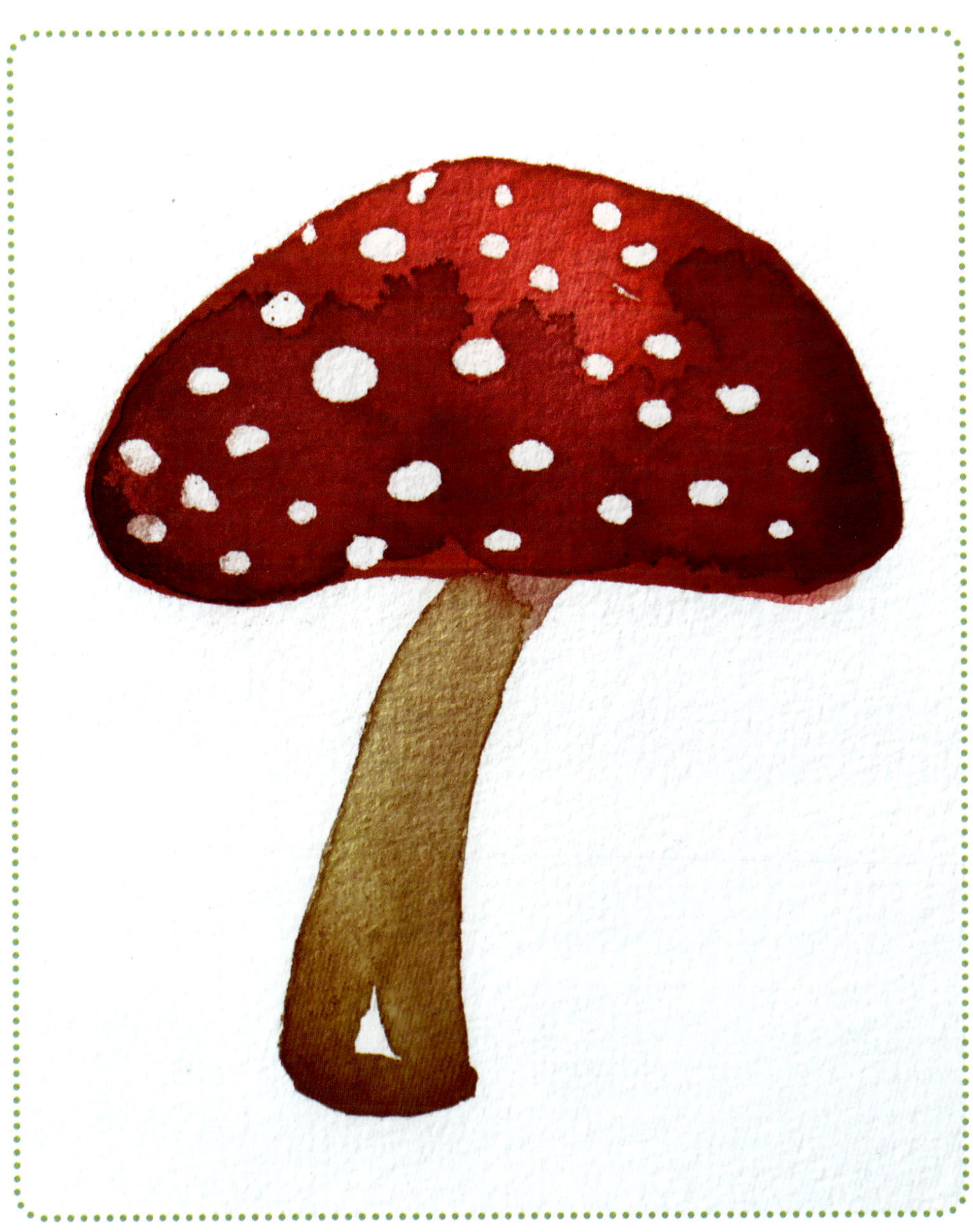

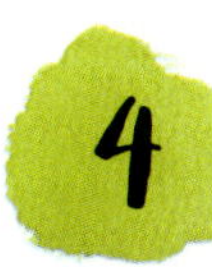

Remove the masking fluid with a rubber cement eraser to reveal the hallmark dots of this special mushroom, which is often depicted in children's fairy-tales.

MOREL MUSHROOM

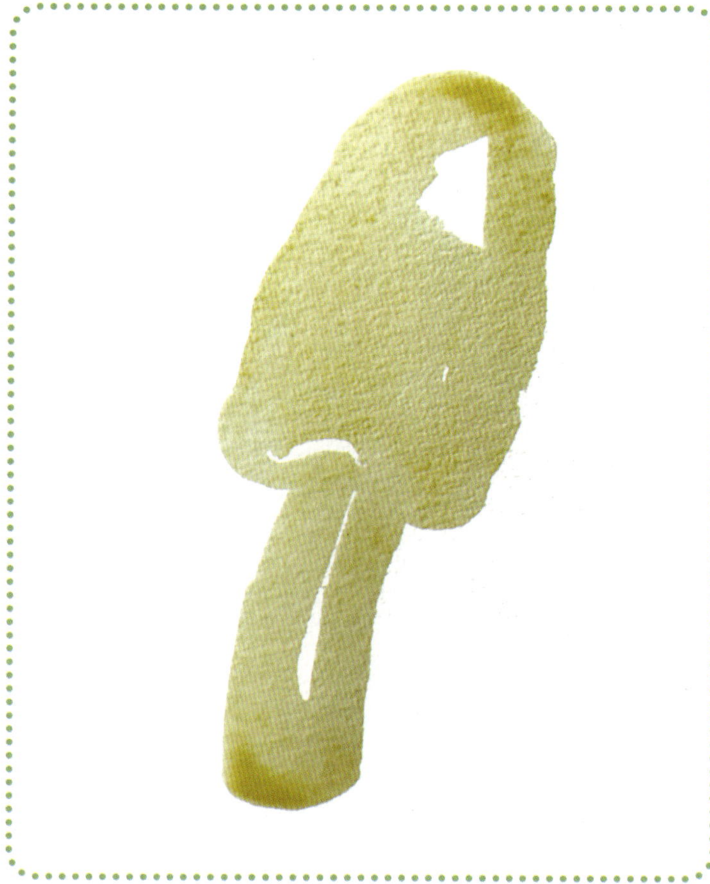

1 With watered-down raw umber, make an elongated mushroom cap and stem, leaving a small white patch of paper in both areas.

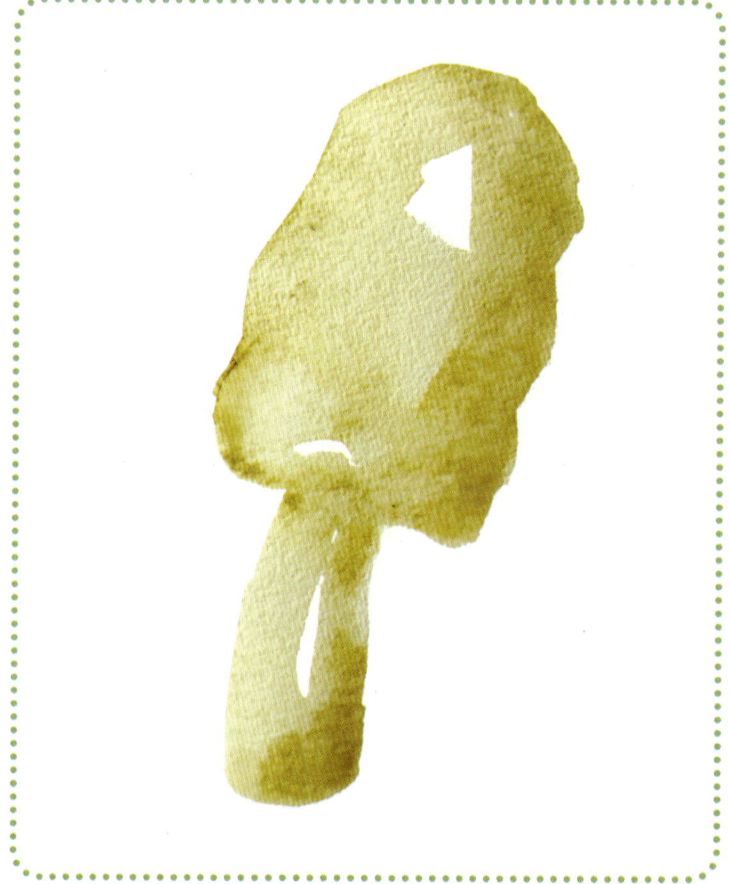

2 While the paint is still wet, use the tip of your brush to create angled edges on the sides of the mushroom cap. Morels have a more geometric appearance than some sloped varieties. Tap some more opaque raw umber into the edges and base of the stem.

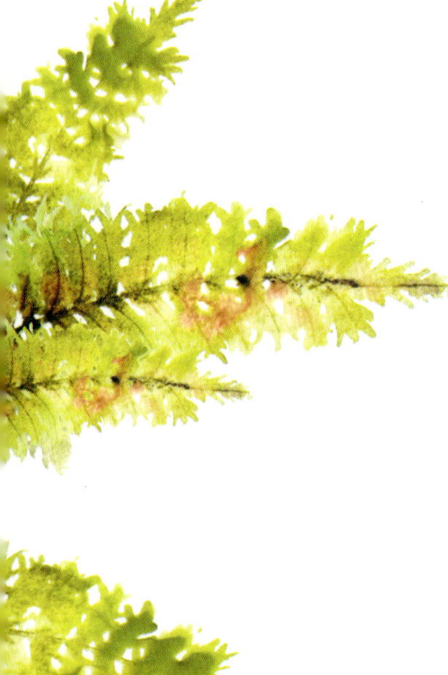

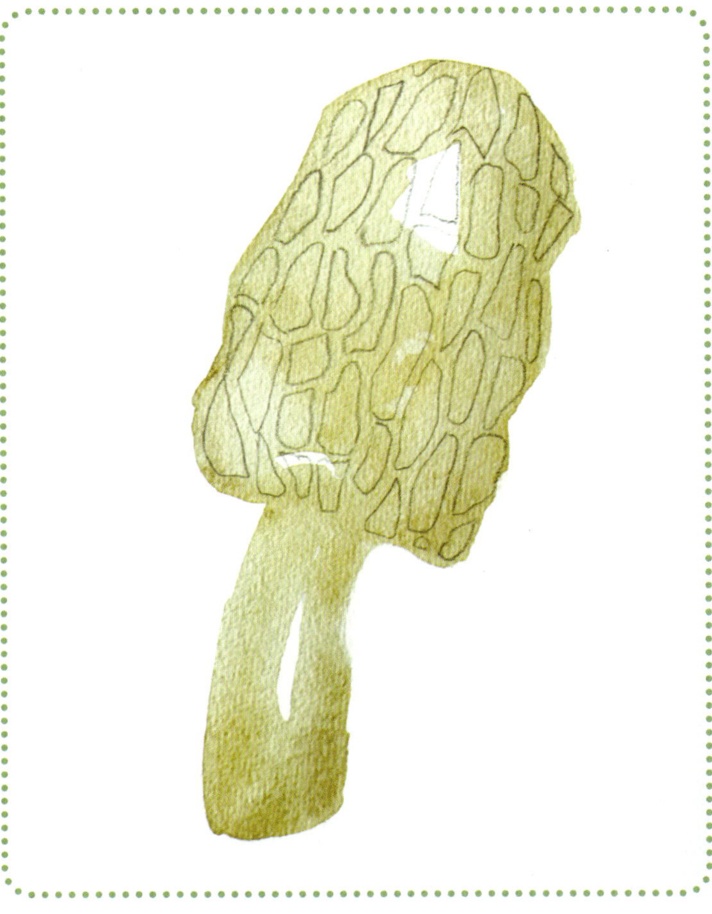

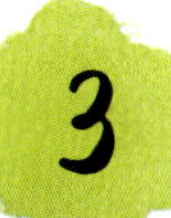

This is a more difficult mushroom to depict, so I've used pencil to sketch the recessed pits and create the honeycomblike pattern in the morel before painting it.

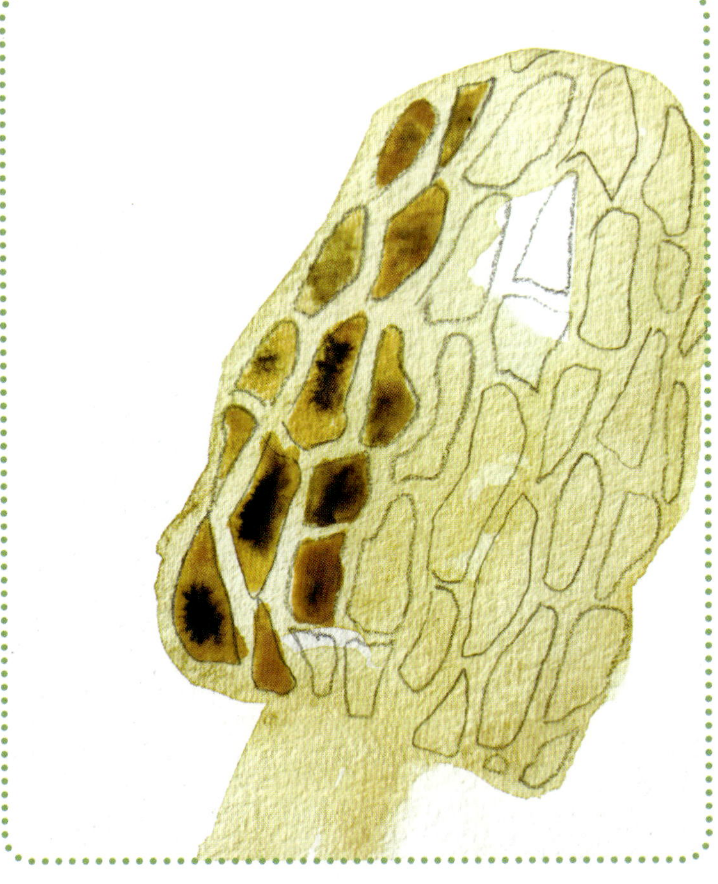

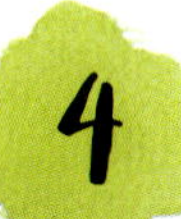

Use the tip of a #4 round brush to apply paint to the pits. Keep the paint mixture wet and tap sepia into the centers of the pits to create the illusion of depth. Complete this step in sections so that the paint doesn't dry too quickly. Let the paint dry completely before continuing.

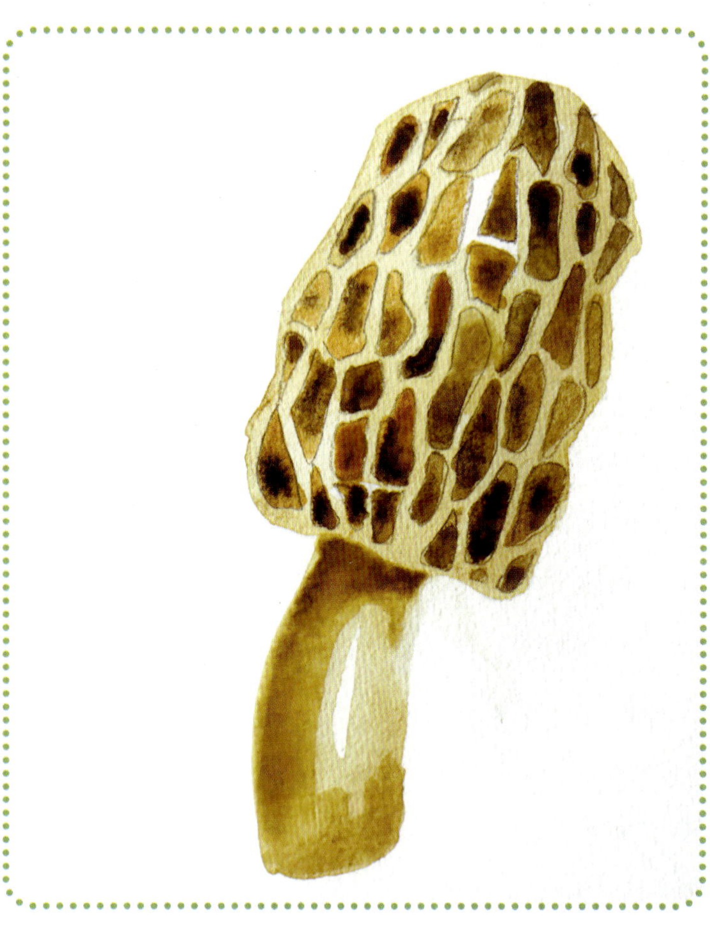

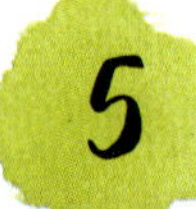

Now let's move on to the stem. Using sepia, create a wash with a #8 round brush. Gently start with the tip of the brush beneath the cap and bring it down along the left part of the stem to the base. This will add roundness to the stem and make the highlight more pronounced. Let the paint dry completely.

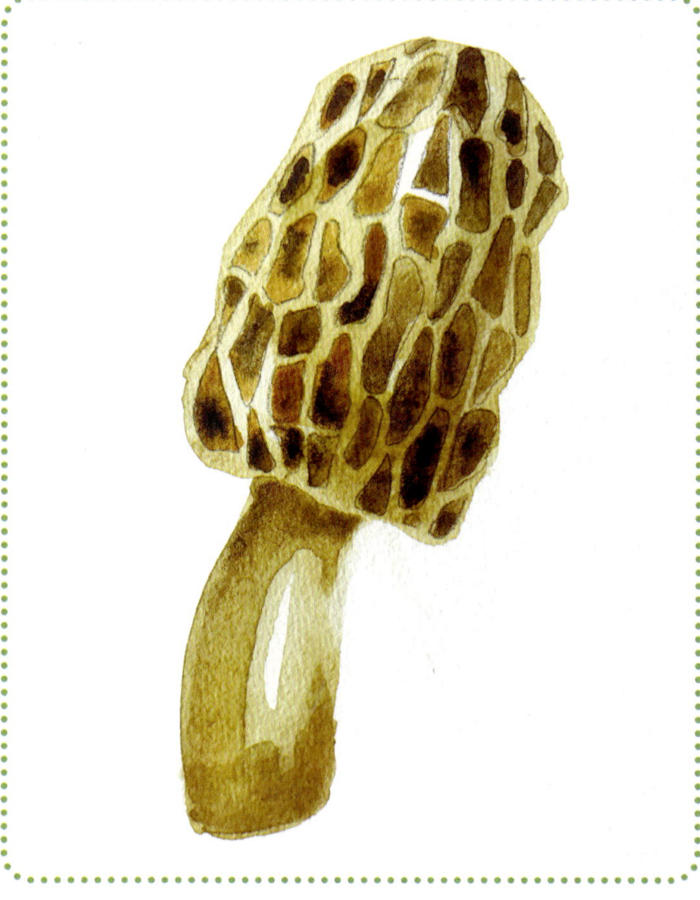

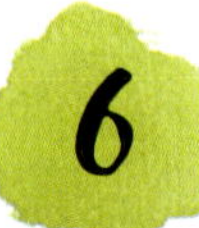

With a #16 Filbert brush and a wash of raw umber, make one broad, vertical swipe in the center of the mushroom cap. This will give the cap a more unified and conical look, and then you're all done!

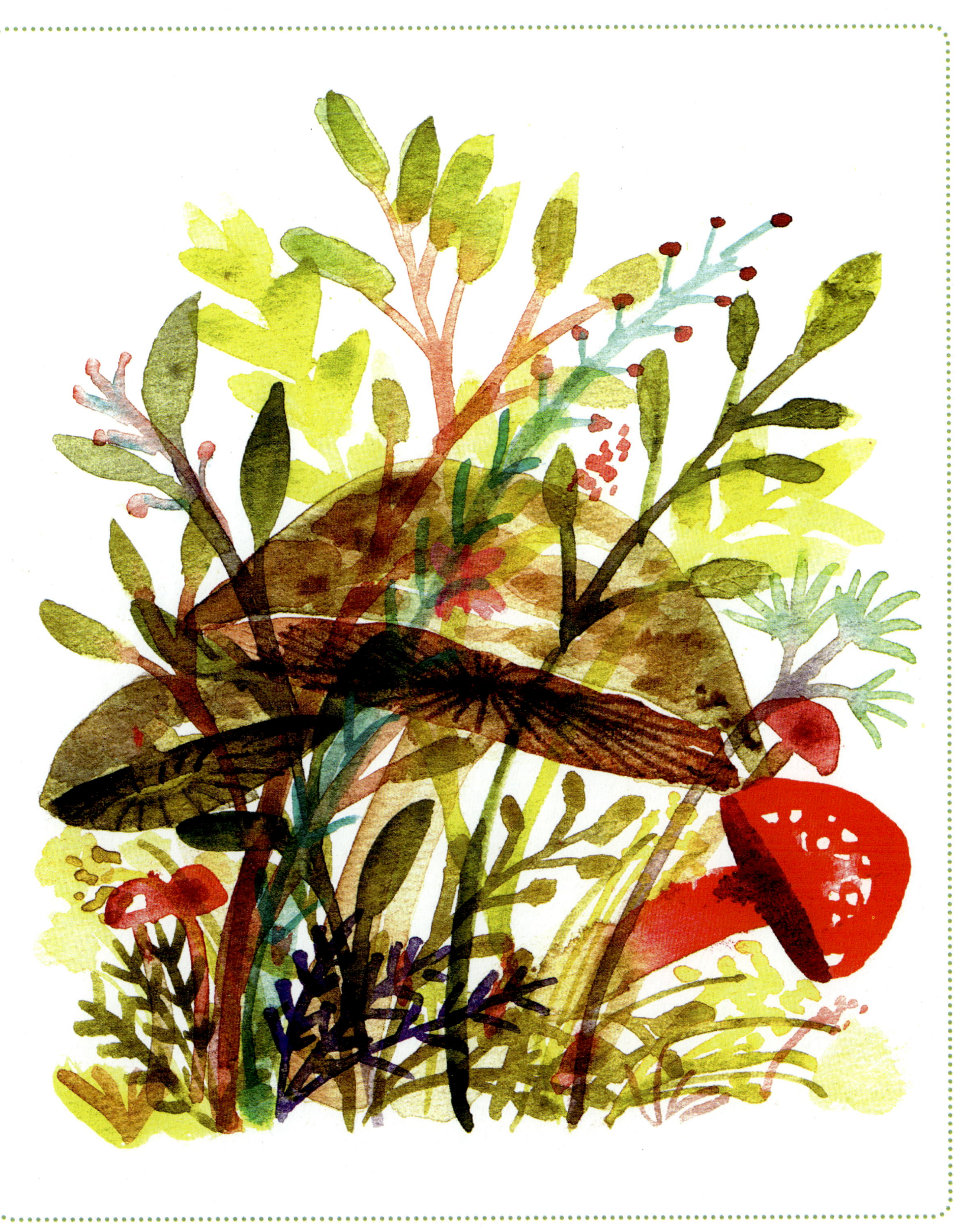

Flowers: Buds, Stems & Blooms

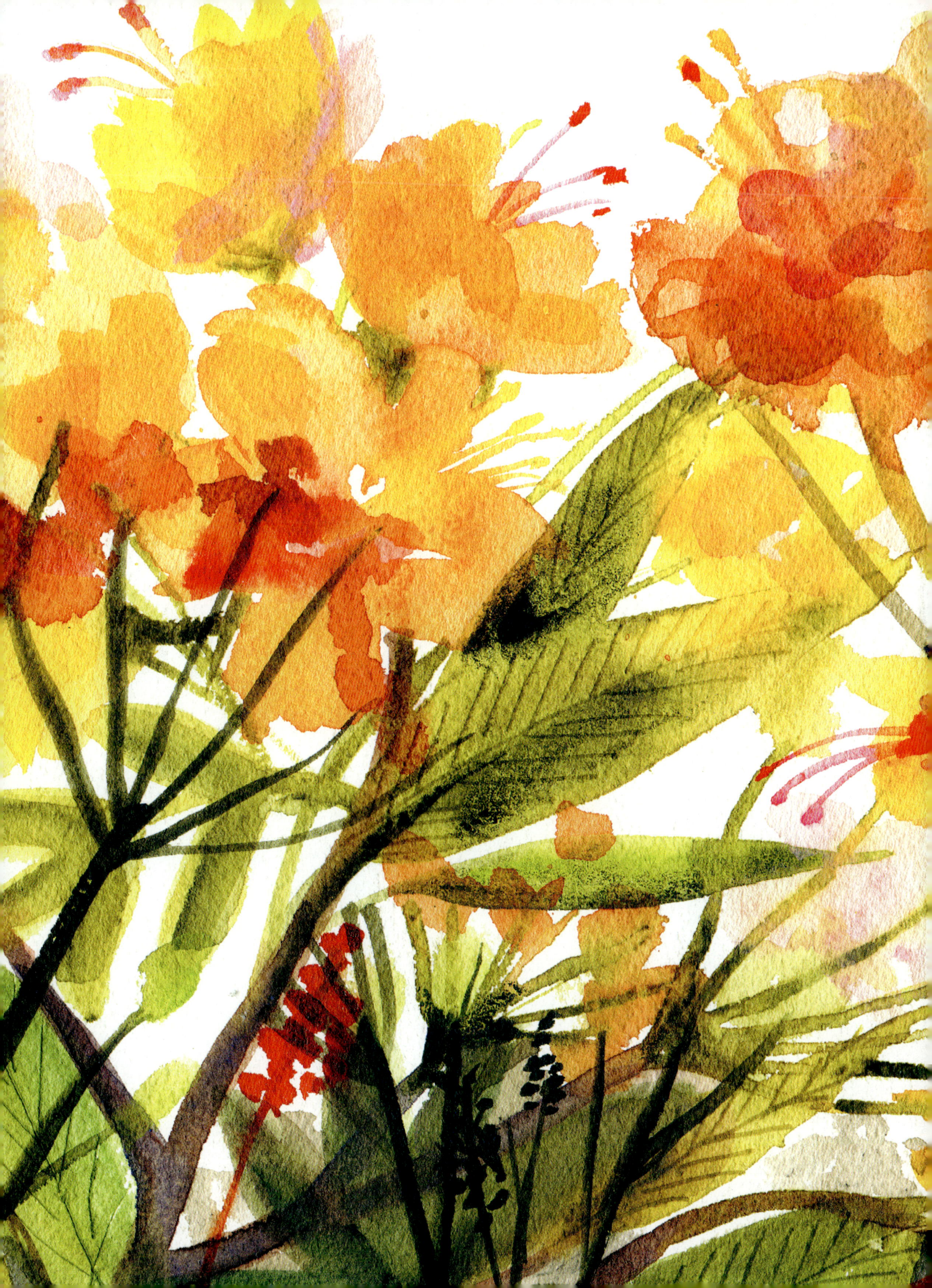

CHILEAN FIRE TREE

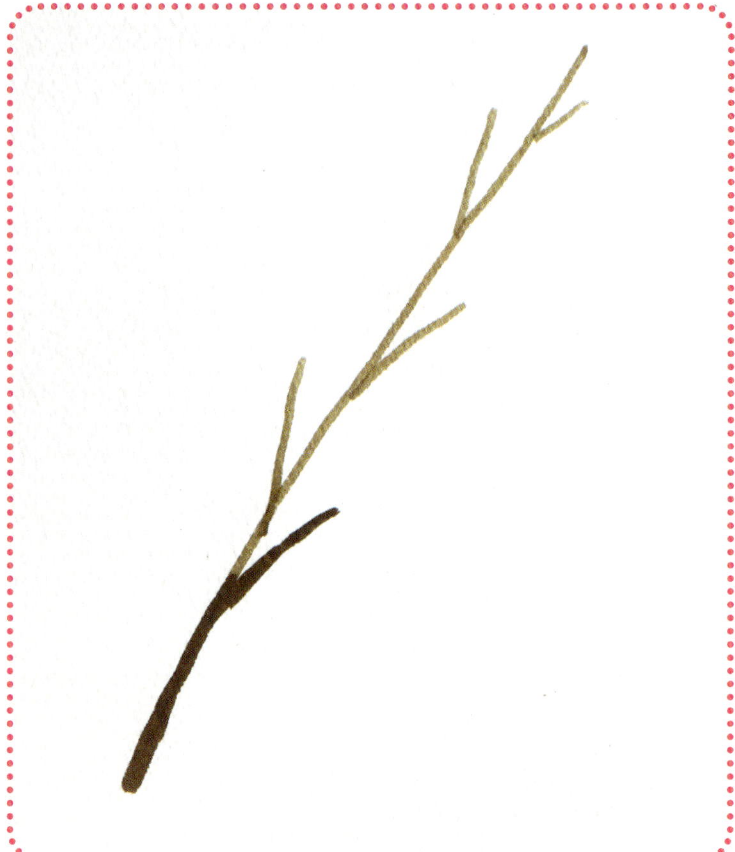

1 With a liner brush and raw umber or another shade of brown, create a simple stem with offshoots.

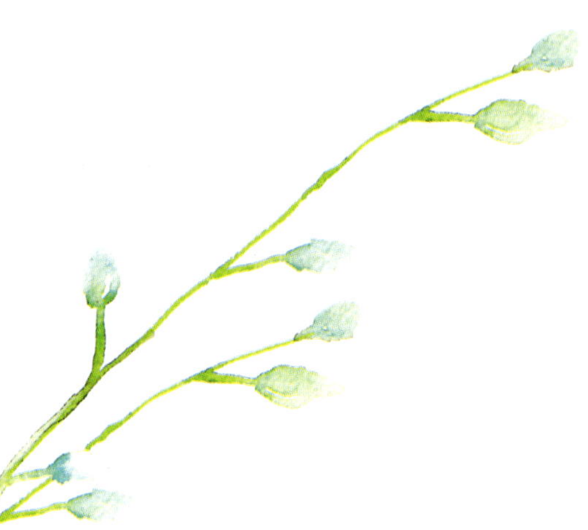

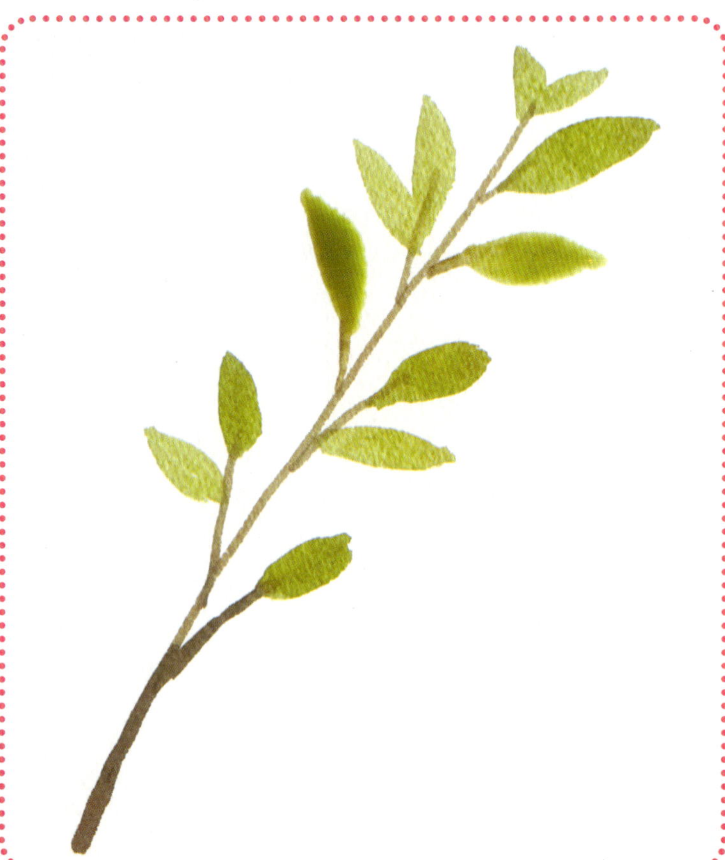

2 Using a #8 round brush, start at the tip of the stem and then move down, pressing to create small petals with the widest part closest to the stem. The greens and browns may meld together if the paint is wet, or the lighter green will overlay the darker stem. Both are fine!

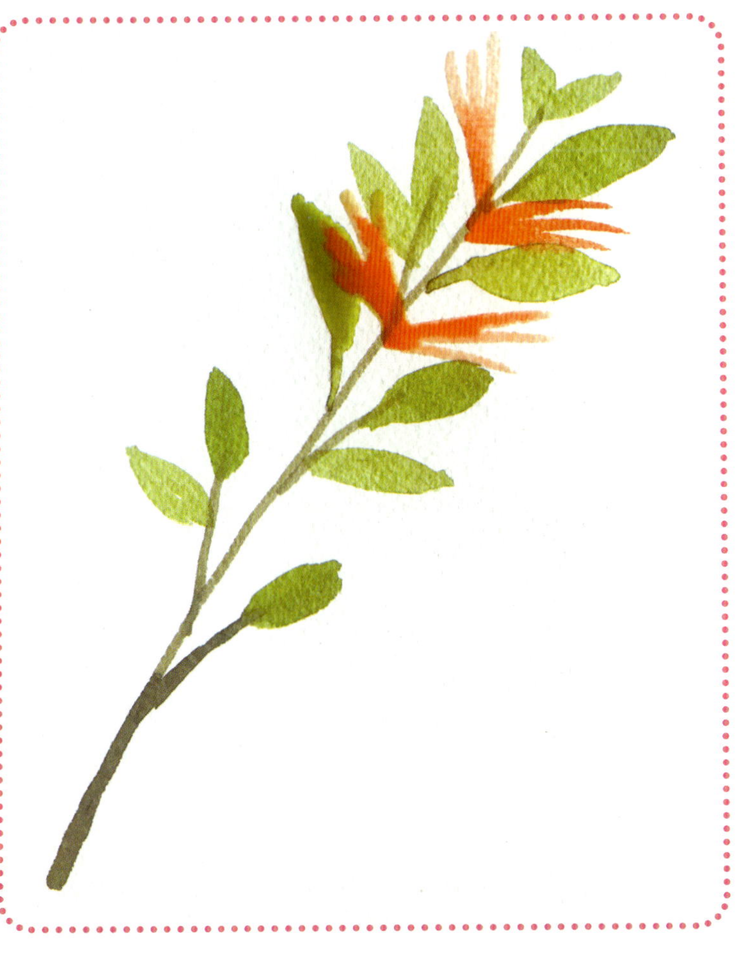

Using the wet-into-wet technique (page 18), load your liner brush with a warm red and begin adding the flowery lobes.

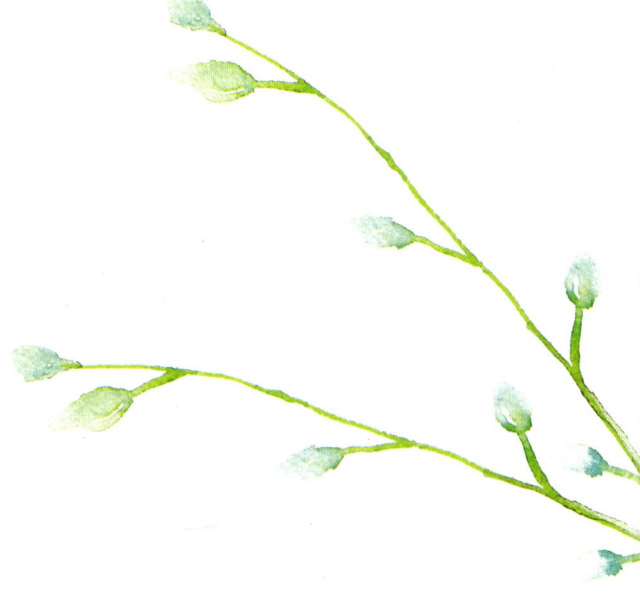

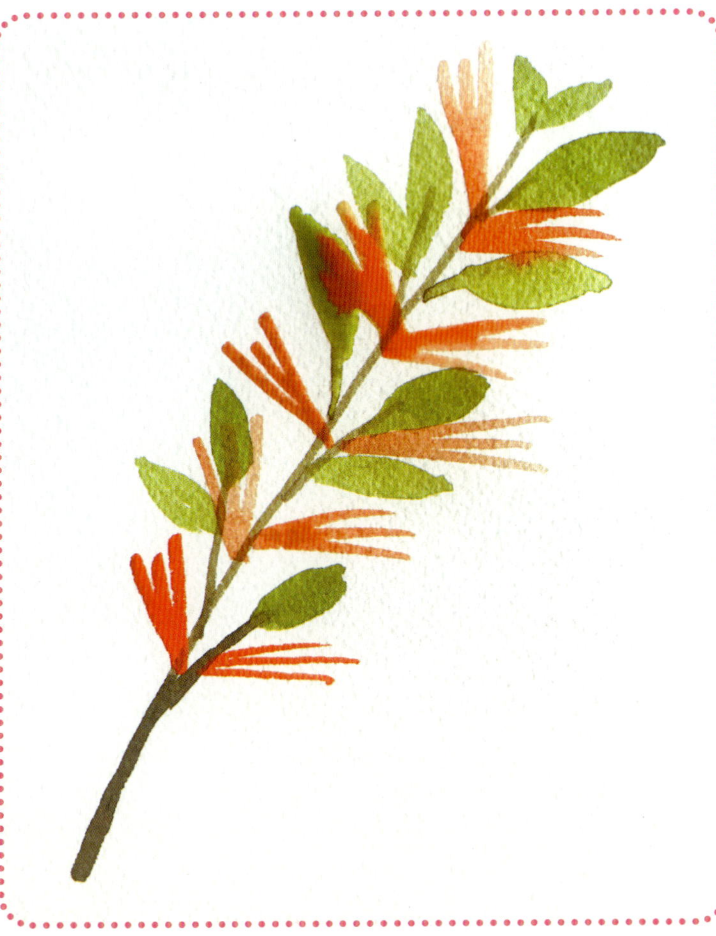

Try alternating an orangey-red with the more solid red to give your artwork some dimension. You can also add more water so that each lobe is a different value.

Add tips to the lobes using the red on your liner brush.

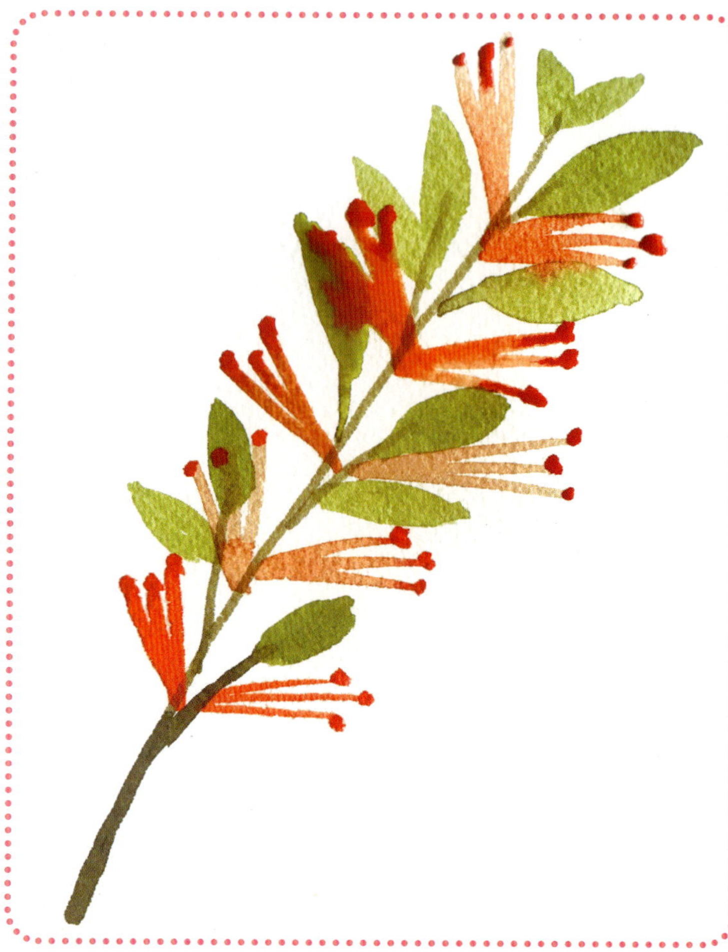

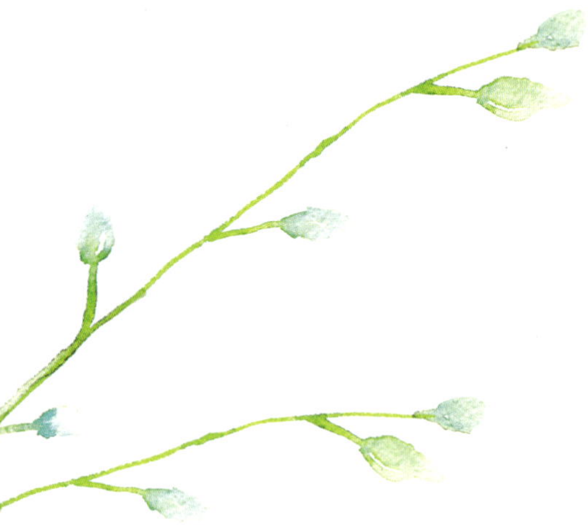

6

Return to the leaves and add a darker green to create more depth.

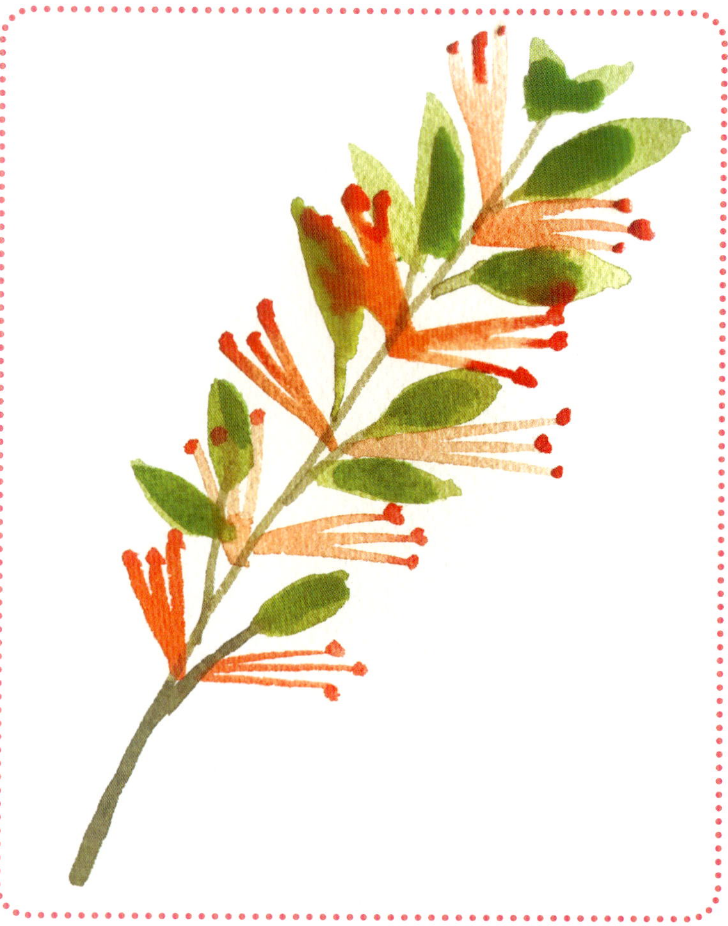

MAGNOLIA BUD

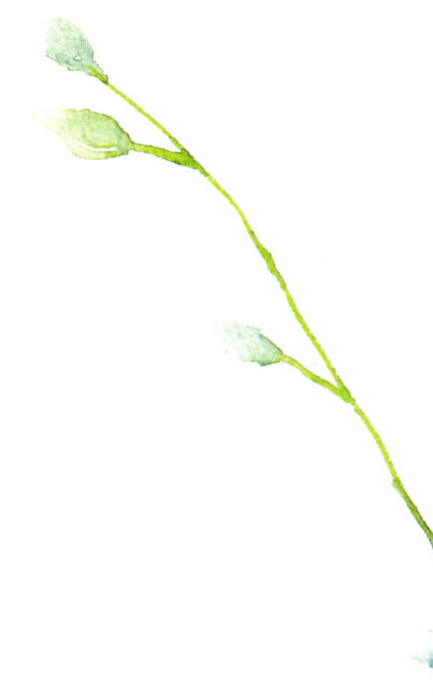

1

With a #8 round brush and a light peachy-pink wash, create a center petal and two thinner petals on each side.

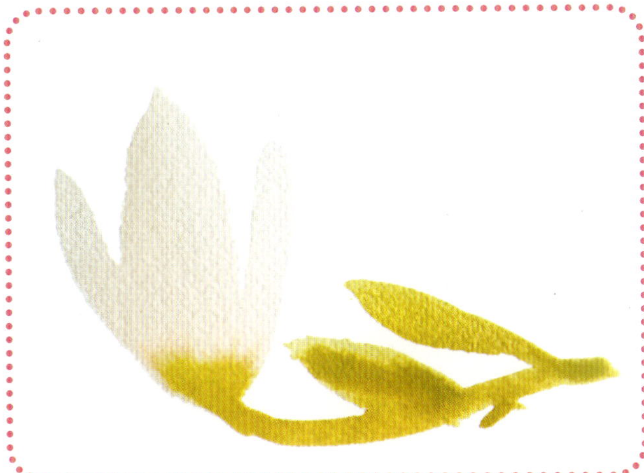

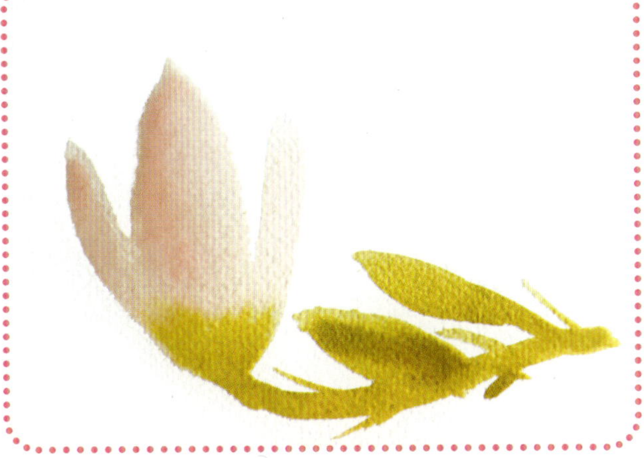

2

While the wash is still wet, add a simple curved stem and a few leaves in green-gold. The green will blend into the pale peach-pink.

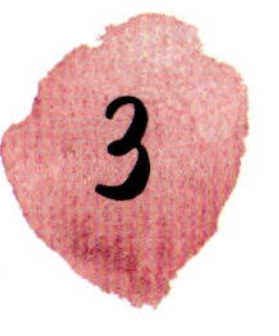

With a bolder shade of pink, delicately tap the #8 brush into the still-wet wash and let the color move about. Do this on each petal.

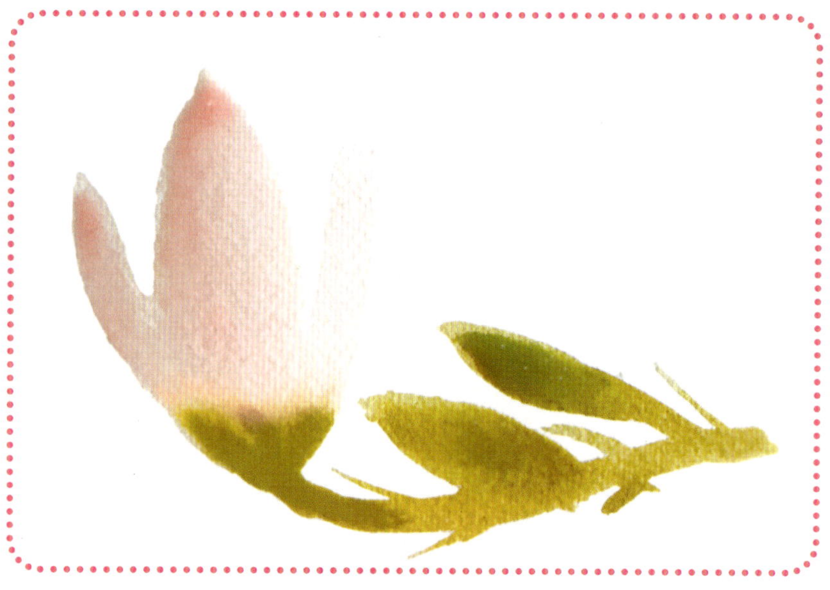

Tap a deeper shade of green into the wet base of the bloom to give it more depth and contrast.

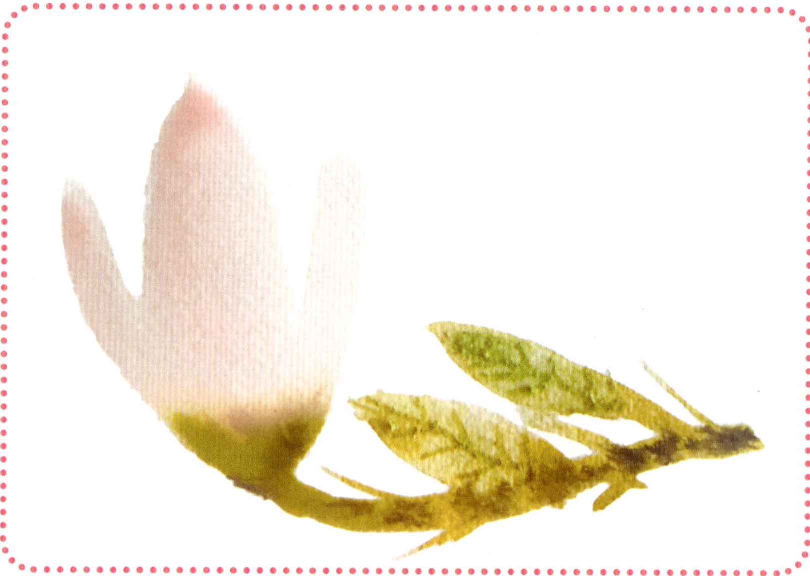

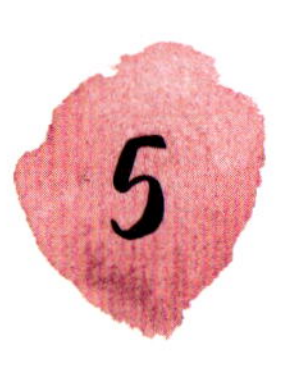

Using a toothpick, score veins into the leaves on the stem.

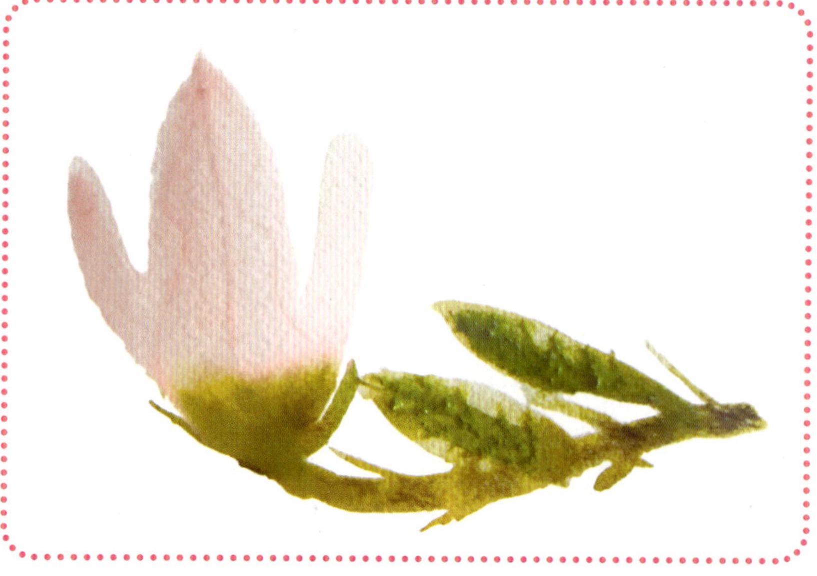

Tap a bit of a dark hue, such as olive green, onto the leaves.

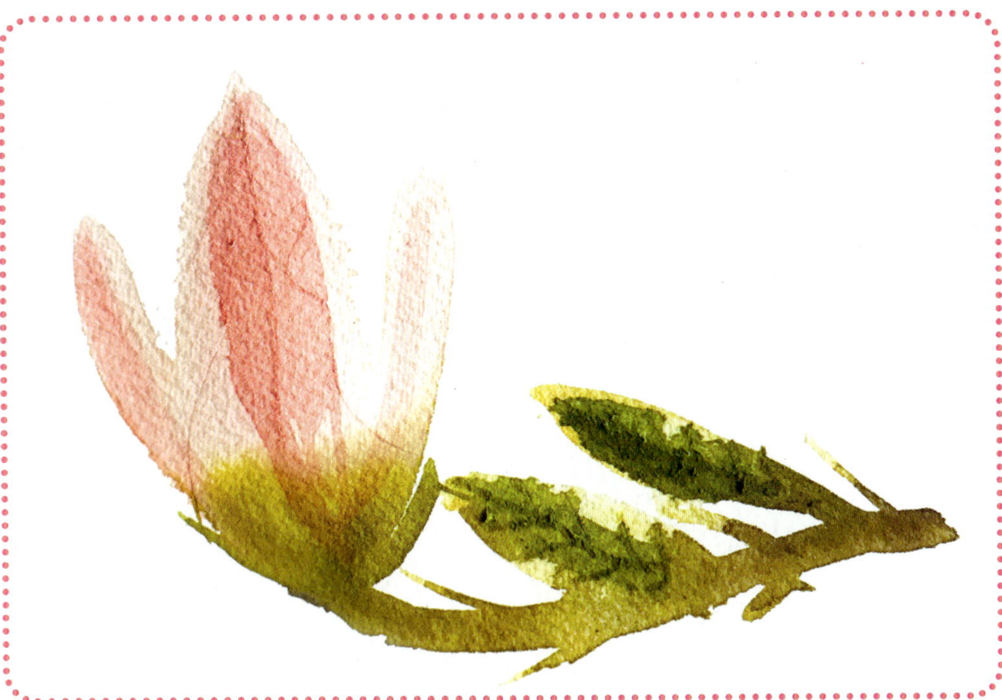

Darken the stem with dark brown to create more definition and allow the leaves to pop.

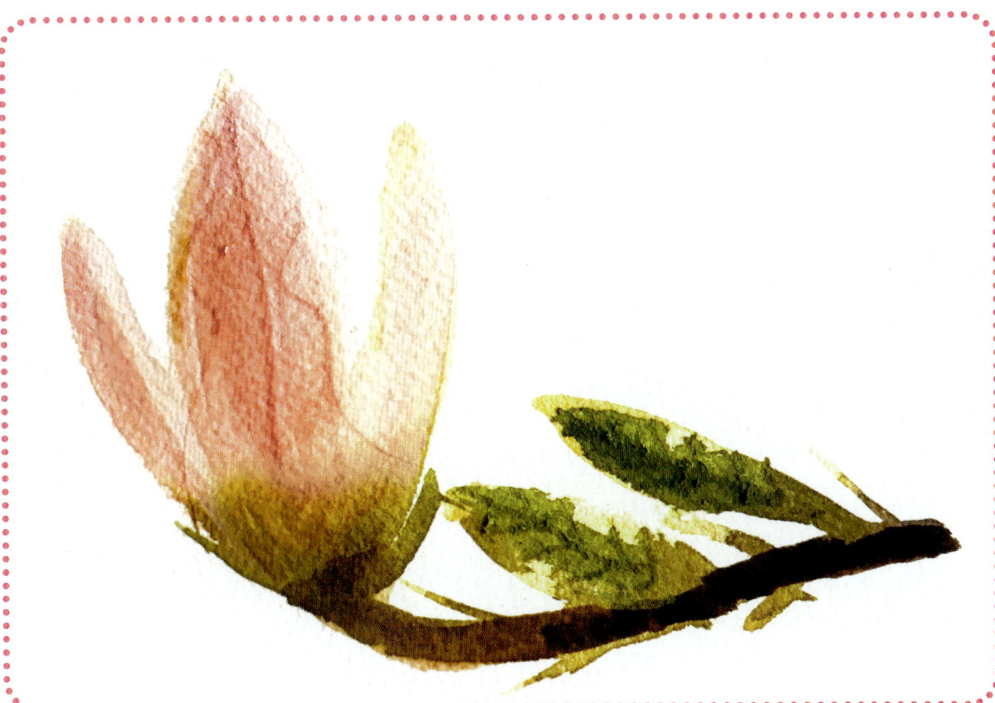

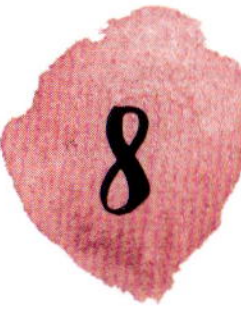

Add a touch more color to the blossom with a wet #8 brush, and then score it with a toothpick to give the illusion of the petal edges curving a bit.

ROSE

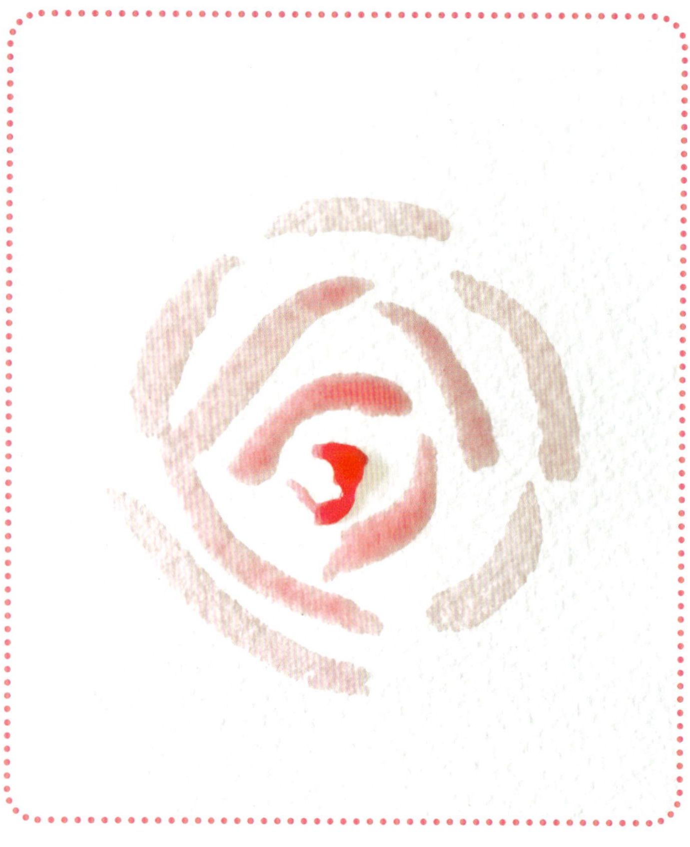

1

With opera rose or another pink pigment and the tip of a #8 round brush, create concentric petal lines to form the tight center of the flower.

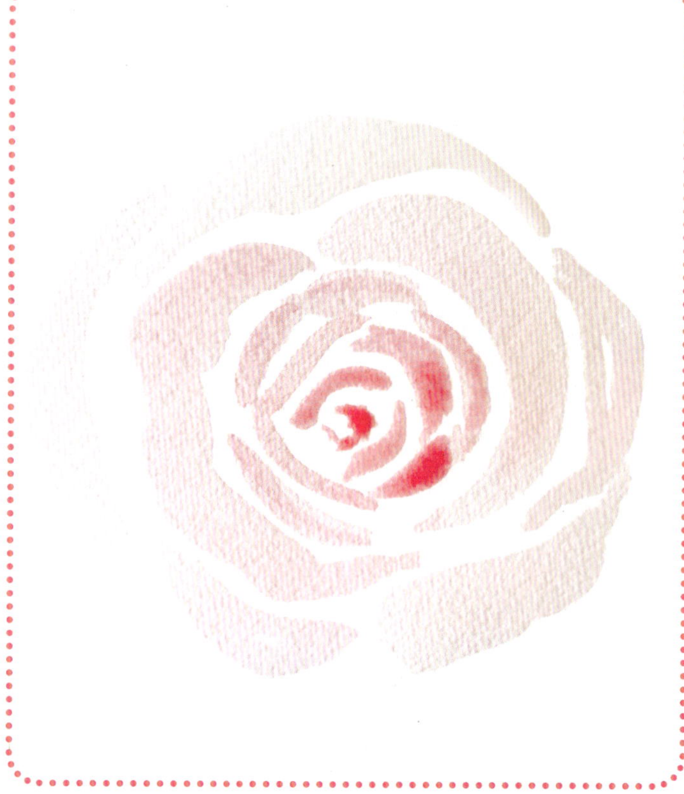

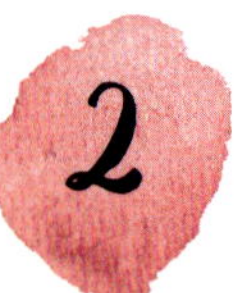

2

Now move from the center outward. Keep dipping the brush in water and gently drag it against the lip of the container to remove excess water. Your rose should get paler as you move to its outer edges.

Add a simple leaf to the outer edge of the rose.

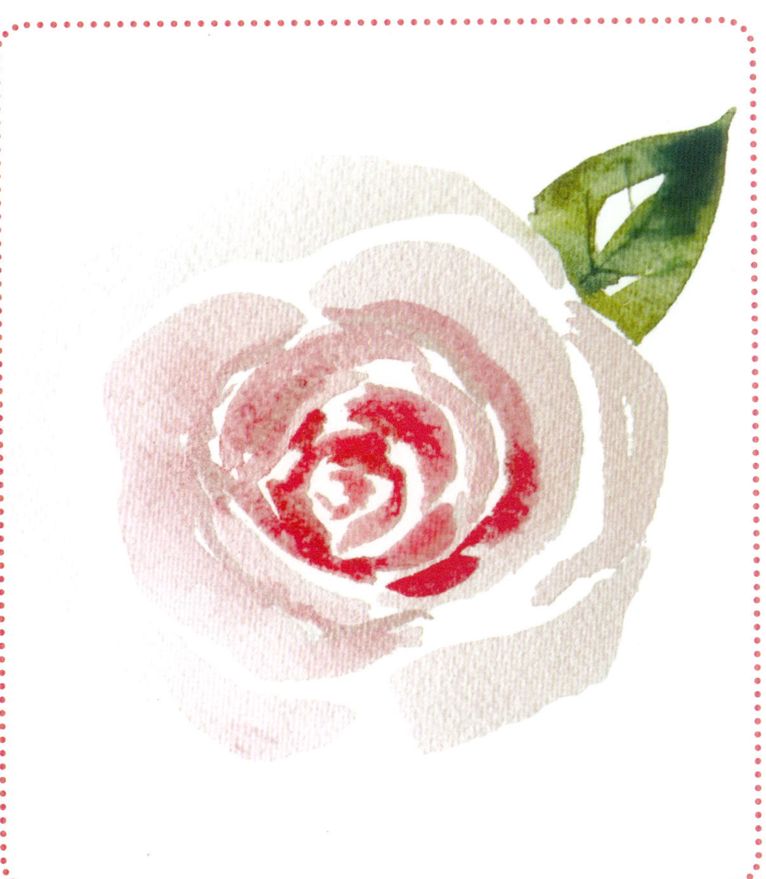

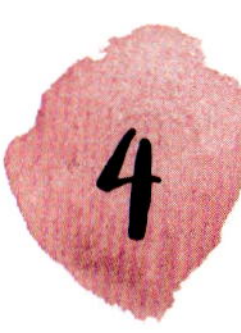

While the petals are still wet, dip more opera rose into the center of the flower to give it a bit more depth. Keep the outer petals pale. You can also add dark green to the leaf and score it to indicate the veins.

ASTER

Make a small circle with cadmium yellow and a #8 round brush.

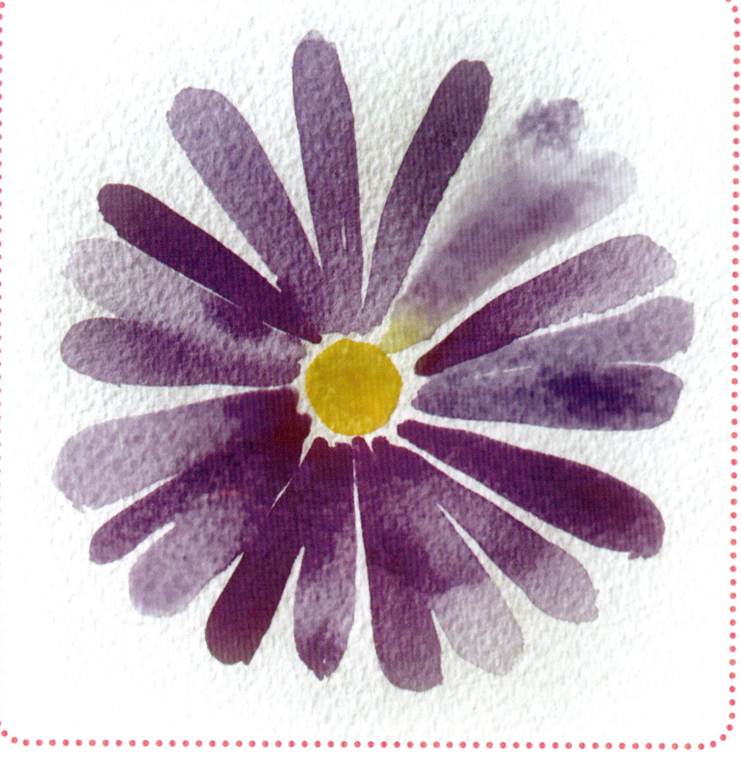

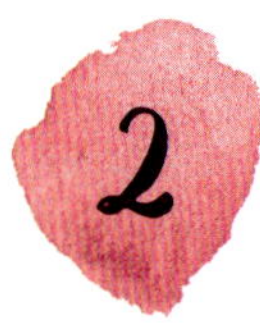

Mix blue or blue-violet to create a colorful hue. Form the petals by pressing the tip of your #8 brush toward the center circle and then pressing it down as you move outward. This will give the petal a tapered shape. Leave a bit of white space between the flower's center and the outer ring of petals to create some "pop."

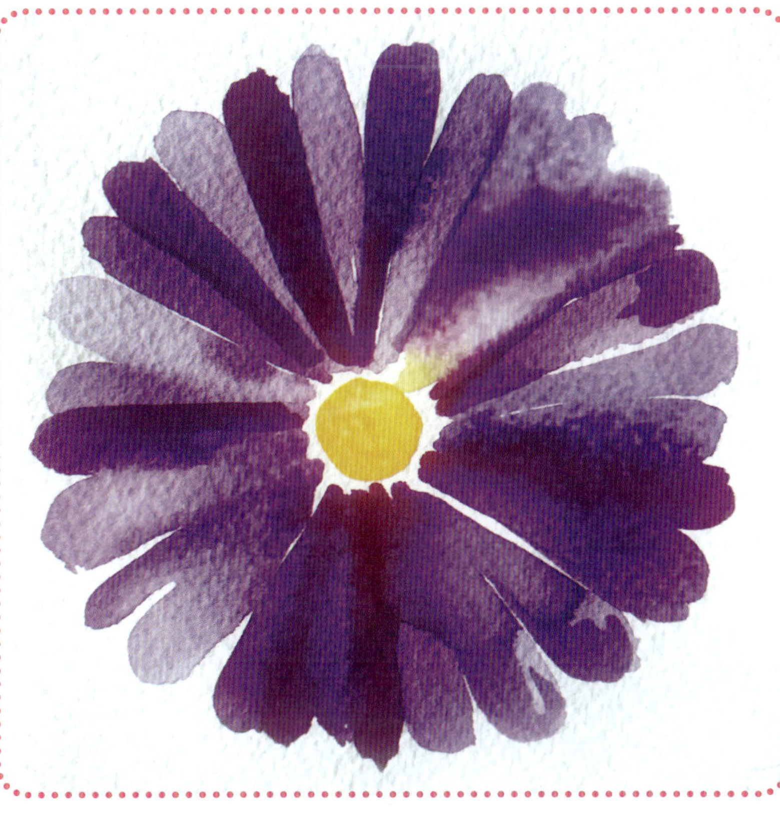

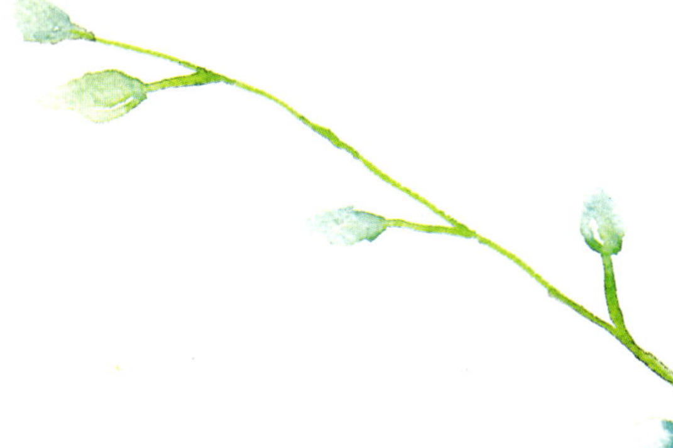

3

Dip your brush in water to create varying levels of opacity in the petals. Continue around the center until you've made the entire flower. You can add more pigment as you see fit; the flower will look more interesting with various values.

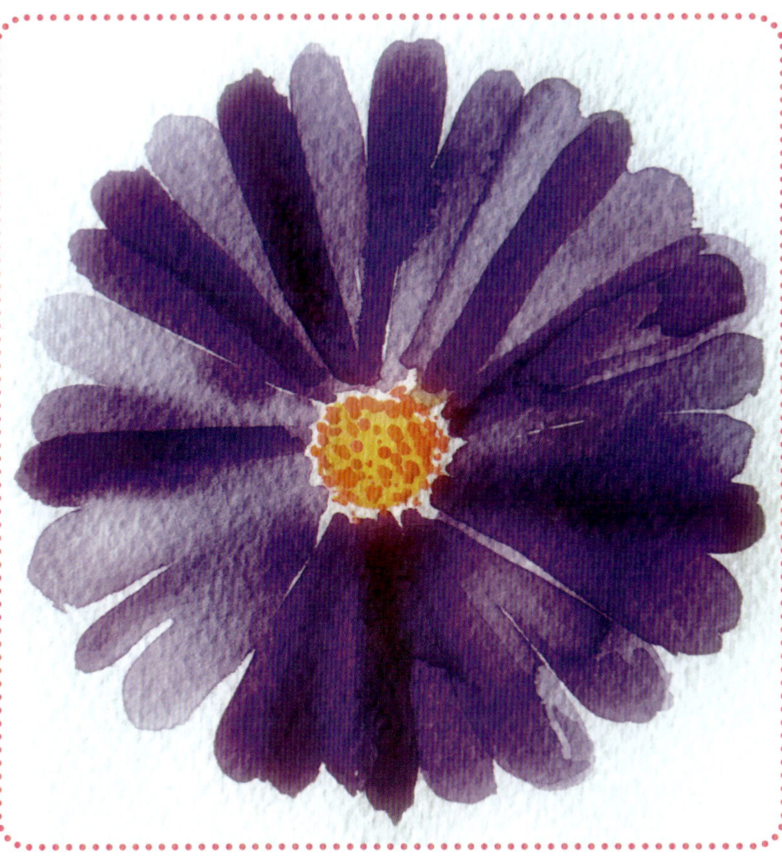

Let the flower dry; then add texture and definition to the center by adding orange stippling with the very tip of your brush.

CONEFLOWER

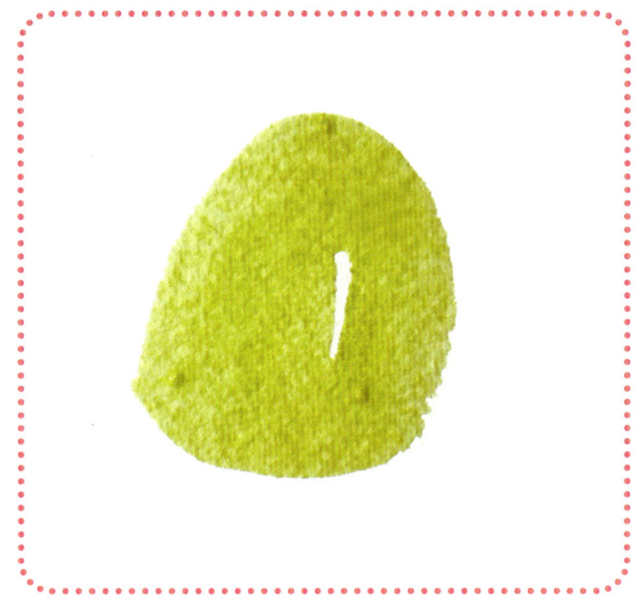

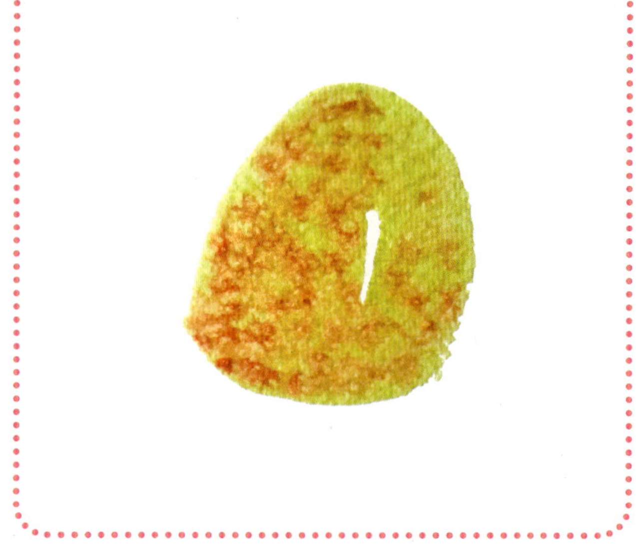

1 Make a dome-shaped cone using a yellowy-green color and a filbert brush.

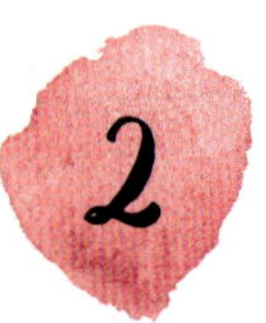

2 While the cone is still wet, use the tip of a #4 round brush to add small orange dots. Allow the dots to bleed into the first color and give the cone some texture.

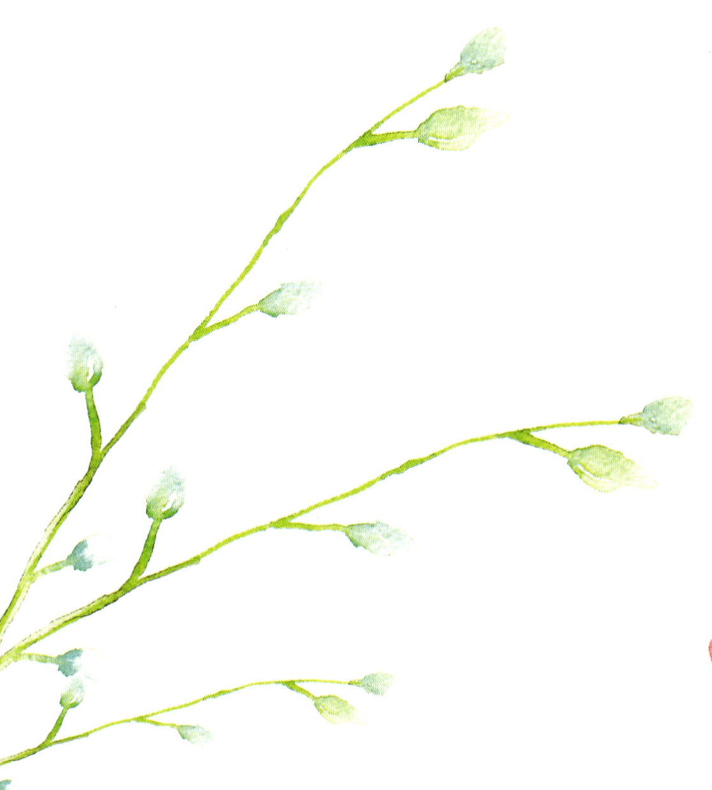

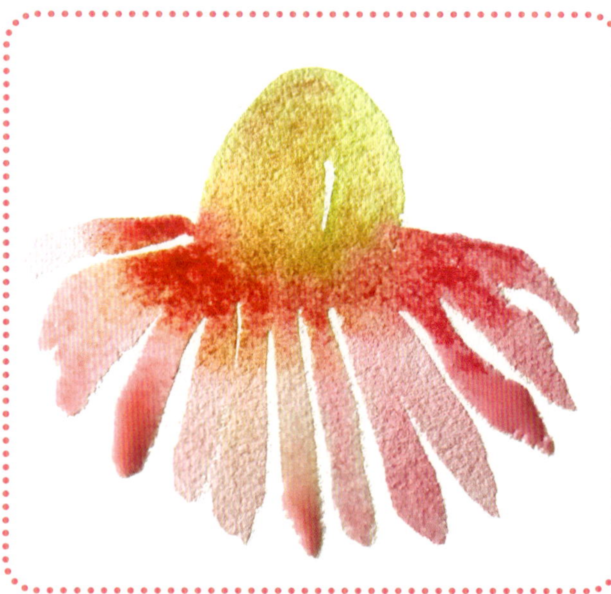

3 Still working while the paint is wet, use the point of a #8 round brush and opera rose to drag the paint down and form a petal. Repeat until you have an arc of pink petals in varying levels of opacity. Remember to keep dipping the brush in water and removing the excess as you go.

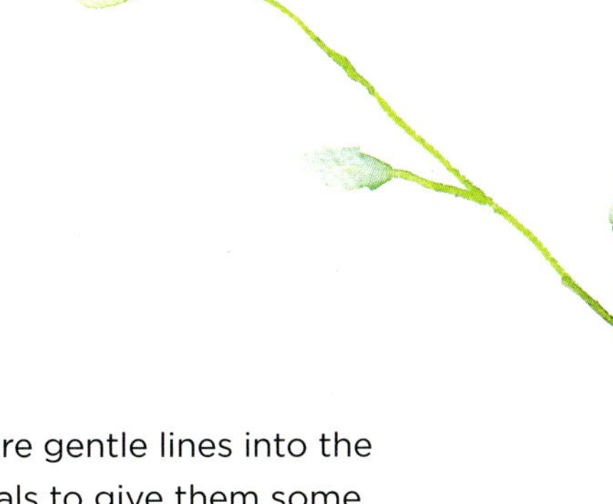

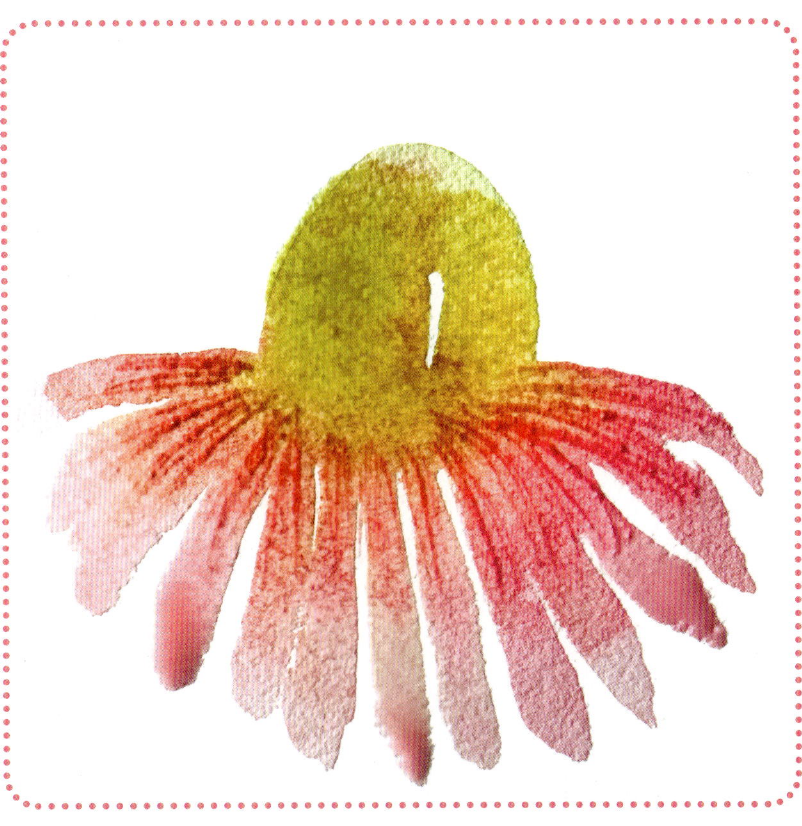

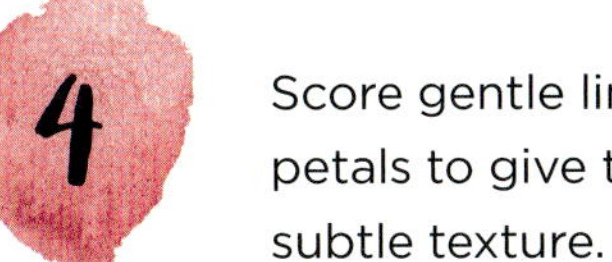

Score gentle lines into the petals to give them some subtle texture.

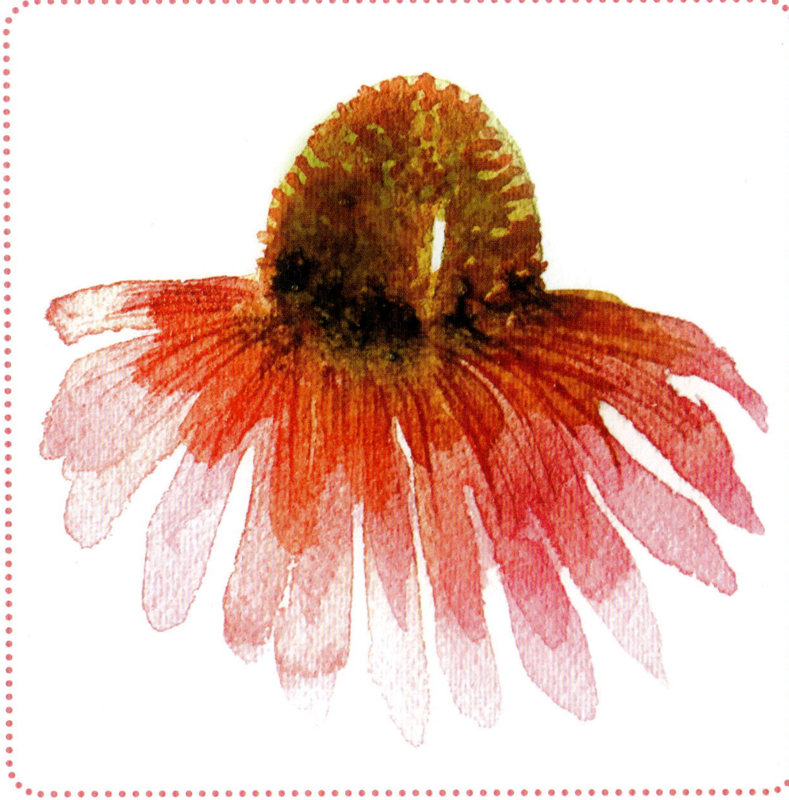

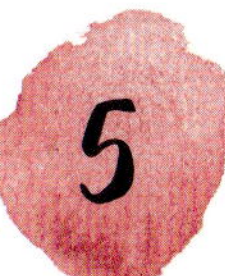

Once the cone is dry, dip the tip of a #8 round brush into orange paint and stipple over the cone. Add denser color at the bottom. While this is wet, add olive green or umber where the cone meets the petals. This will give the flower some depth.

CHERRY LAUREL

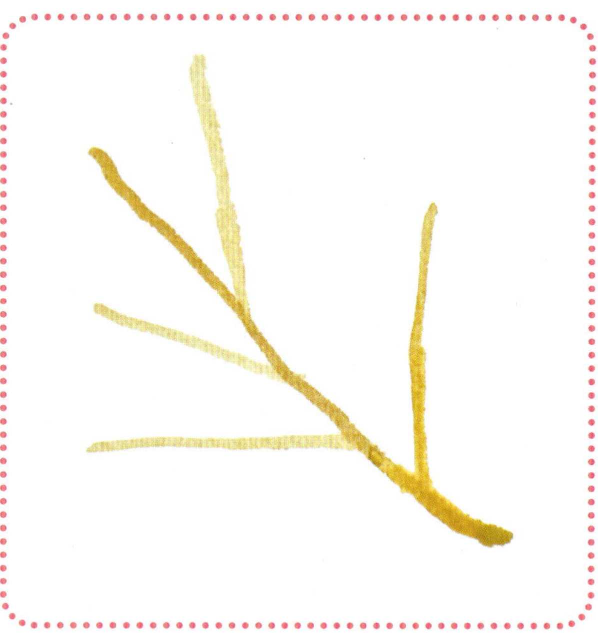

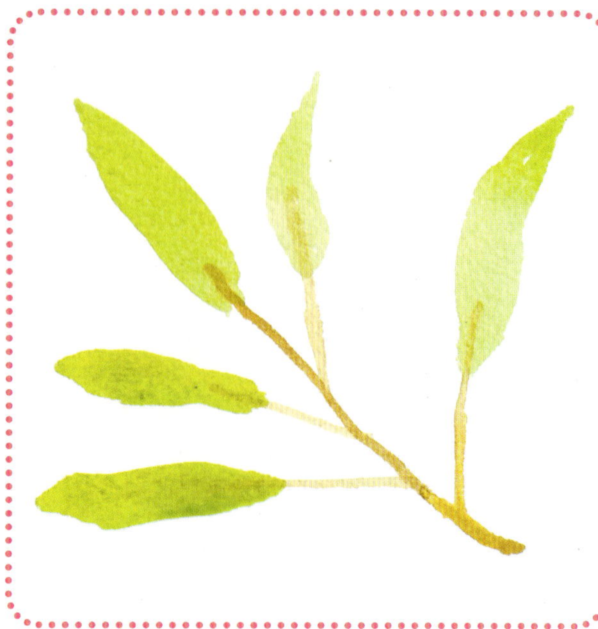

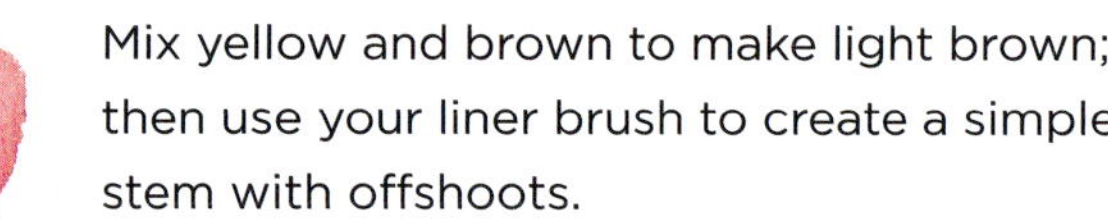

1 Mix yellow and brown to make light brown; then use your liner brush to create a simple stem with offshoots.

2 Use your #8 round brush to create tapered leaves. Start with the very tip of the brush and move toward the stems, applying more pressure as you go. Wiggle the brush around to give each leaf different curves.

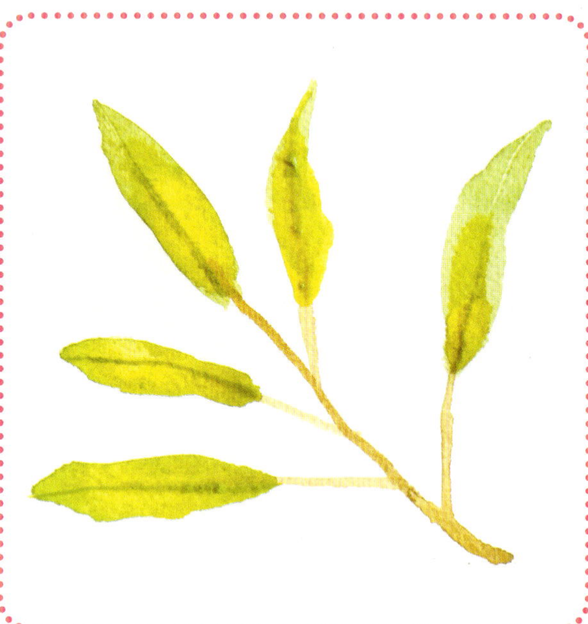

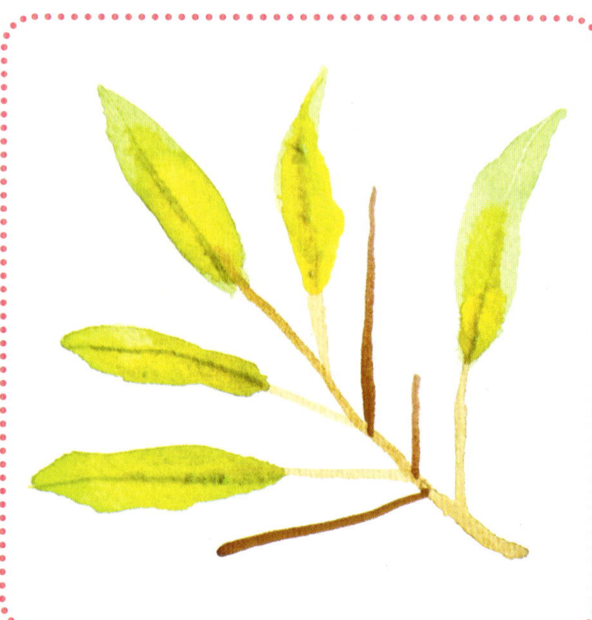

3 While the greens in the leaves are still wet, score the centers with a toothpick to create veins.

4 Now add darker brown stems using your liner brush. These will hold the berries.

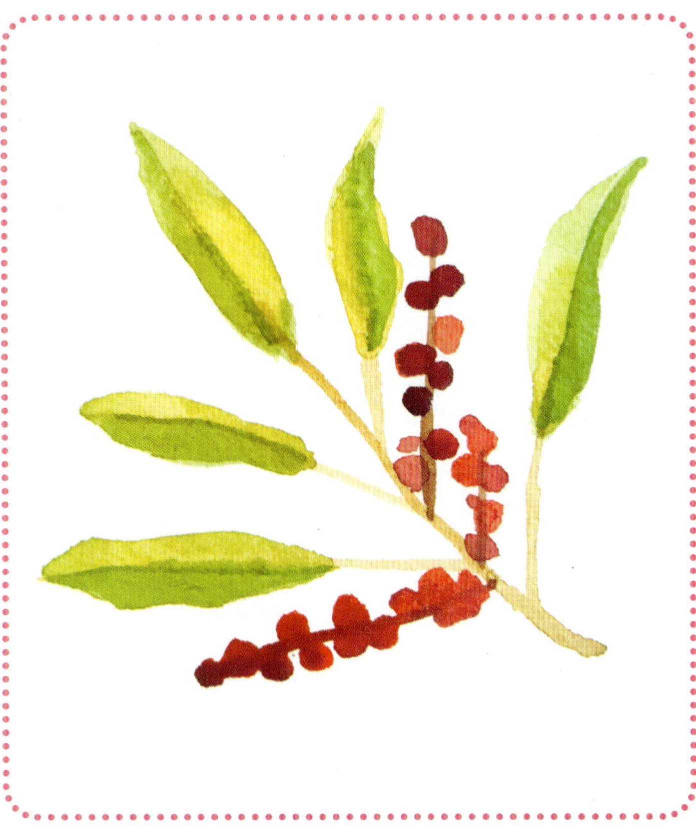

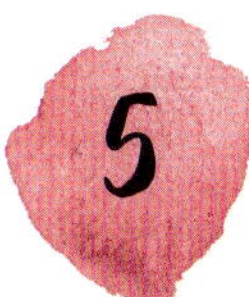

Dip the tip of your #4 round brush into alternating shades of red to create the berries. I've used an alizarian crimson as well as a sanguine red, but really, as long as you have one darker shade and a lighter one, you can use any reds in your palette. Now that the greens have dried a bit, add some darker green to one side of each leaf.

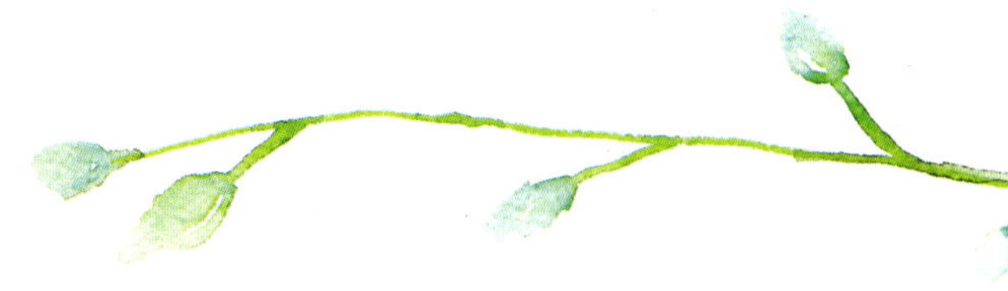

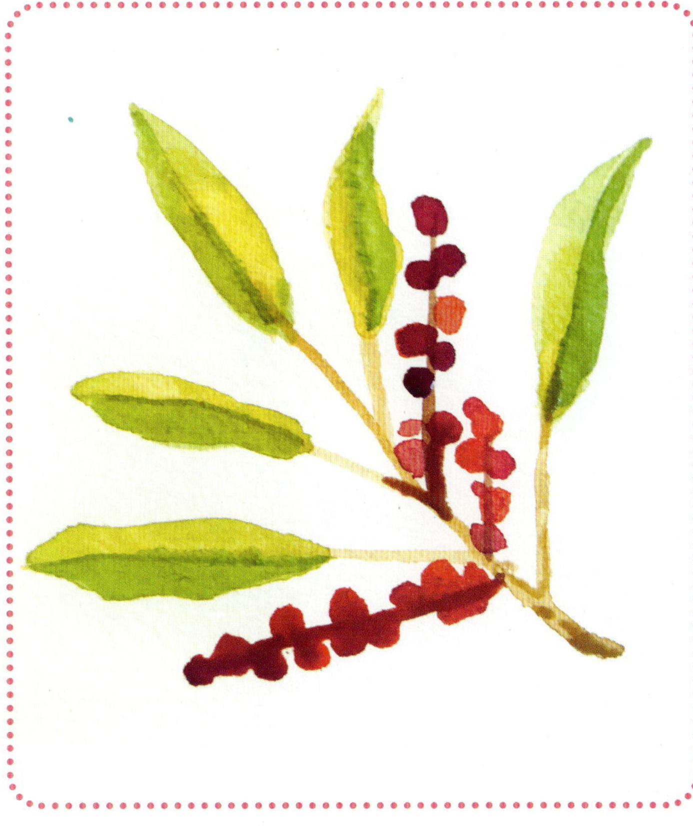

Fine-tune your work. Add a bit of darker brown to the base of the stem to give it the illusion of coarser texture. You can round out the berries with your liner brush, but make sure not to go overboard with any outlines—keep them organic!

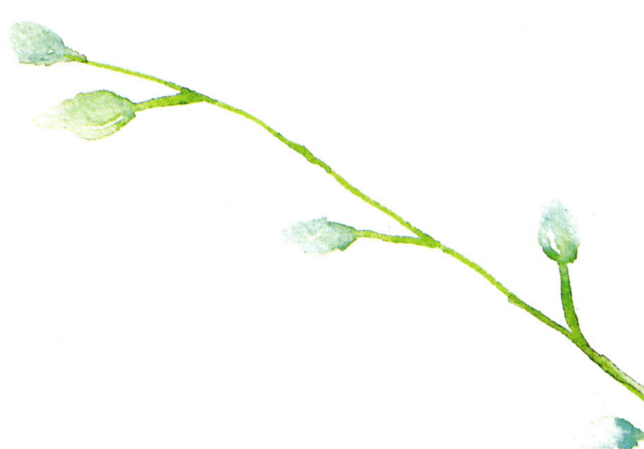

TIGER LILY

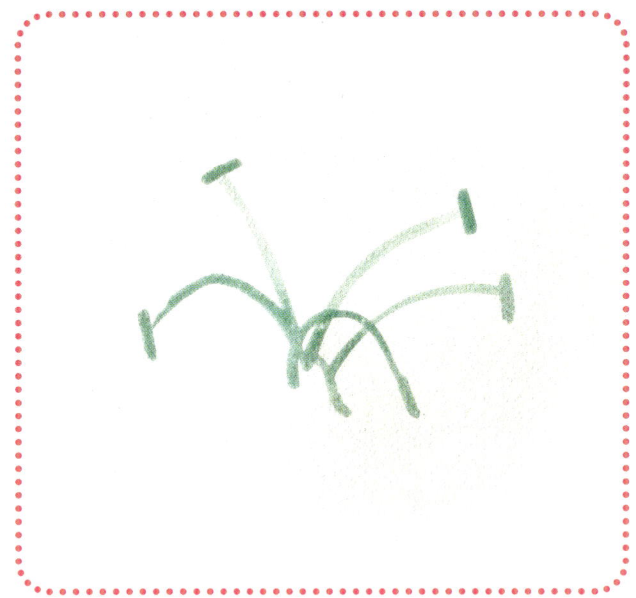

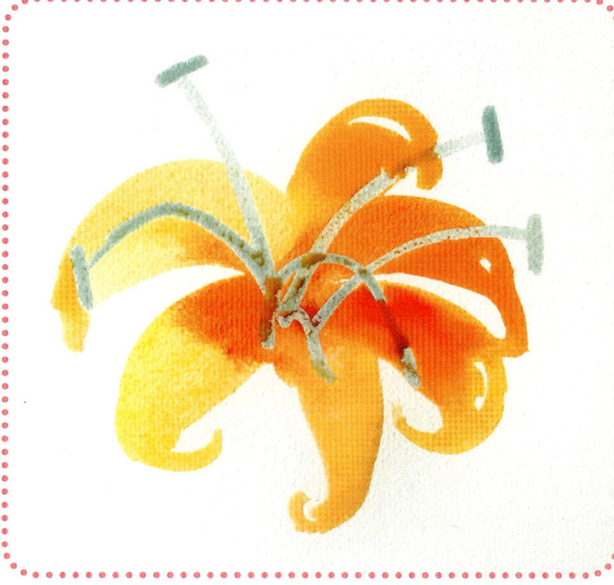

1 Using a small, inexpensive brush dipped in masking fluid, draw several arched lines in the center of your paper. Add small lines at the end of each arched line. These lines will save white space for the stamens and help you map out the painting.

2 Make the six petals of the lily with a #10 round brush and orange pigment. Think of the petal shape as a freeform ellipse with a small curled bit underneath. Then tap red into the still-wet wash and let the paint travel. Lilies have beautiful, vibrant colors, and this is always a fun step!

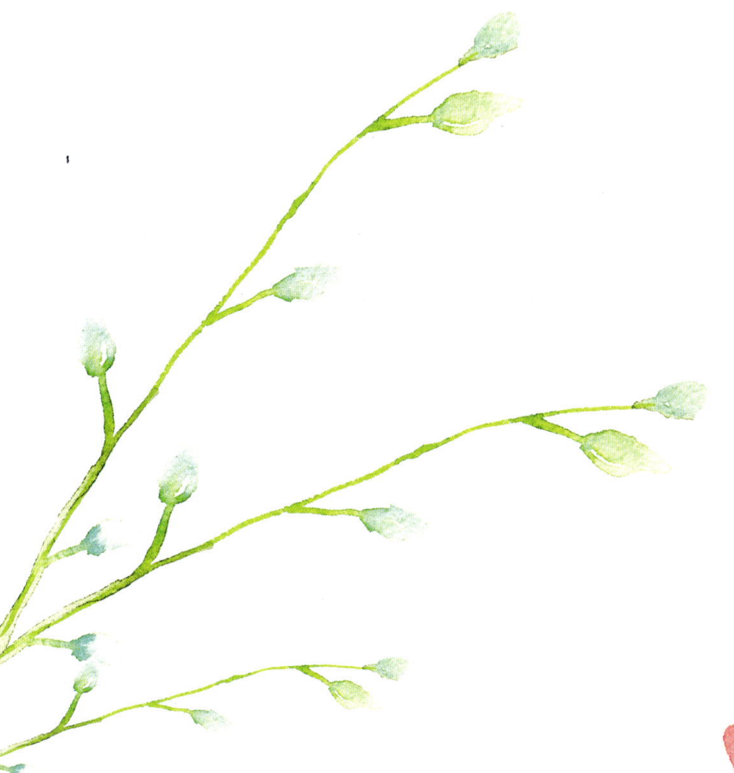

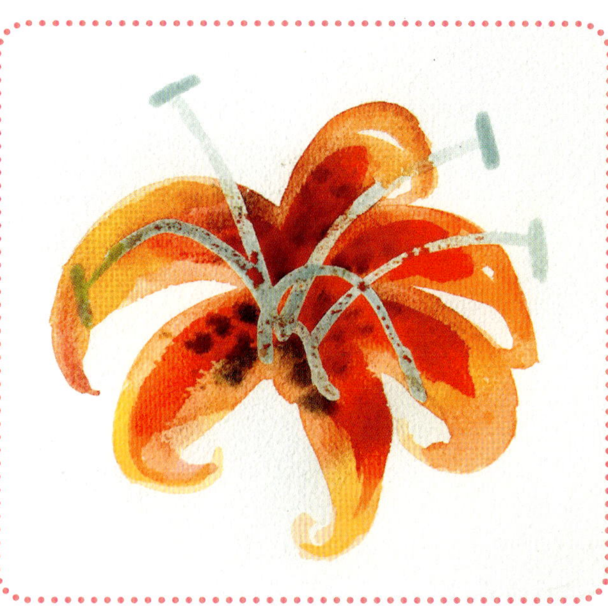

3 Add crimson and burnt umber hues in the center of the flower to give it depth.

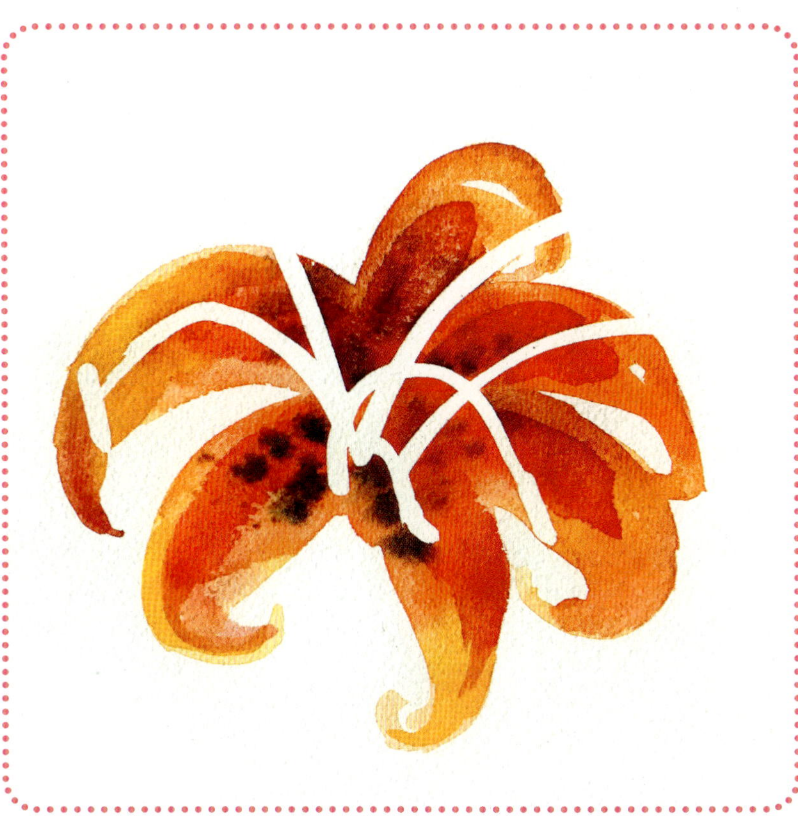

Let the paint dry completely. Then remove the masking fluid with a rubber square or very clean, dry fingers.

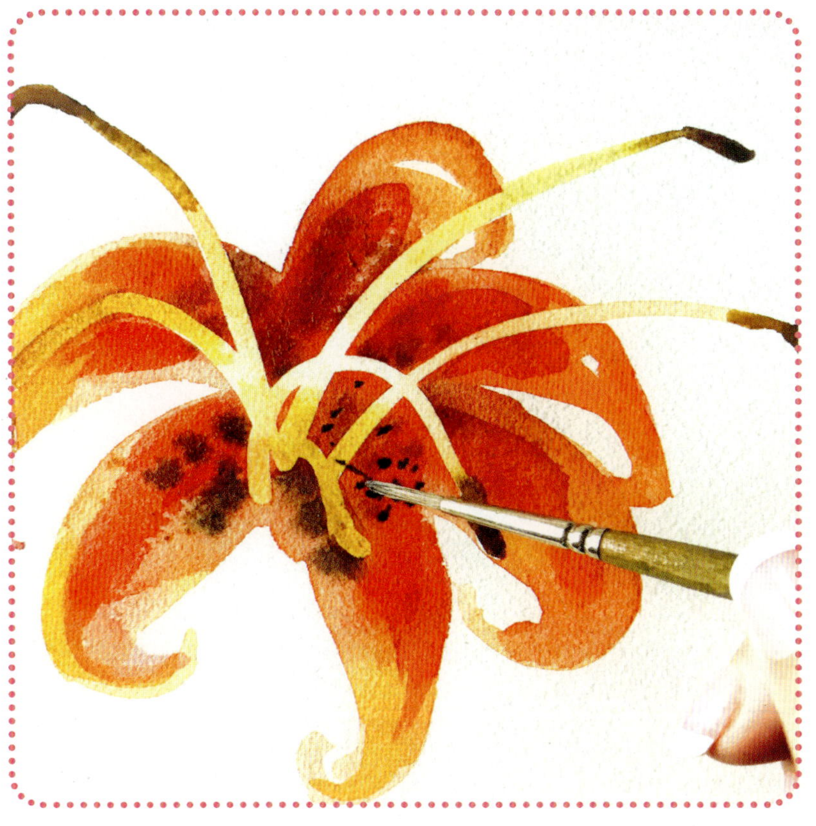

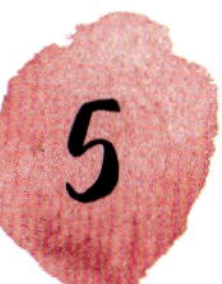

With a liner brush and watered-down yellow paint, fill in the stamens. While the paint is still wet, tap your brush into burnt umber and create the ends of the stamens. The color will run on its own. Tap the point of your brush on the petals to give them their telltale spots.

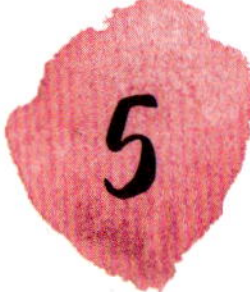

Continue tapping until all of the petals are covered with spots. Alternate the sizes to make the flower look more natural. You can also tap a bit of water into the spots to make the edges blur a bit.

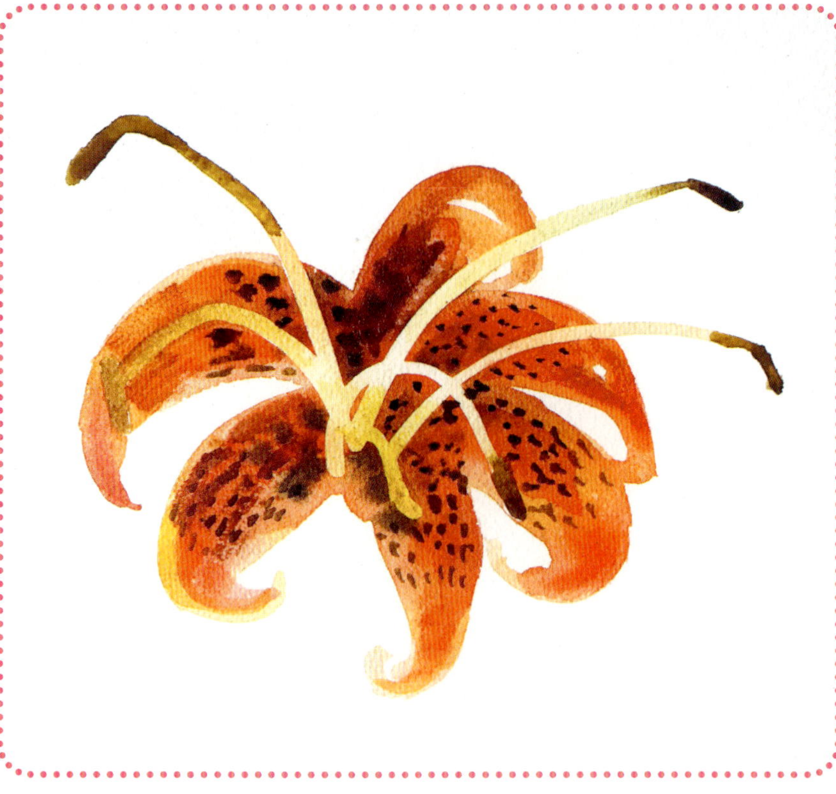

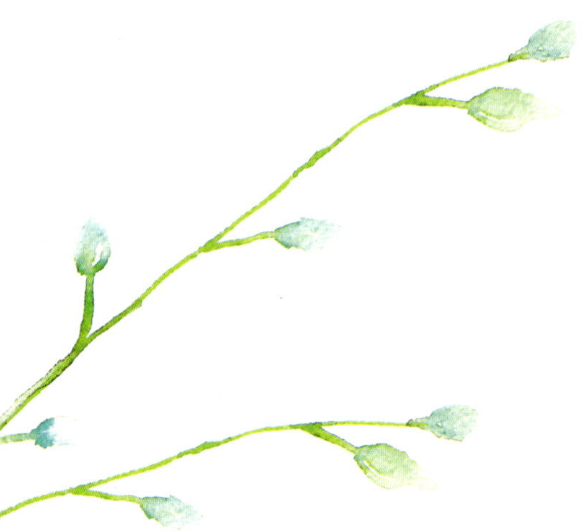

Finish by refining the details. Use more burnt umber to emphasize some of the darker areas in the center of the lily. You can also go back and add subtle shading with the drybrushing technique (see page 21). Dip a very stiff brush into red pigment and blot until the brush is almost dry; then scrape the brush along the outer edges of the petals to give them a bit of texture.

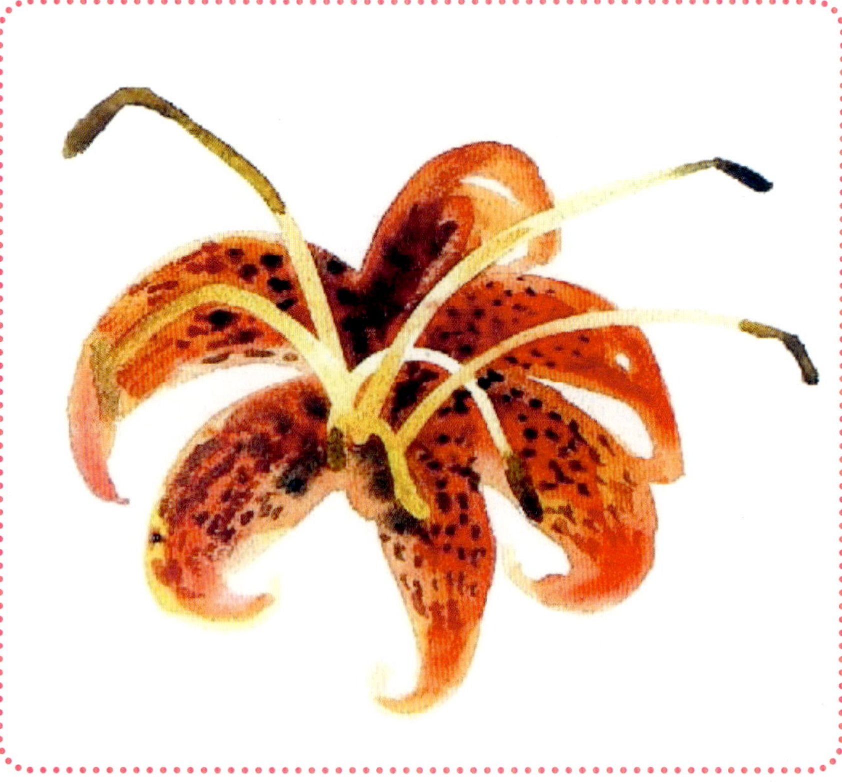

HOLLYHOCK

With pale pink pigment and a #8 round brush, make a watery circle, leaving a bit of white in the center. Then tap in watered-down violet with the tip of the brush. Use excess water and the tip to round out and define the petals on the edge of the circle.

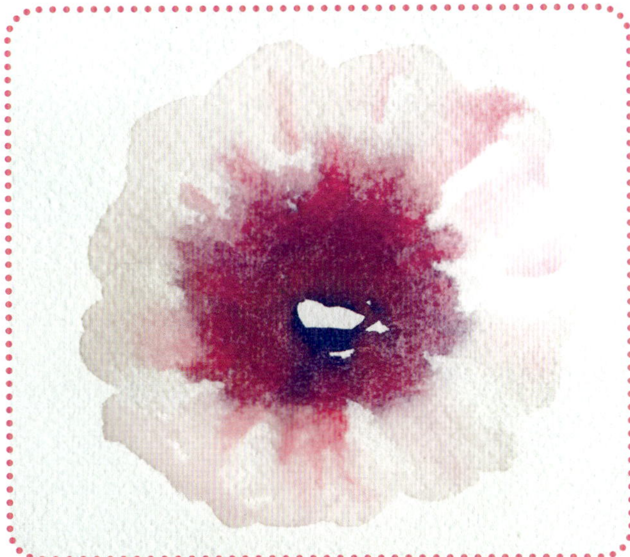

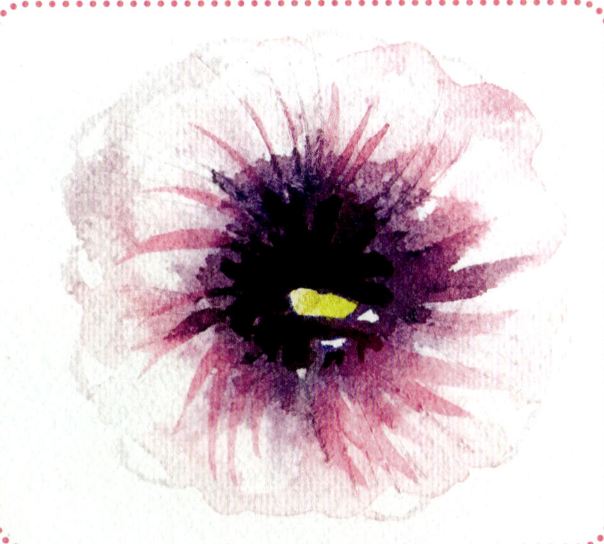

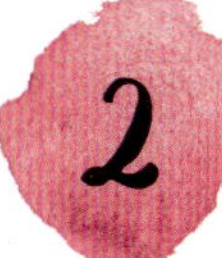

Dip a #8 round brush into violet or violet mixed with crimson, and tap into the wet center. The pigment will immediately extend outward and bleed. If it runs too far, you can use a cotton swab to blot around the violet color to stop it. Now use the tip of your brush and a rosy-pink color (I've used opera rose) to make little lines from the center out. This will give a boost of color to the pale petals. Let the paint dry completely.

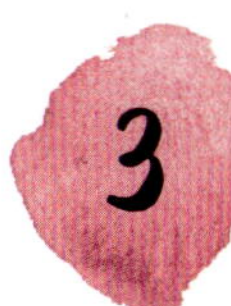

Add definition to the core of the flower by mixing violet and crimson with a touch of black. Tap all around the reserved area to create more depth. Rinse your brush and use a vibrant pink like opera rose to add more lines to the petals. Now mix a bit of yellow with green-gold and fill the center of the flower. While this area is wet, tap with a toothpick to add texture. The pigment will fall into the recessed areas of the paper. If necessary, repeat any of these steps to give the flower depth.

PEONY BUD

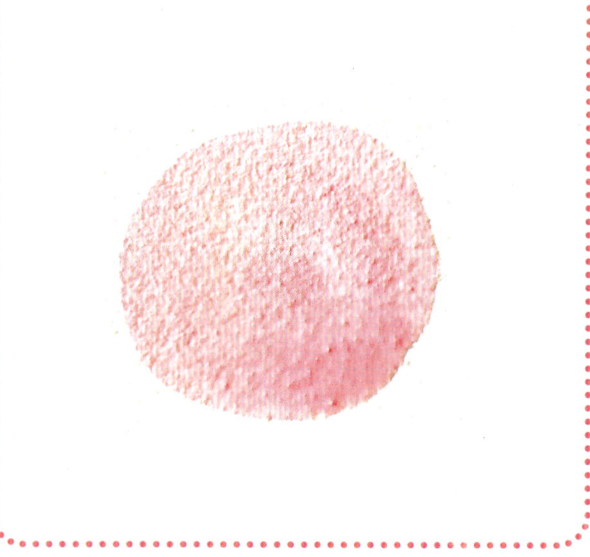

With a round or Filbert brush and a wash of pale pink, make a circle.

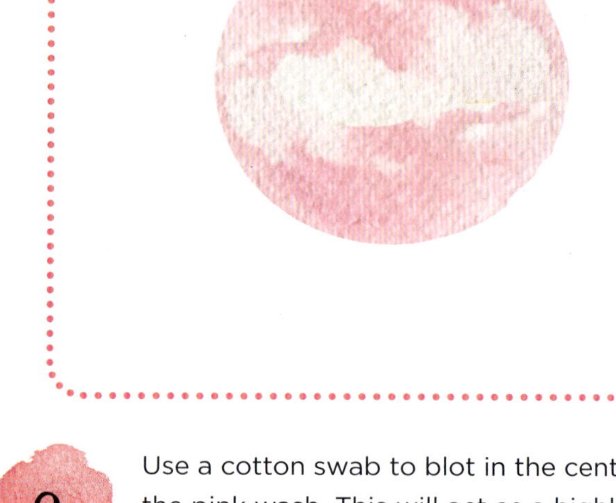

2

Use a cotton swab to blot in the center of the pink wash. This will act as a highlight for the bud. If you move the swab gently from side to side, you can create the illusion of a petal effect.

I like to tap extra pigment where the stem joins the bud and where the leaves join the stem.

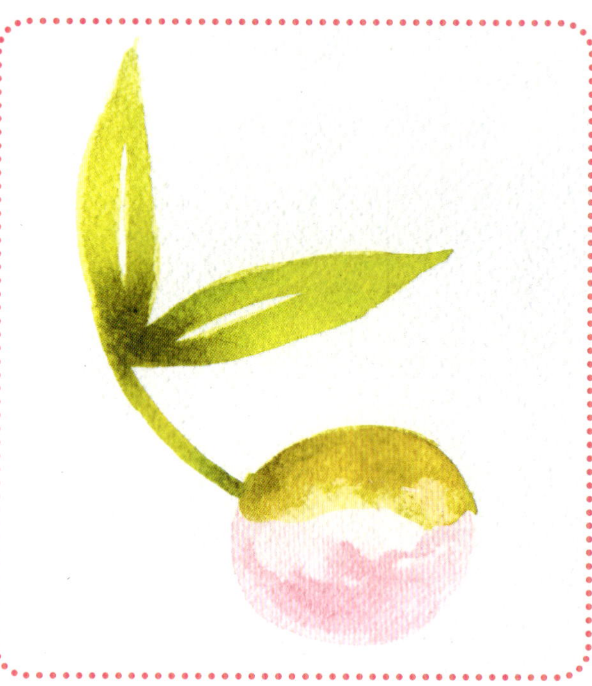

3

Dip a #8 round brush in green-gold pigment and make a small, watery cap on top of the bud. Add a stem and thin leaves, leaving some white space in the center of each.

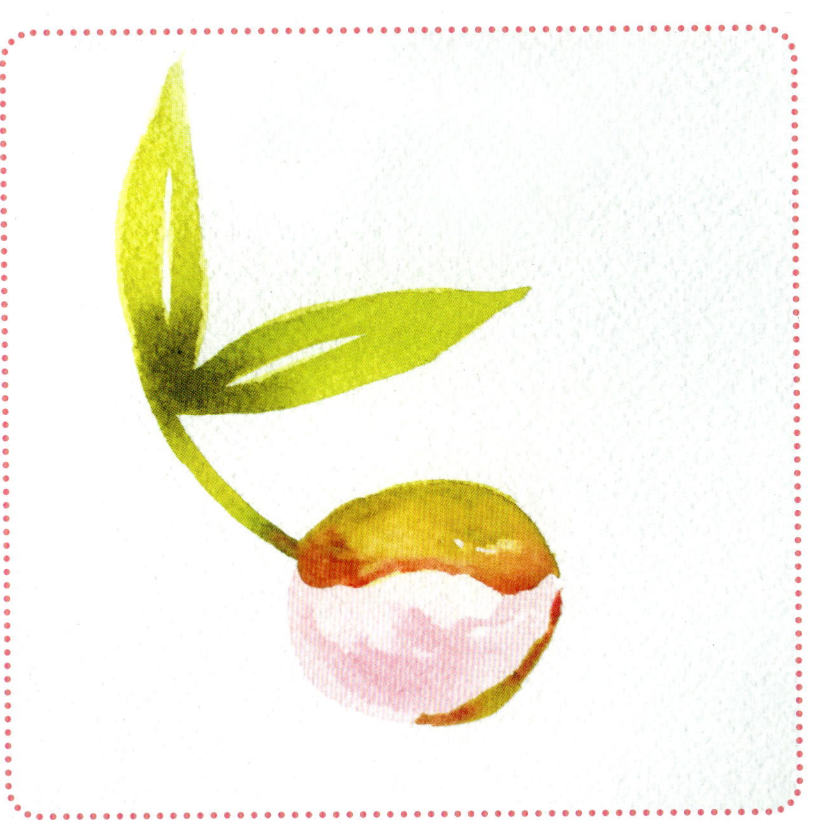

Tap a bit of rose into the bottom ridge of the leaf cap and the bottom of the bud, and let the water move the paint about.

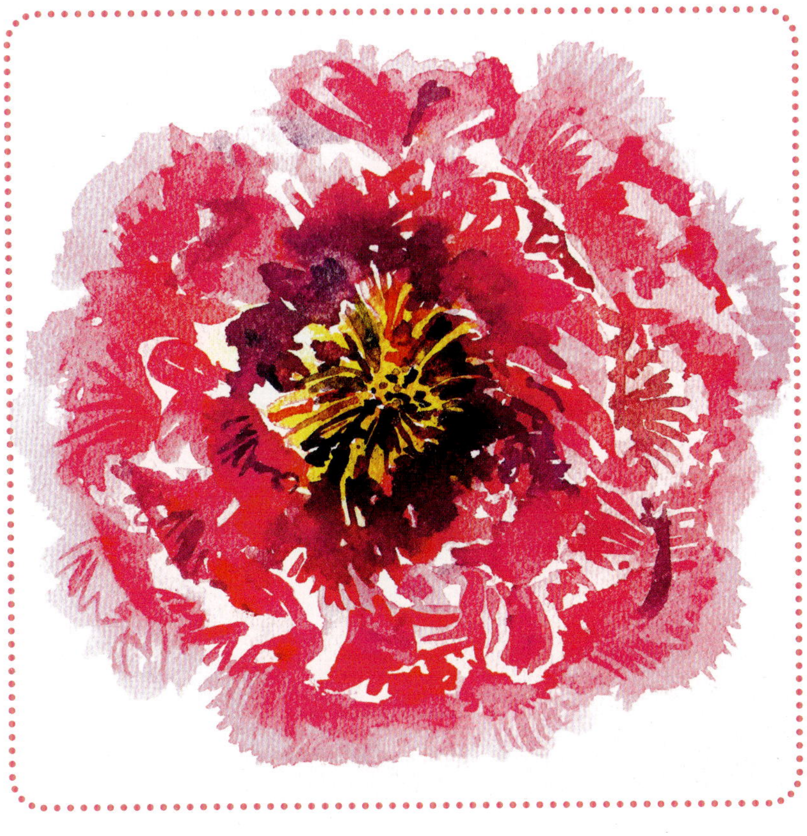

HERE'S A PEONY IN FULL BLOOM!

COLUMBINE

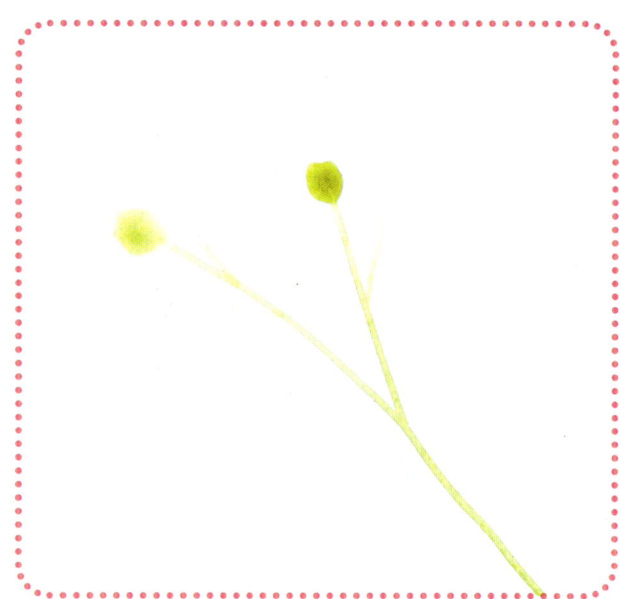

1 With a liner brush, draw a simple stem with green-gold paint. Add one or two offshoots, and cap these with small green circles.

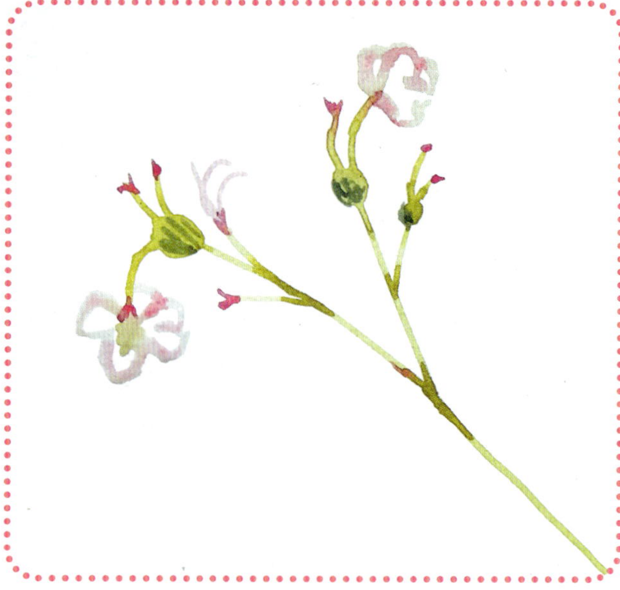

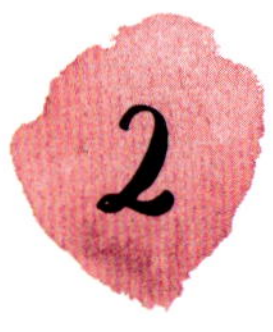

2 Add tiny offshoots in pale pink, as well as small, simple flowers. While the paint is still wet, tap rose pigment into the tips of the offshoots and let the water move the paint around.

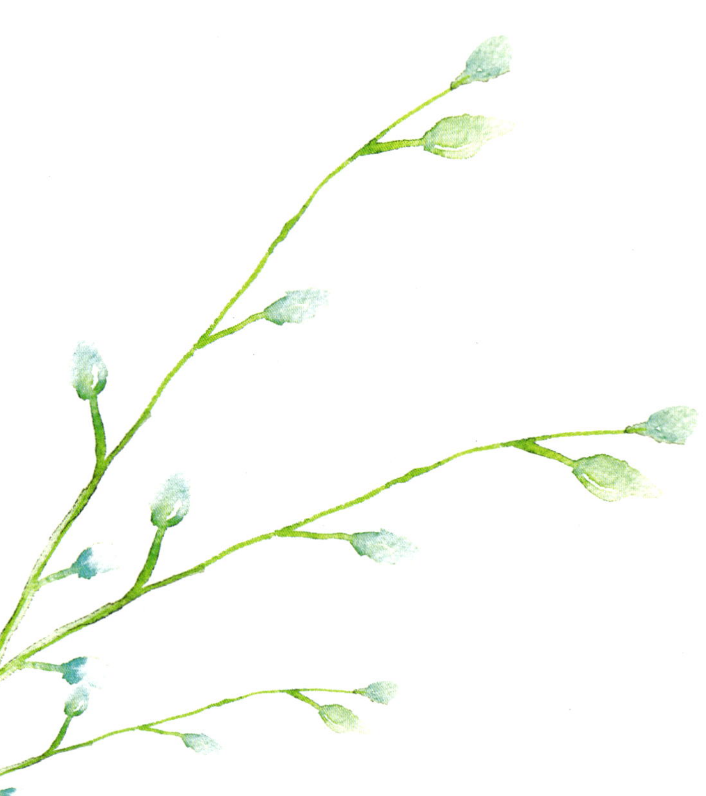

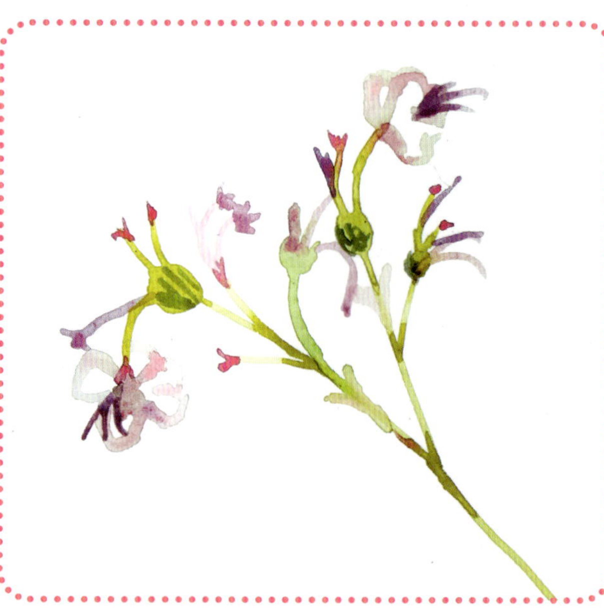

3 Tap some violet into the wet flowers; then tap green-gold into the areas where the stems meet. This will create more dimension and shadows where the stems join. Using your smallest brush or a toothpick, drag small lines out from the centers of the flowers to form the anthers.

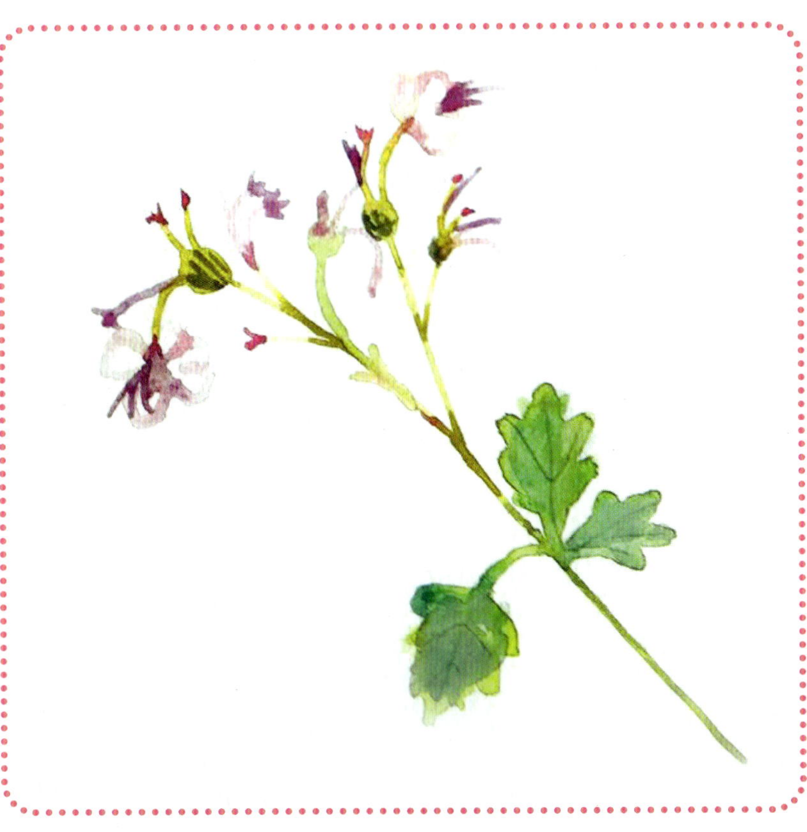

Give the green areas a bit more contrast and texture using a liner brush; then add leaves to the base of the stem. Columbine leaves look a bit like oak leaves; score them with a toothpick to indicate the veins.

Reserve a little white space when painting flowers or leaves to add a natural highlight to your subject matter. White space (or negative space) gives the work room to breathe and the colors just seem to pop more. To achieve this technique, you can use masking fluid (see page 20) or just leave bits of the paper bare.

Critters: Birds, Squirrels & Chipmunks

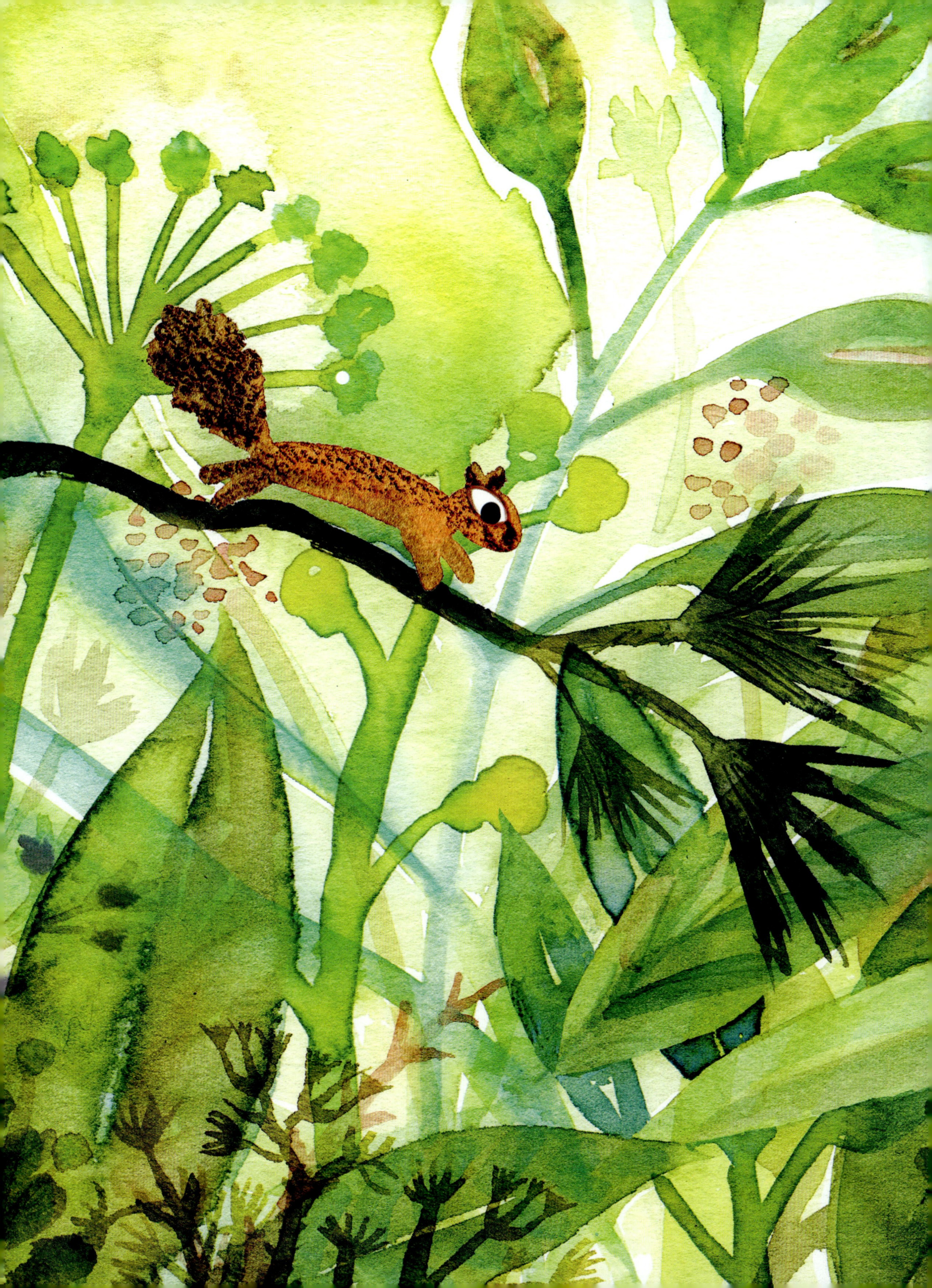

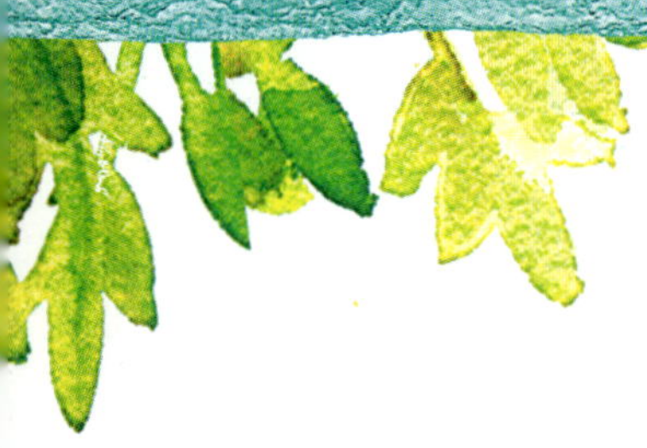

YELLOW WARBLER

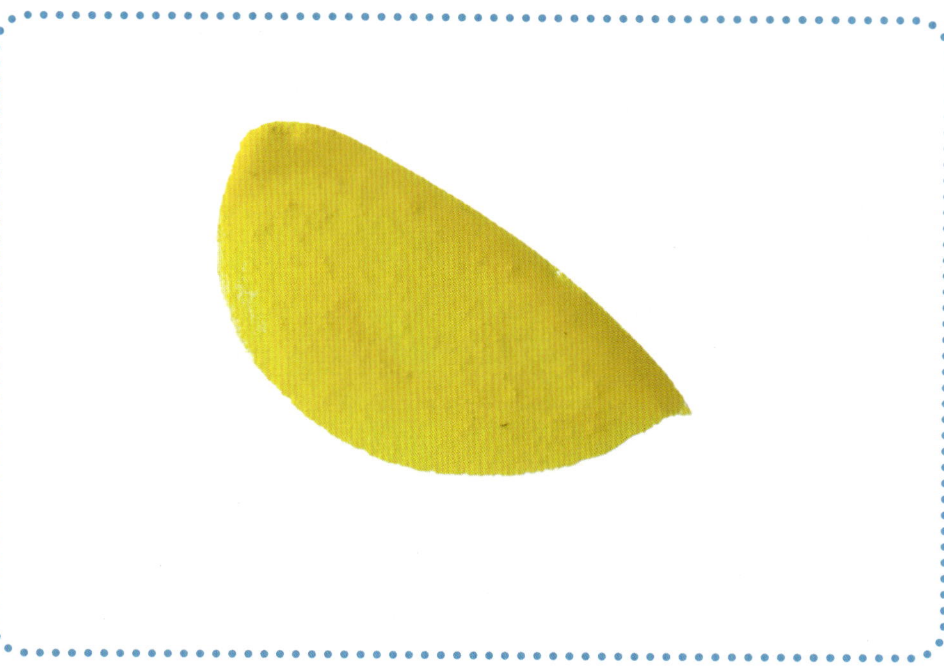

1 Using lemon yellow paint and a #10 round brush, create the body of the bird consisting of a simple oval shape with a straight edge on top.

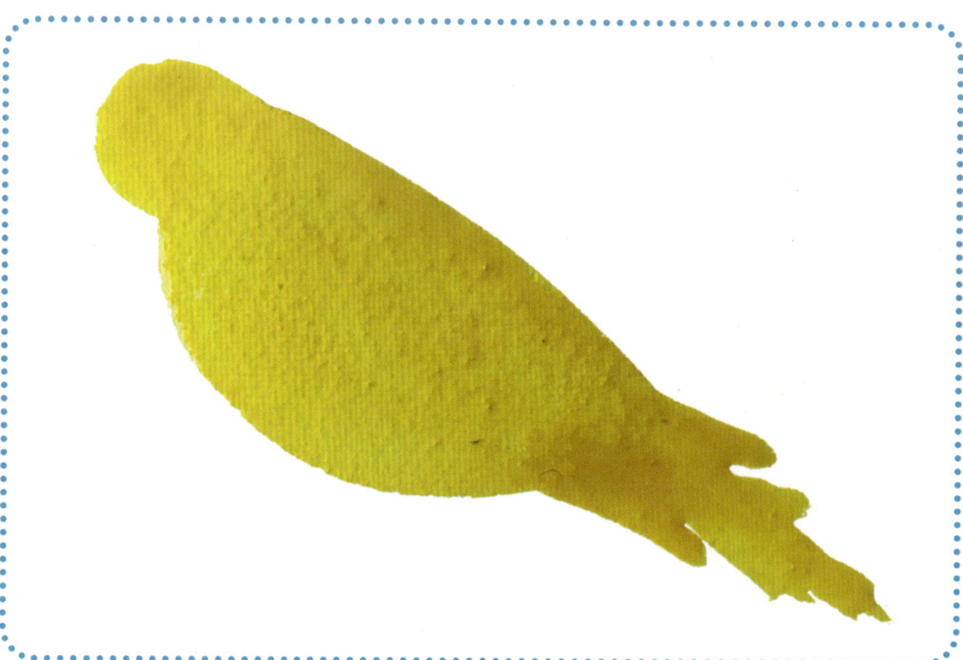

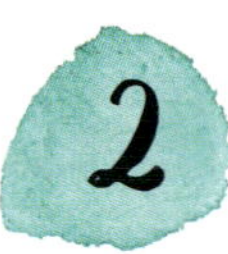

2 Now add a small circle for the head, with half of the circle inside the oval you already created. Add tail feathers with the tip of a #10 round brush.

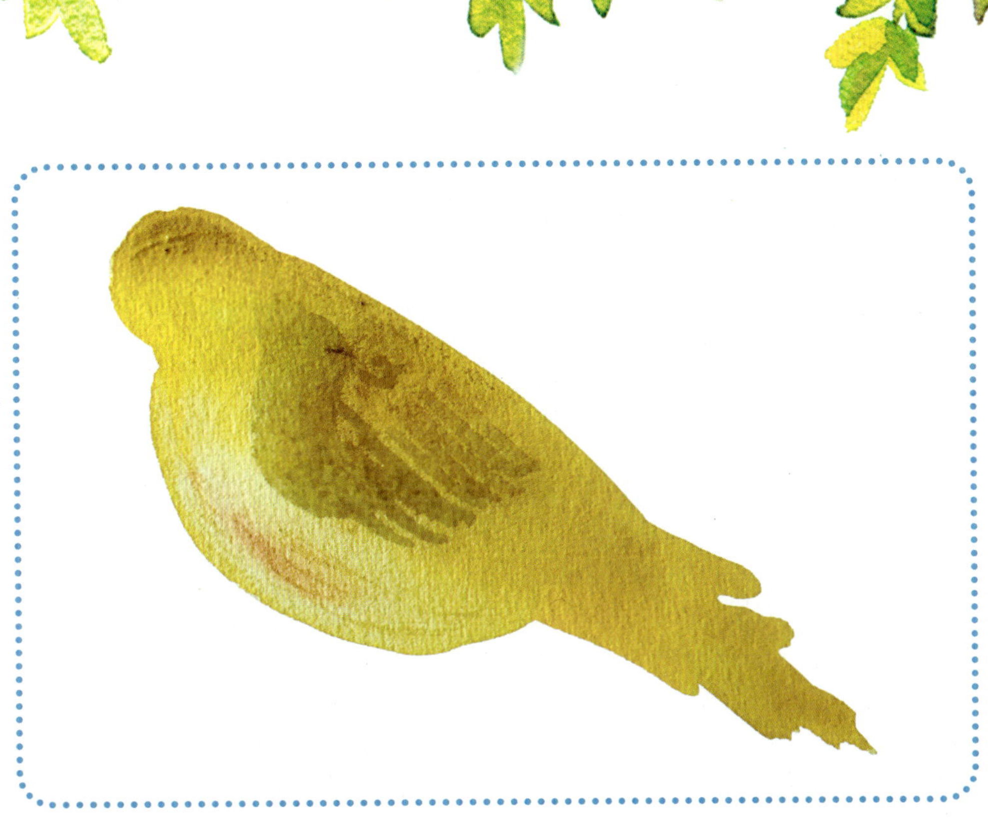

3

While the paint is still wet, dip the tip of the brush in raw umber and touch it down on the top of the bird's head and in the wing area. You can drag the brush delicately here to create a striped appearance if you wish.

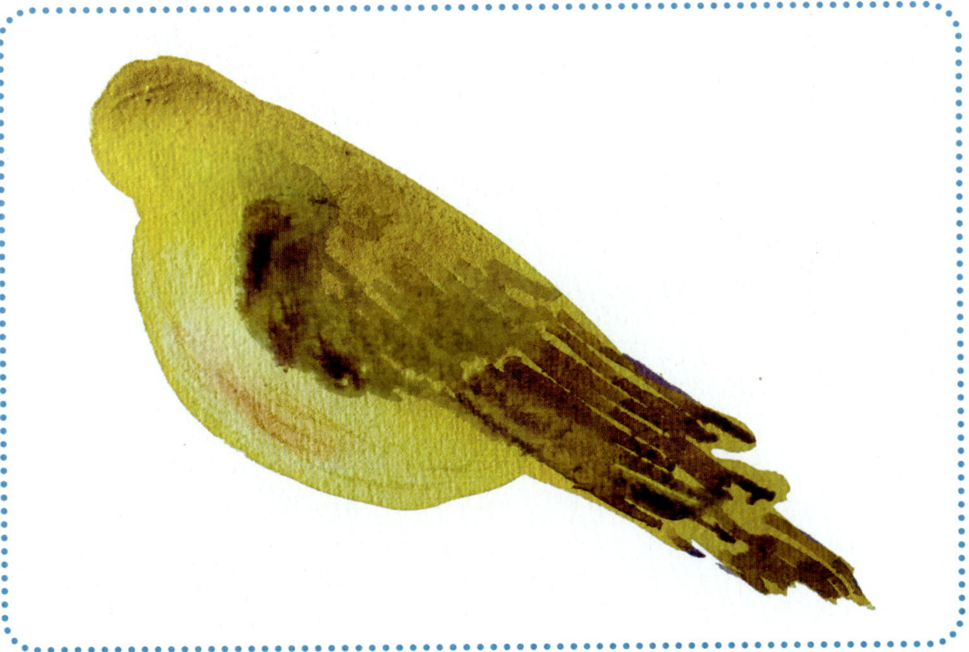

With the paint still wet, add violet to the wing and tail feather areas. Dot paint at the bottom of the wing and let the water move the paint. Use the tip of the brush to create stripes in the tail area.

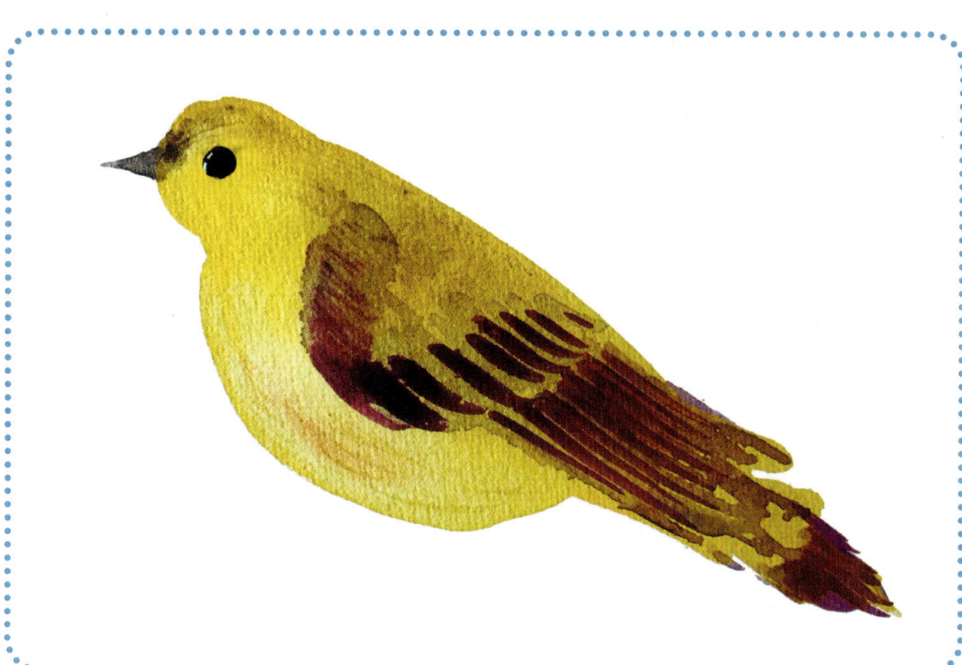

5

Now it's time to add a beak. With a little neutral tint and a touch of Prussian blue, use the tip of a liner brush to form a small triangle at the front of the bird's head, giving it a bit of curve. Once the body of the bird is dry, enhance the intensity of violet in the wing and feathers using the same techniques. Let the paint dry completely.

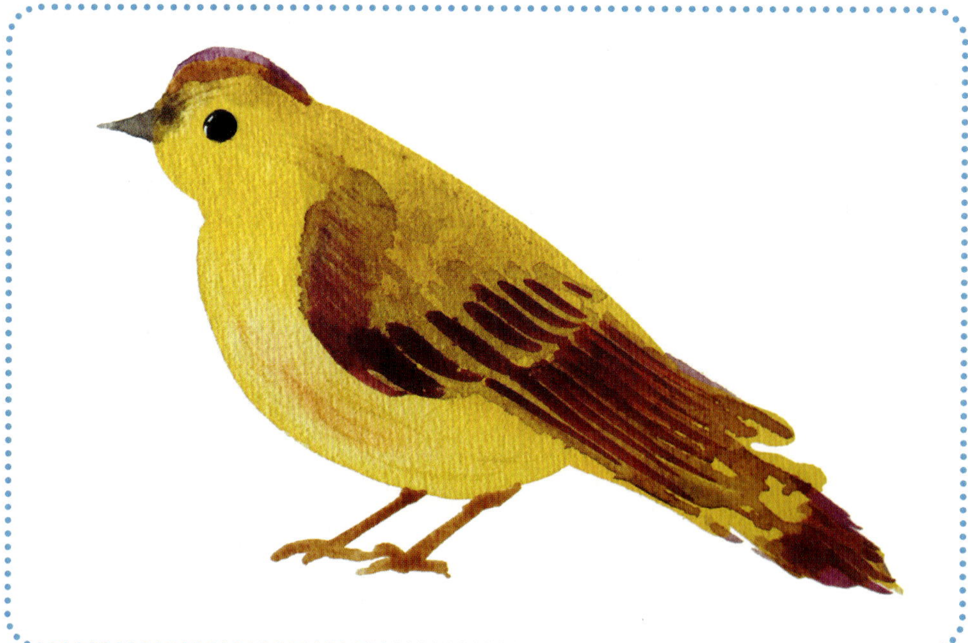

Give your little bird feet! Using two diagonal lines and a mixture of orange and yellow, drag a liner brush down from the body 1 inch. Then add two curved lines in the front and one in the back to form each foot.

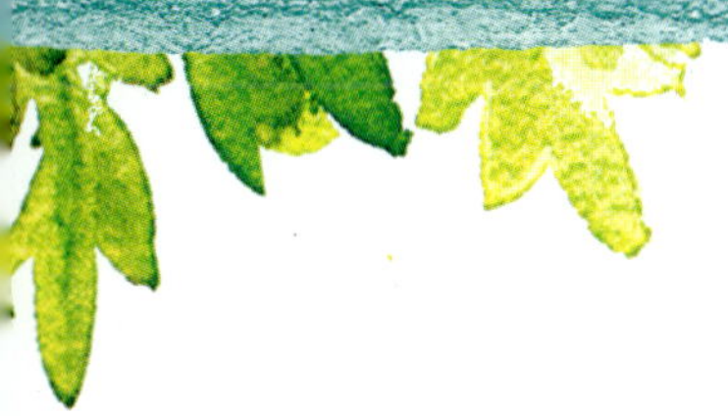

WOODPECKER

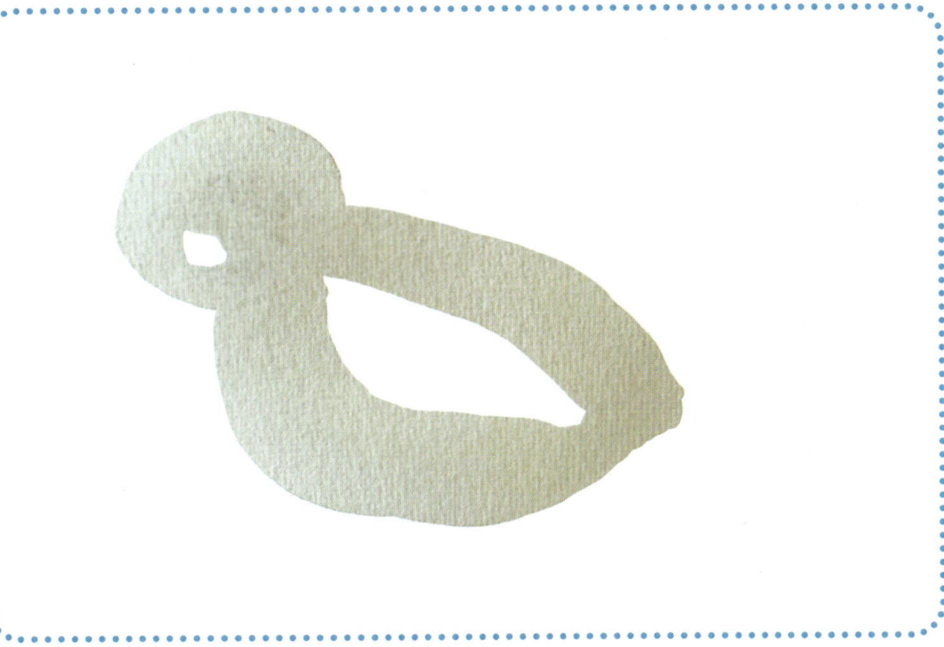

Using a warm gray mix (I've watered down some black and added a tiny touch of lemon yellow) and a #10 round brush, form a basic bird shape consisting of a small circle and an oval, leaving some of the wing free from pigment. The white of the paper will act as a highlight.

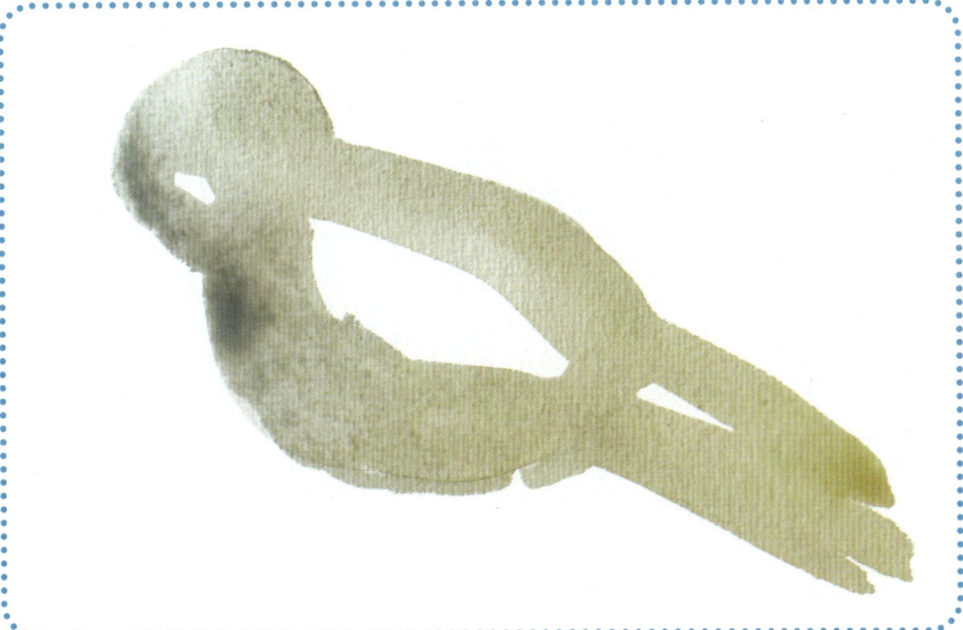

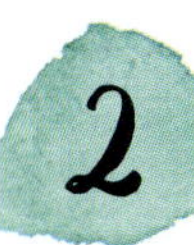

Drag the tip of a #10 round brush off the body to create the tail.

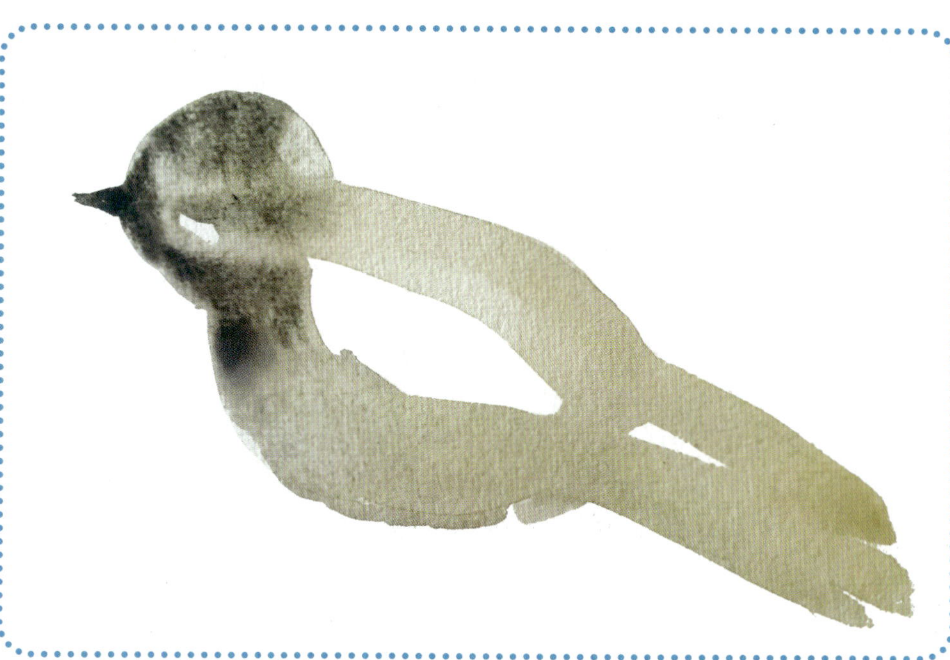

3

While the paint is still wet, add the contrasting pattern to the bird. Start lightly to gain a sense of how the water will make the pigment travel. Use the liner brush and black paint to make a quick beak, and then coax the black color into the head and breast of the bird.

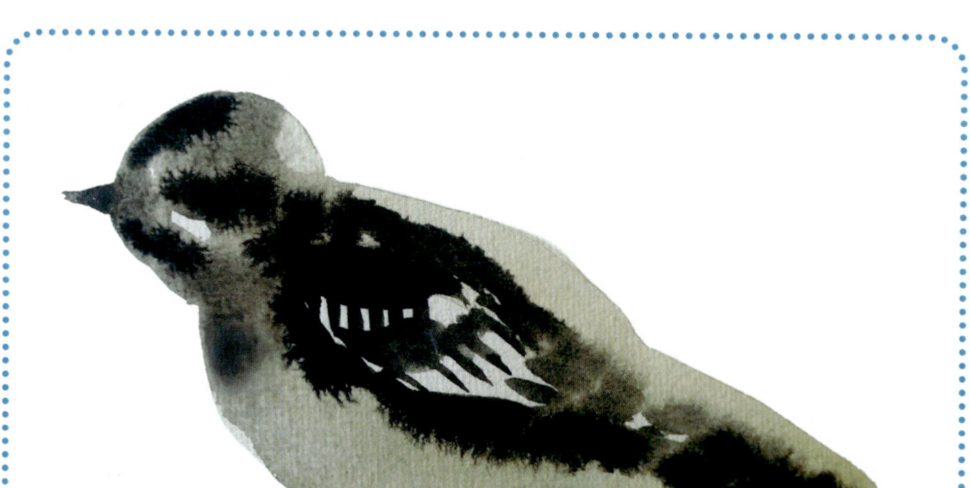

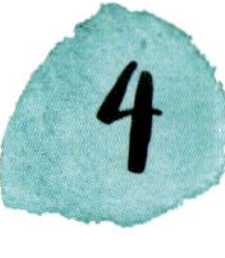

Now it's time to get bold! Load the tip of your brush with black and tap the paint into the wing and tail feathers. This is a fun step and it's exciting to see how the pigment moves and blurs in some places. You will see how the areas left white by the paper now pop against the black!

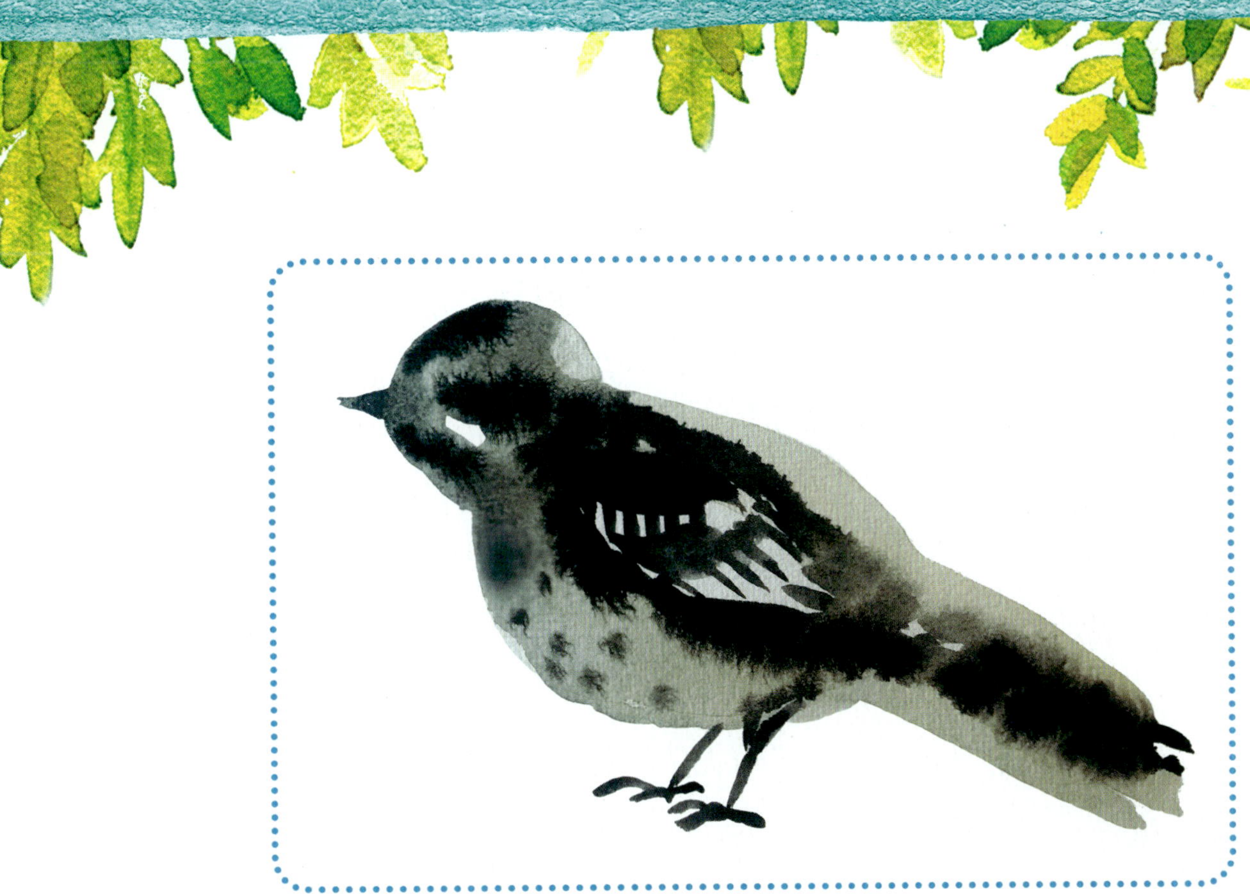

5

It's time to add feet to the woodpecker! I've used gray and black.

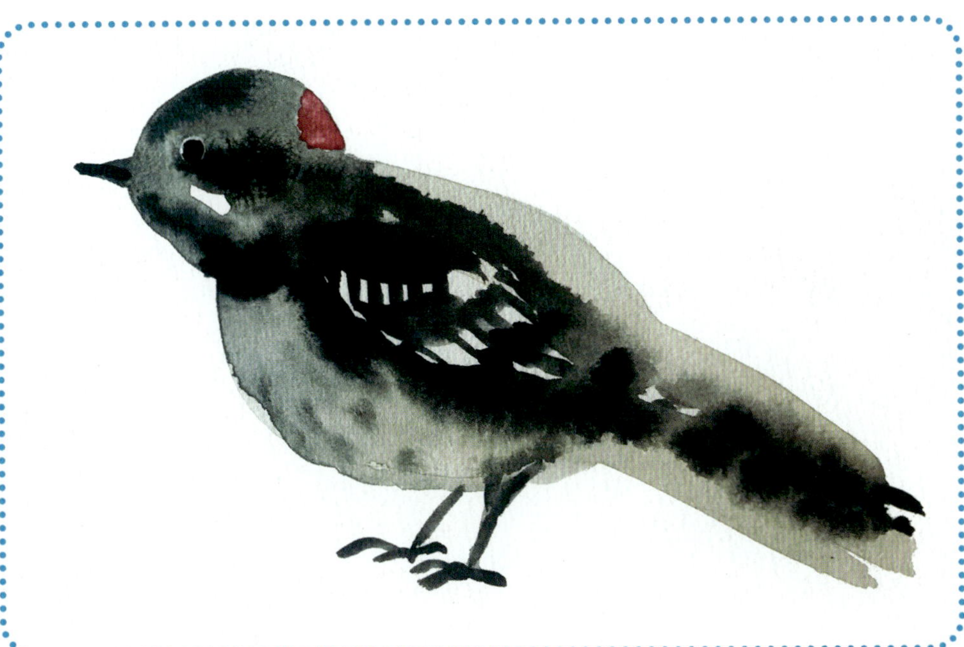

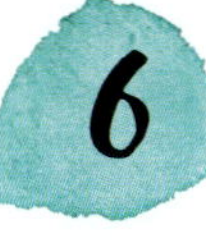

Dilute some black paint and add soft lines to the breast to give it more texture. Then add the iconic punch of red to the back of the bird's head. Using your liner brush, outline a tiny circle for the bird's eye; then fill it with black.

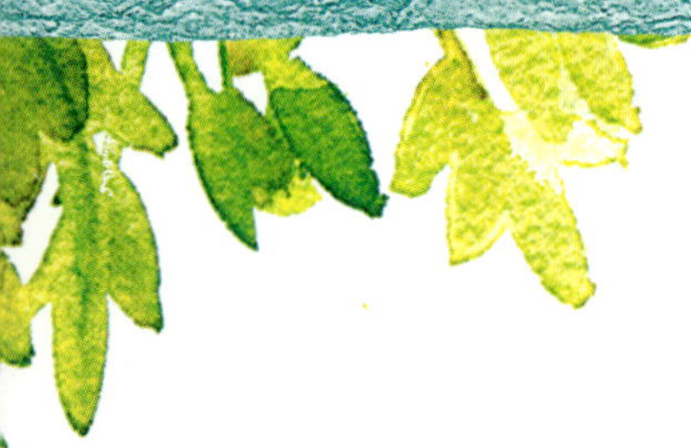
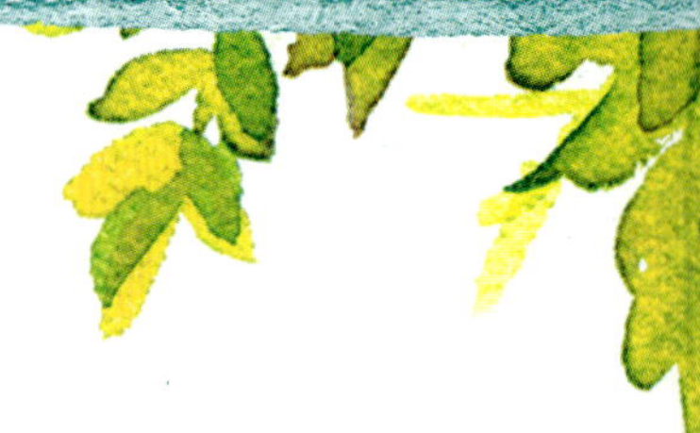

AMERICAN ROBIN

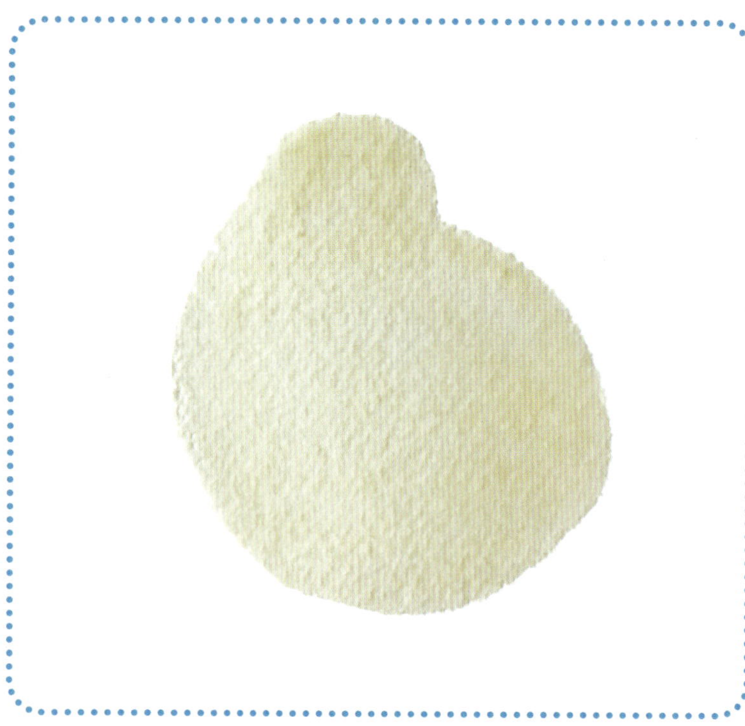

Using dirty water and a #10 round brush, form an oval with a circle on top. The circle can be just slightly left of center.

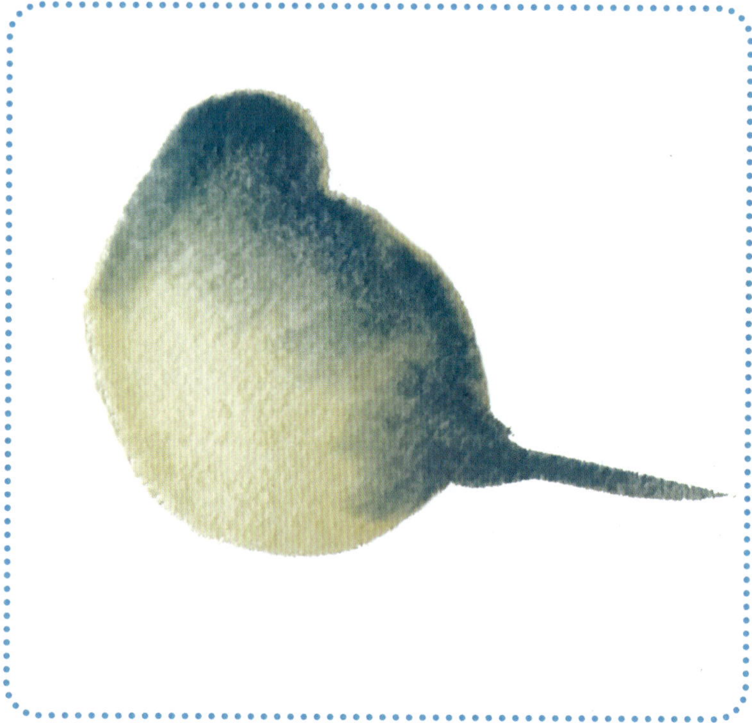

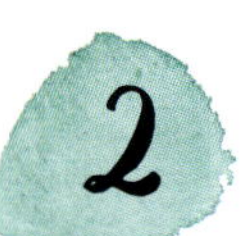

Dipping your brush in cobalt blue, tap into the wet bird shape from the outer edges. I've moved from the breast to the top of the head and then down along the back and into the tail.

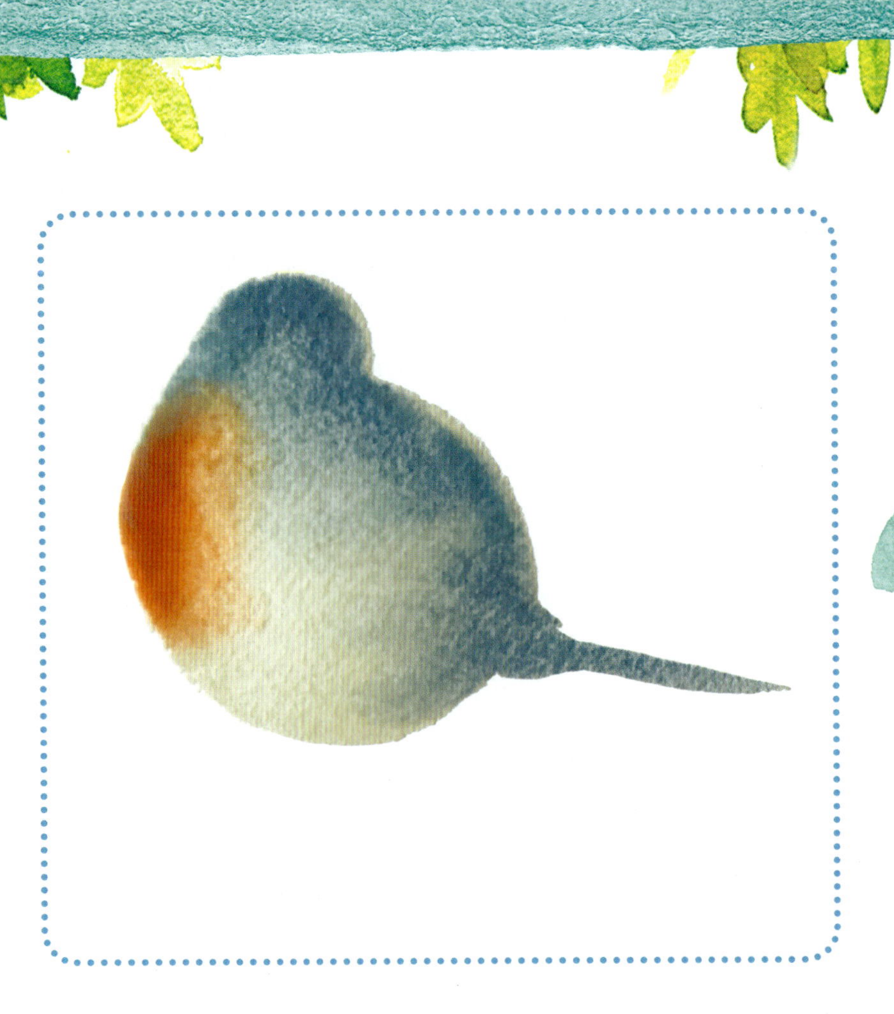

3

While the paint is still wet, dip your brush in a red-orange mix and tap deeper into the breast area. Let the paint dissipate on its own to create subtlety. If you need to coax the paint a bit, add more water to your brush.

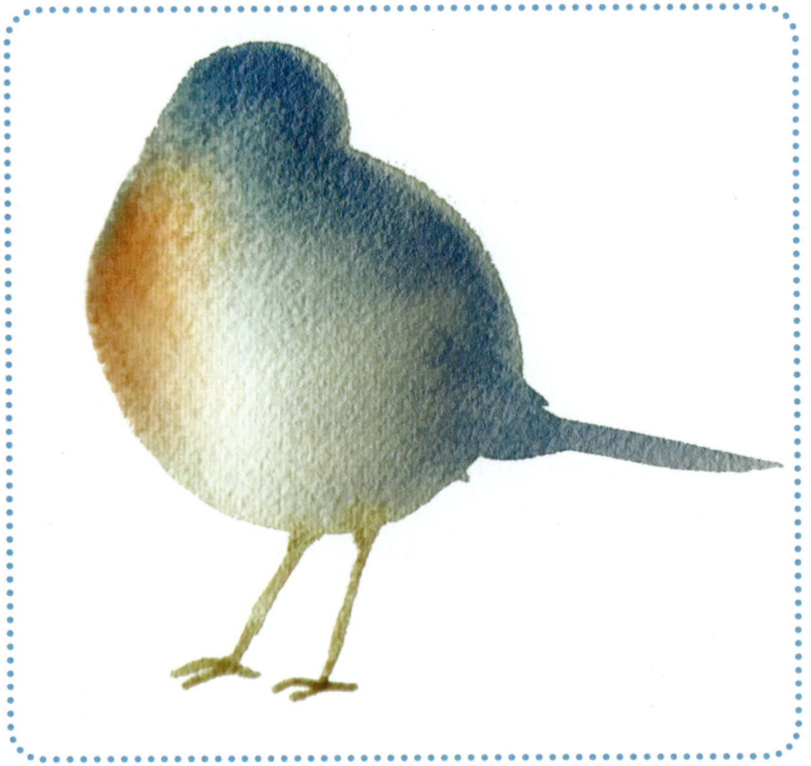

4

Time to add some legs! I've mixed up some brown-orange and let the pigment bleed gently into the robin's body. I like that effect, but you can wait and let the body dry first if you prefer. Let the paint dry completely.

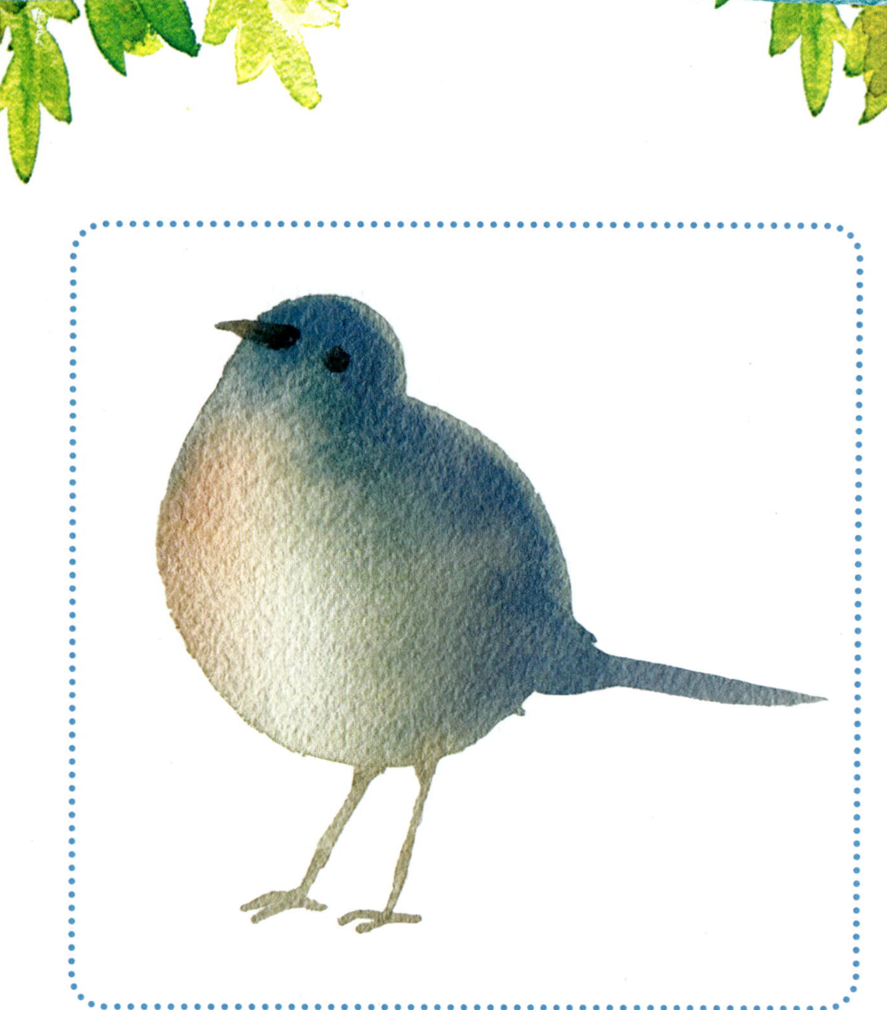

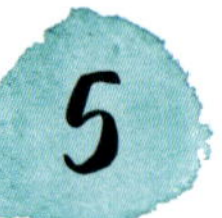

Add a beak and an eye with a liner brush and diluted black.

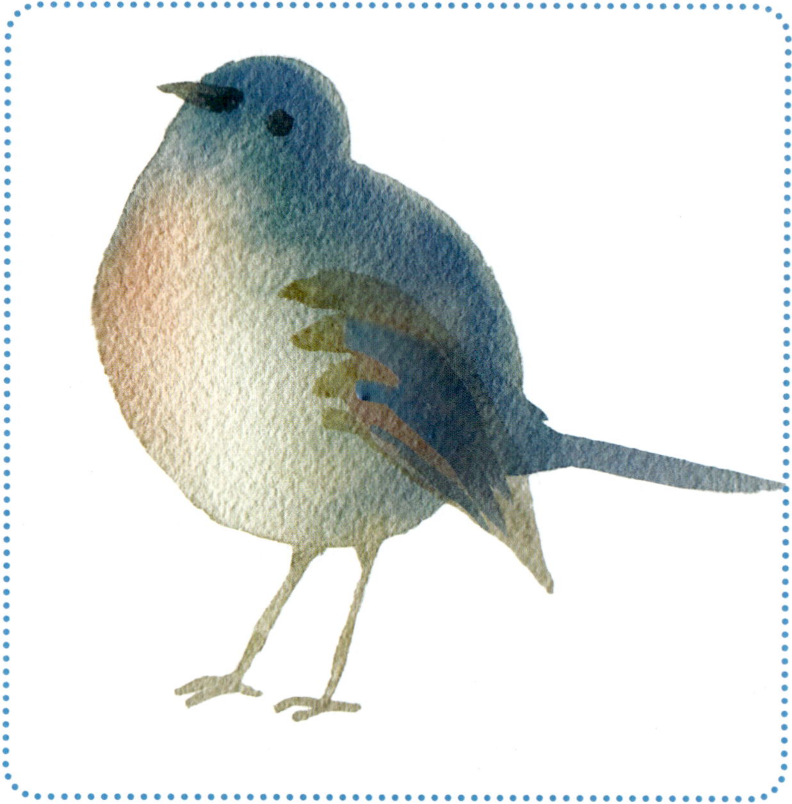

To finish, mix up some of the brown-orange with a touch of blue and give the robin a wing. I've dragged the tip of my #10 brush from left to right, applying less pressure as I move. To add more definition to the wing, you can go back in with some blue lines once the paint is dry.

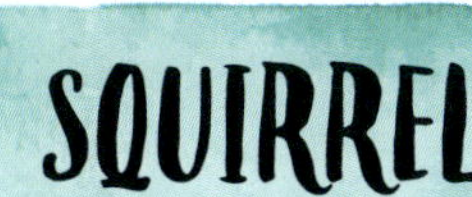

SQUIRREL

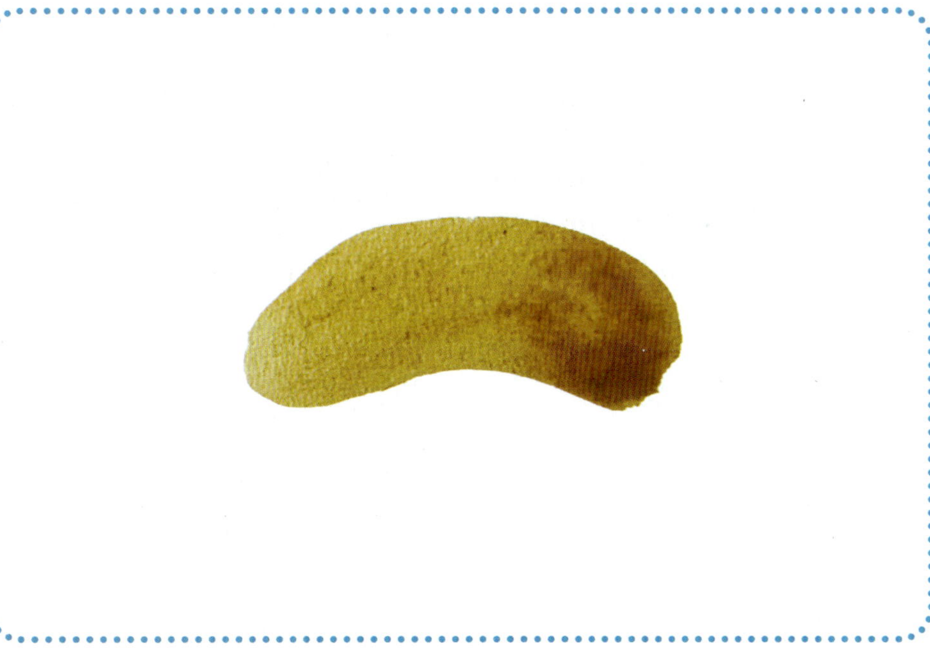

1 With a #10 round brush, create a simple arced sausage shape in a warm orange-brown to form the body of the squirrel.

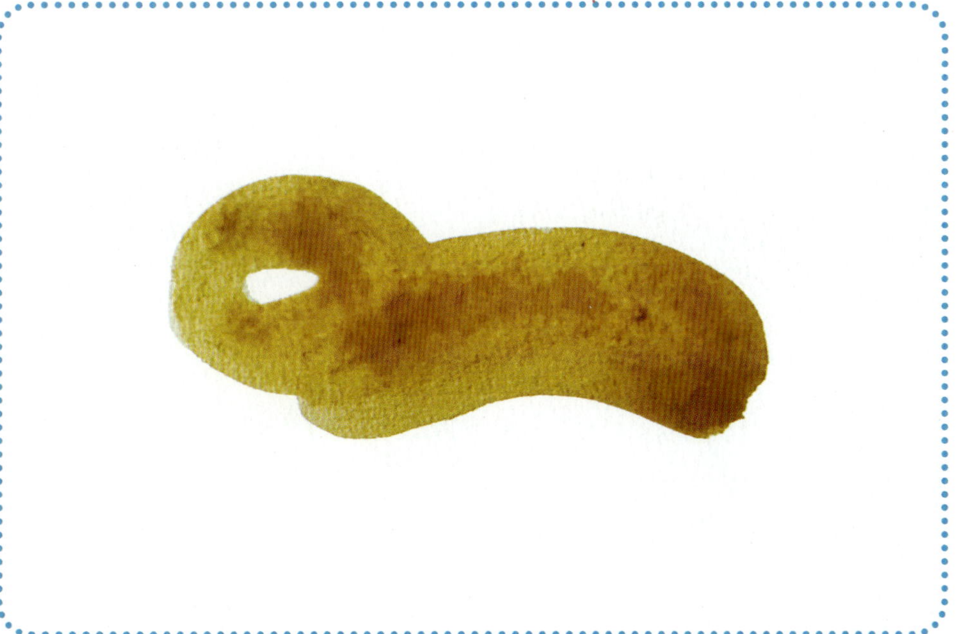

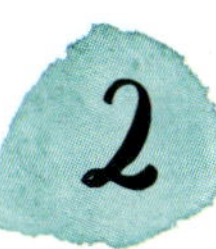

Now add an oval-shaped head, leaving a bit of white space for the eye that will come later.

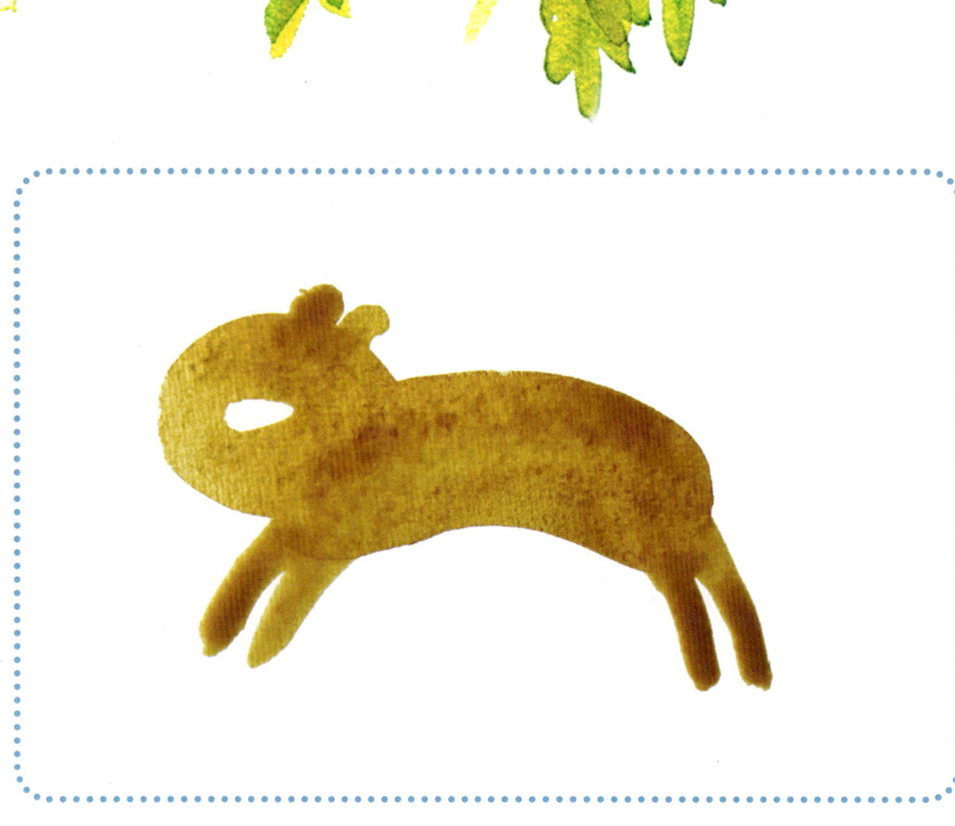

3

Using the same brown, add two small ears and four simple legs.

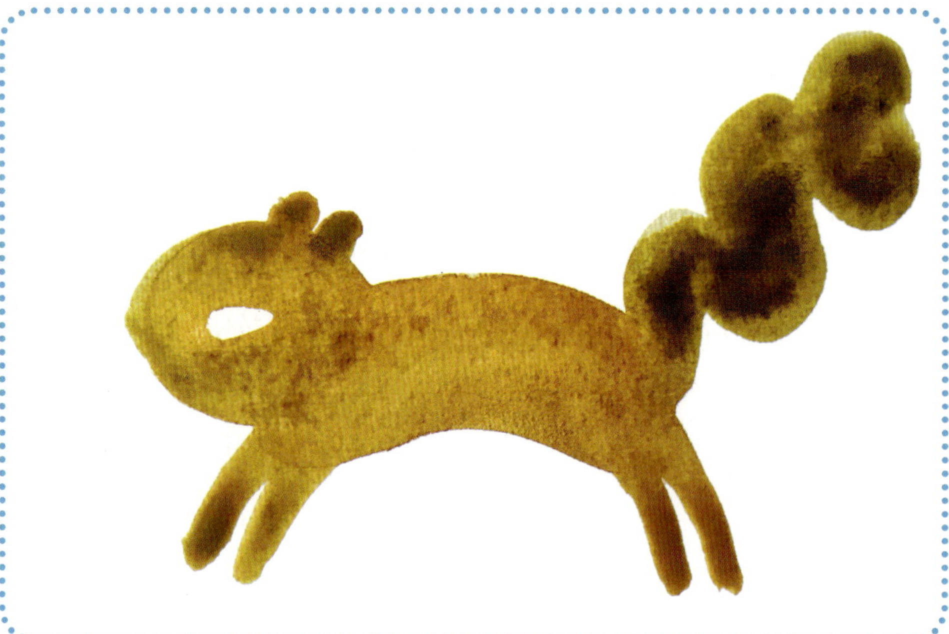

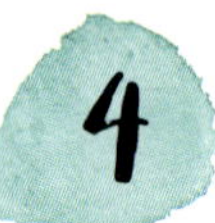

While the brown paint is still wet, tap sepia into the ears and tail to give the squirrel some depth.

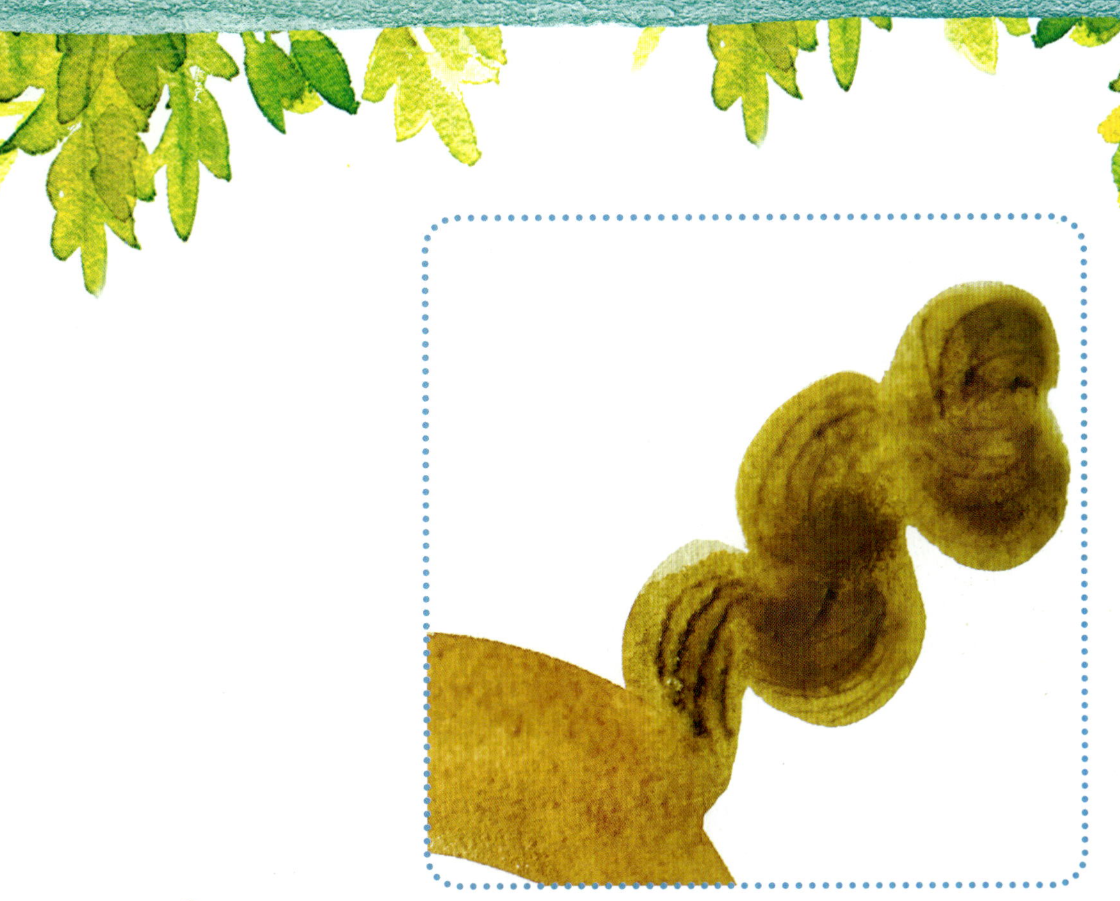

5

While the paint is still wet, focus on the tail and use a toothpick to draw curvy marks in the direction of the different segments of the tail. This will give it a bushy appearance and a whimsical quality.

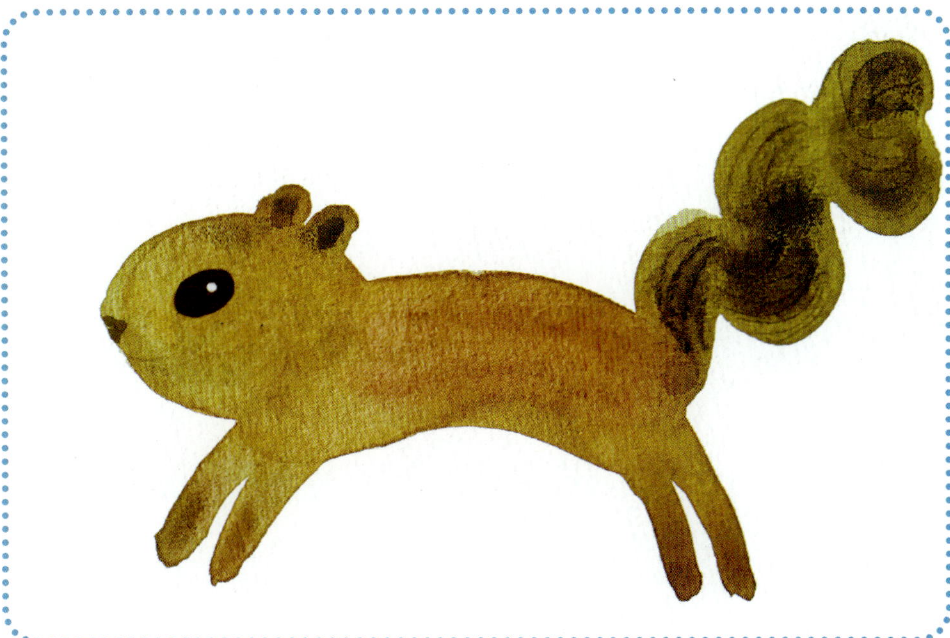

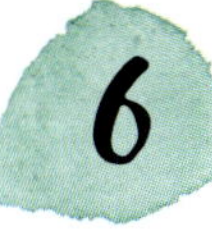

Now add a small, almond-shaped eye. I've used sepia, leaving some of the paper white for a highlight. Add a tiny nose and you're all done!

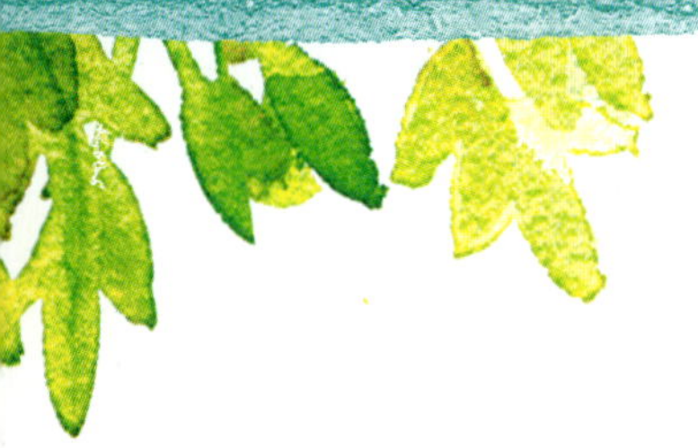

CHIPMUNK

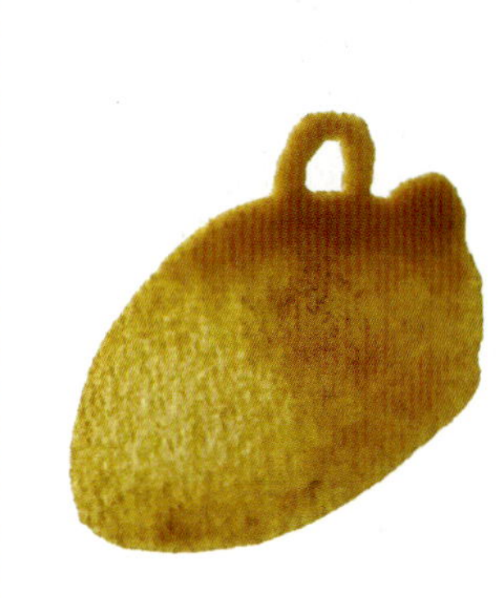

Use a #10 round brush and orange-brown pigment to create a simple almond-shaped head. Add two ears, with the back one in outline.

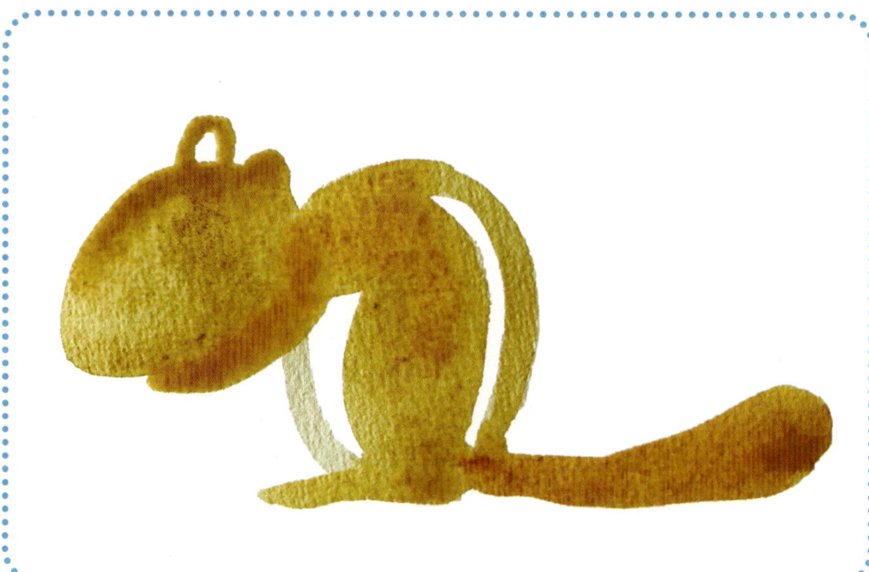

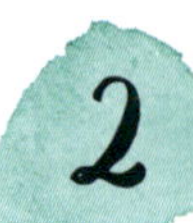

Now add the body. Think of it as an oval with the bottom flattened out. Leave two highlights inside: one in the belly area and one along the spine. Take a moment to run your round brush just under the head to create an arm. Now make a simple foot by dragging some of this wet pigment out from the body with a liner brush or the tip of a small round brush. Make a tail by applying a bit more pressure as you move left to right.

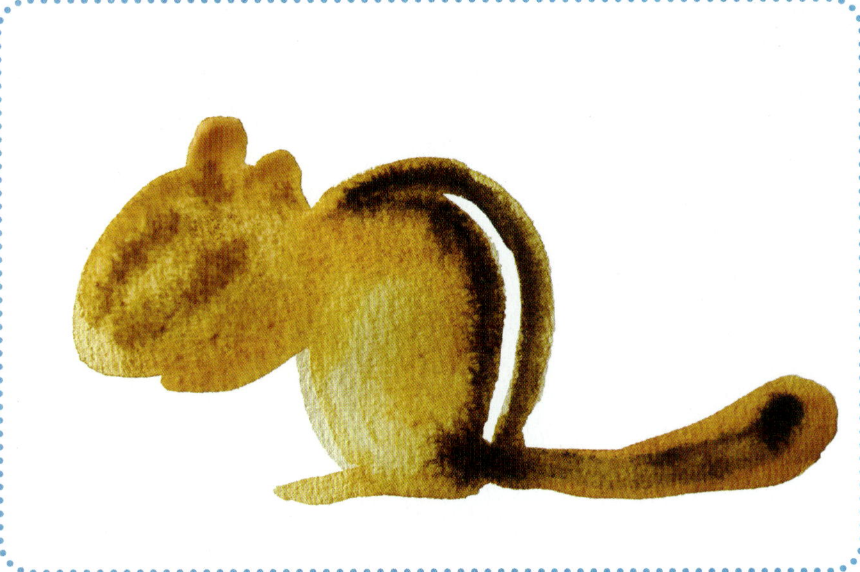

3

While the pigment is still wet, dip your brush in sepia paint and tap the brush on either side of the saved white area along the spine. Now tap the brush at the base of the tail and along the center and tip. I've also added an additional wash of the body hue to give the chipmunk's face more markings and depth.

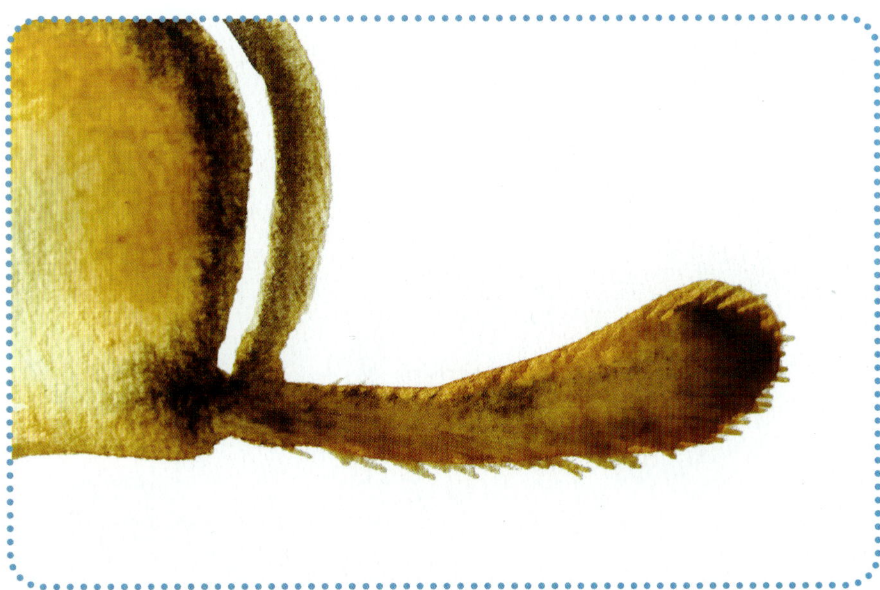

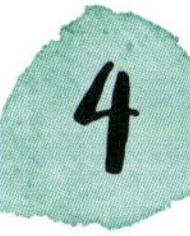

Here you can see some detail in the tail. Use a toothpick to score little hairs from the center of the tail outward. This will give the tail movement and a bristly texture.

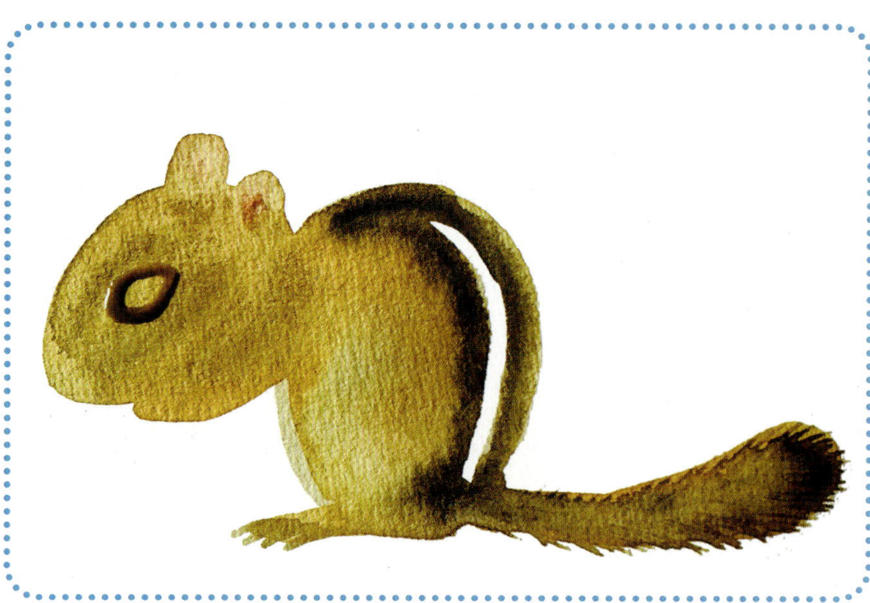

5

Now let's create the eye. Using a liner brush and sepia paint, create a small almond-shaped outline that follows the angle of the head. Also lightly add a touch of soft pink to the inside of the ears. Define the chipmunk's little feet with a liner brush and a darker brown hue.

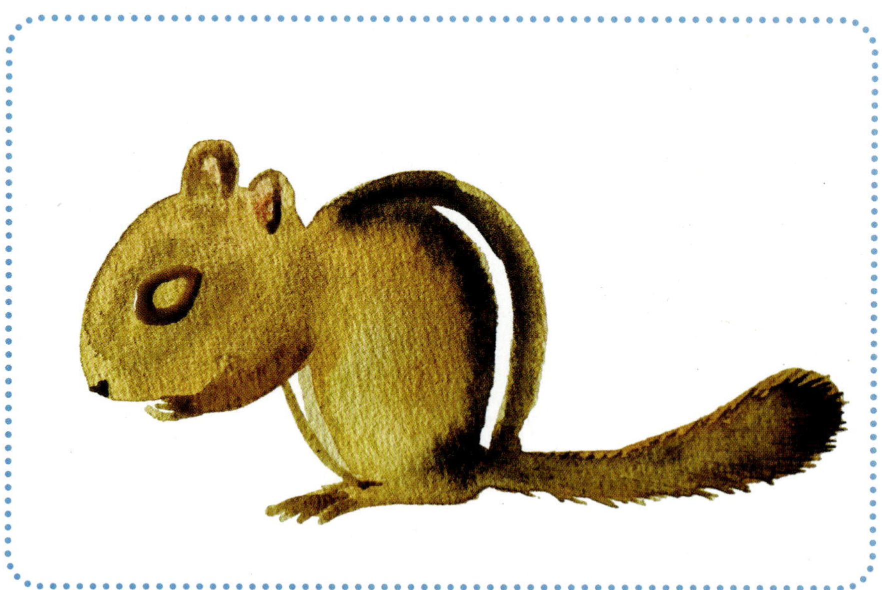

Line the ears to give them definition. Use a shade just slightly darker than your original body hue, such as umber. Define the chipmunk's arm by adding an additional wash of brown and small fingers with the liner brush.

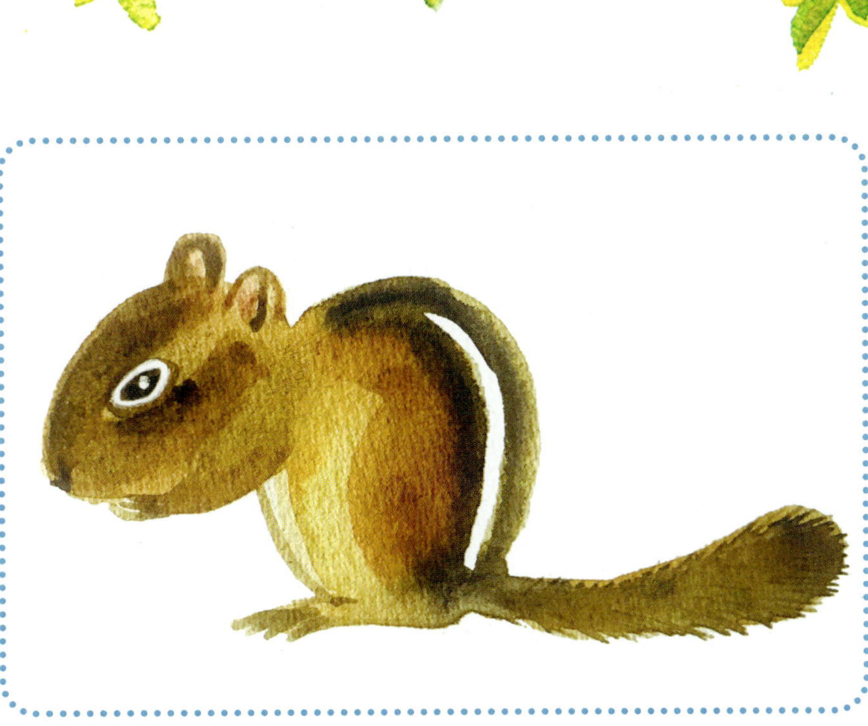

Using a small brush and sepia paint, finish the eye. Let this dry. Add a small nose in the shape of a tiny triangle. While the paint dries, define the chipmunk's hip by adding a bit more orange-brown.

Once the eye is dry, dip your liner brush into a tube of white. If the paint is too dry, add the tiniest bit of water. You need just enough to rim the outside of the little eye.

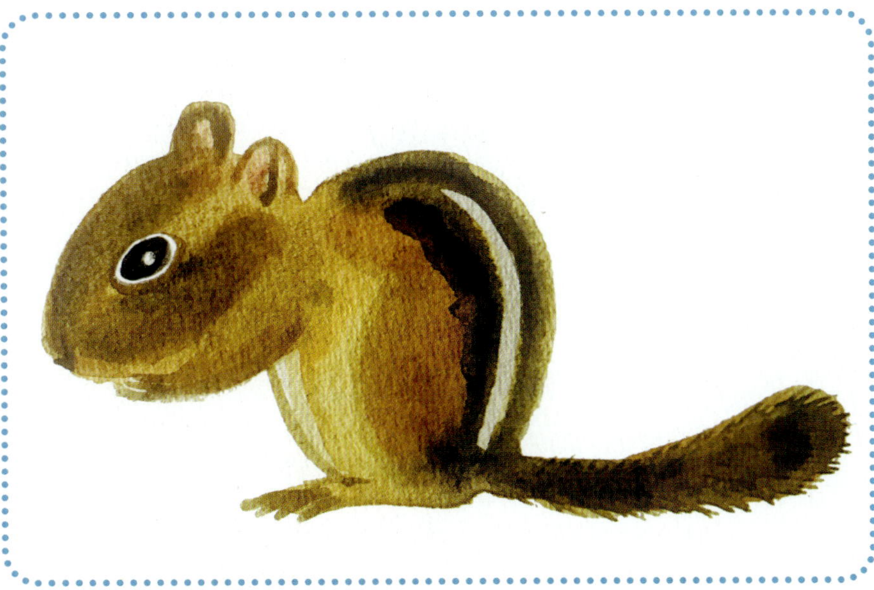

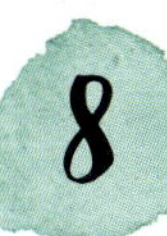

In this final step, you may elect to darken some areas. I want the chipmunk's stripes to really stand out, so I've added a bit more sepia to the lower stripe. I've also defined the eye some more with an additional application of sepia. How does the chipmunk look now? Feel free to make any additions as you see fit.

Seasonal Bits: Leaves, Pods & Thistle

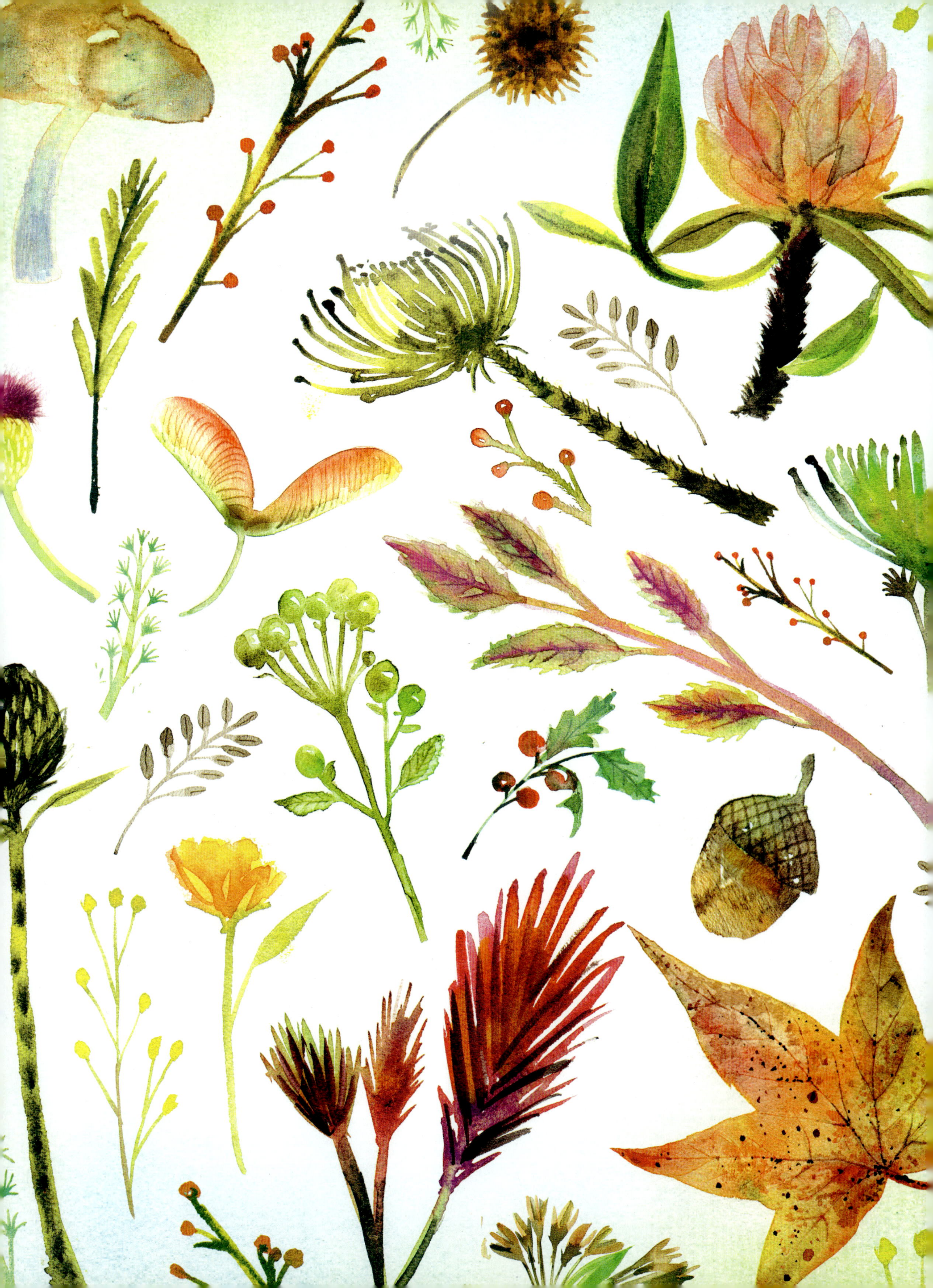

BEECH LEAF

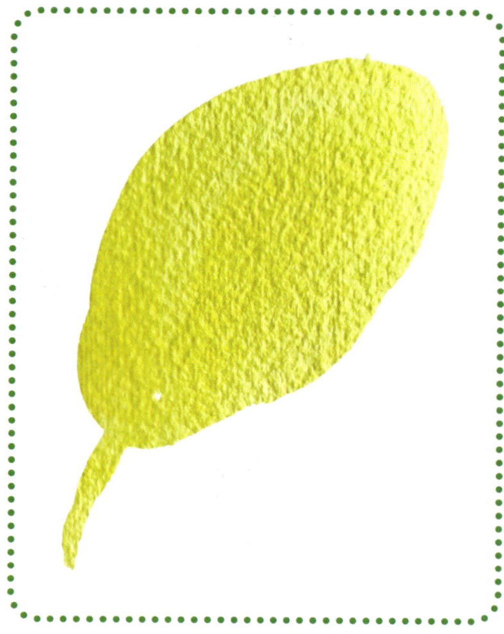

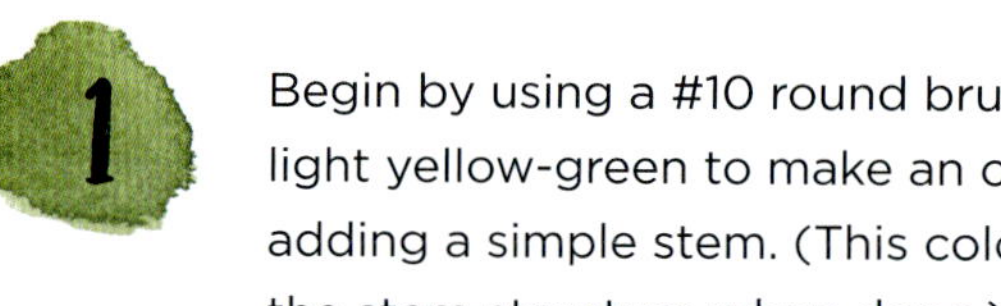

1 Begin by using a #10 round brush and light yellow-green to make an oval shape, adding a simple stem. (This color will form the stem structure when done.)

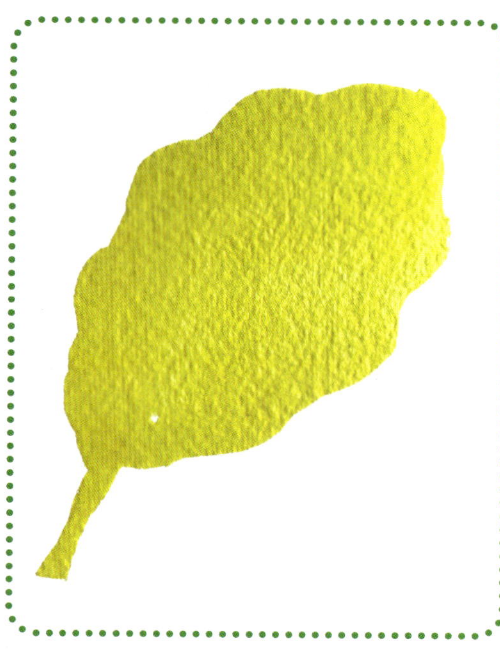

2 Next, define the oval by creating a scalloped edge with the tip of your brush.

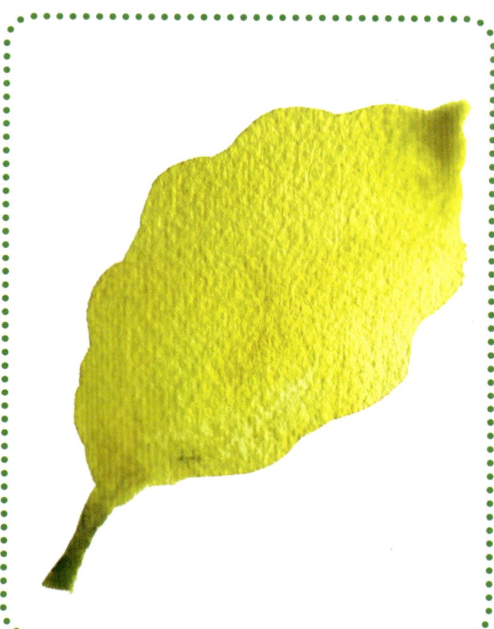

3 Add a point to the tip of the leaf with a slightly darker hue of green, and tap this into the bottom of the stem as well.

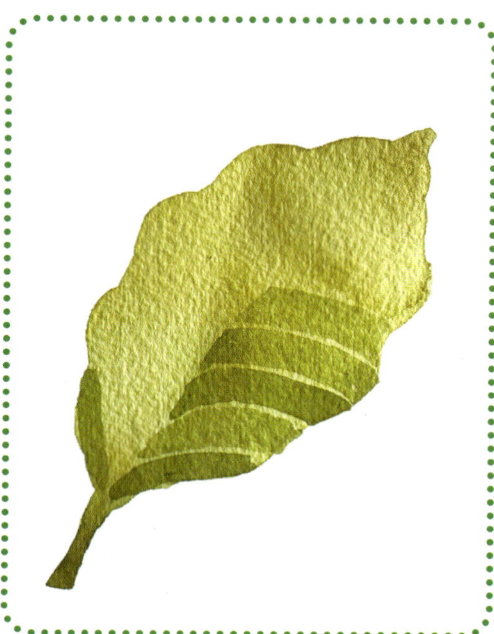

4 Begin to paint the sections of the leaf using negative-space painting. You can alternate values of green to give the leaf visual interest.

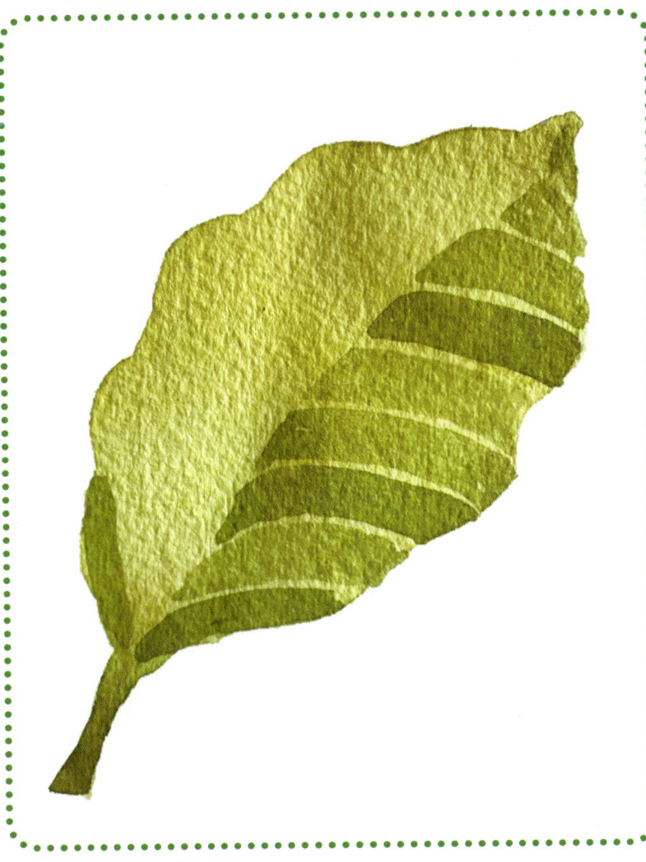

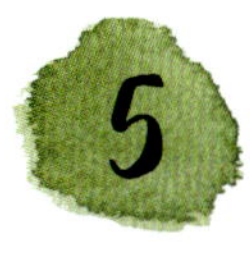

Continue on the other side of the leaf, keeping the center section of light green clean so that it forms the vein in the middle.

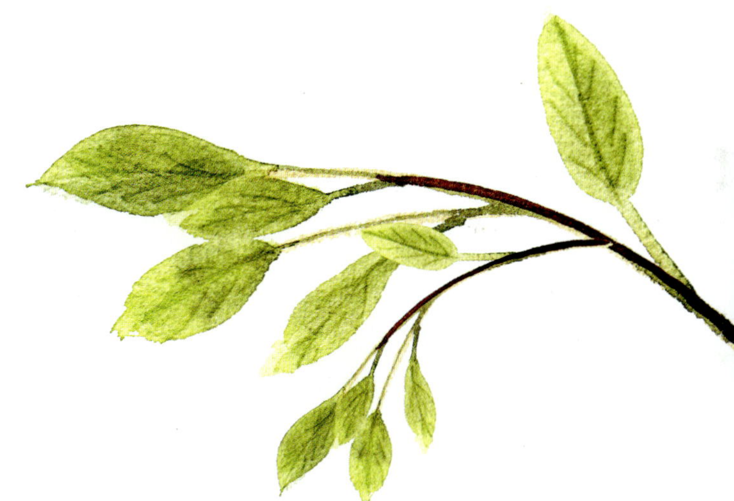

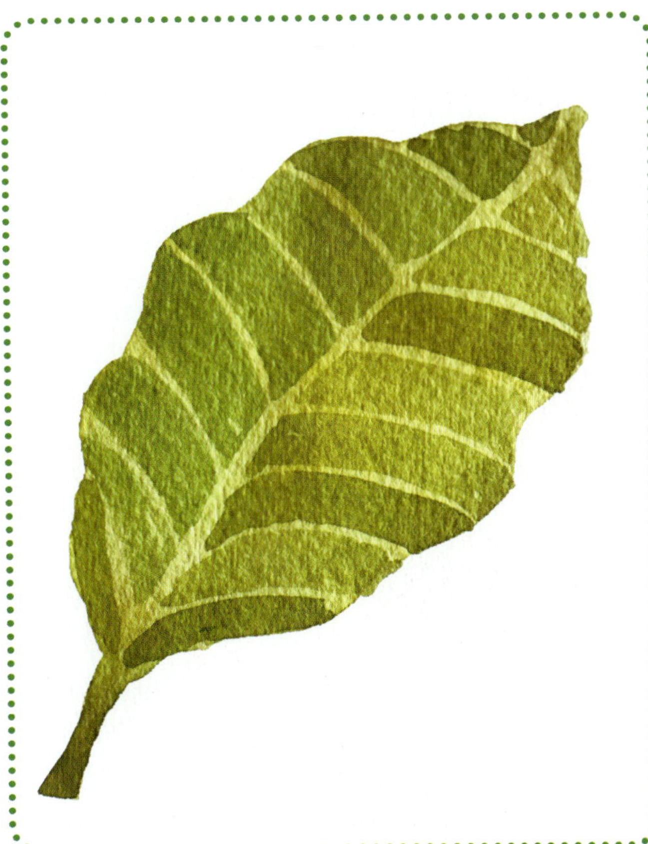

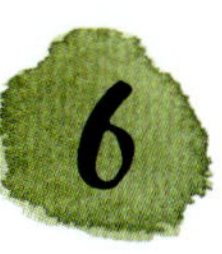

Fill in the leaf until you reach the tip. While the paint is still wet, you can tap some darker green paint into the little valleys by the center stem to add dimension.

EVERGREEN SPRIGS

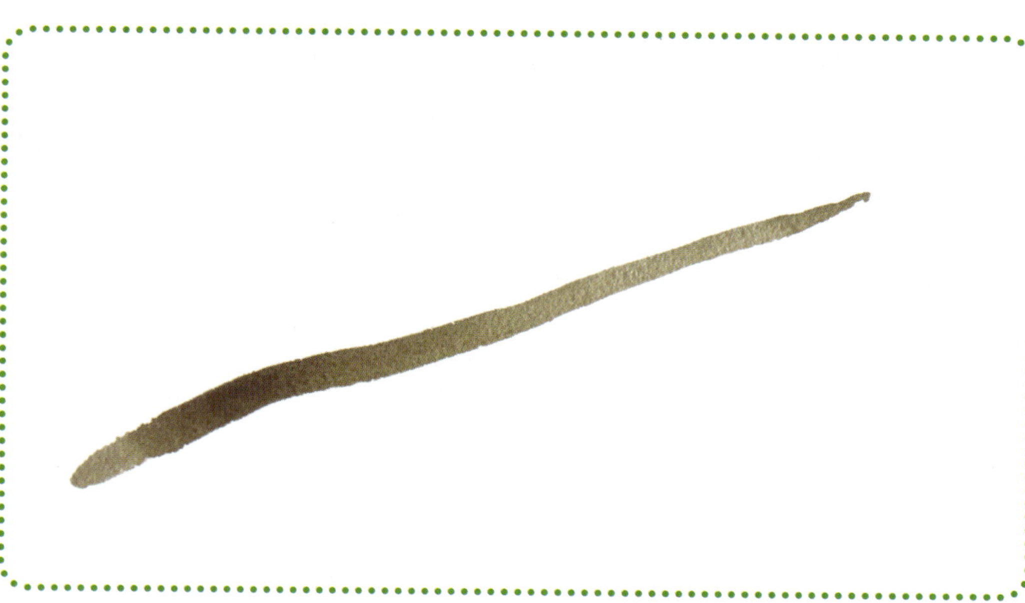

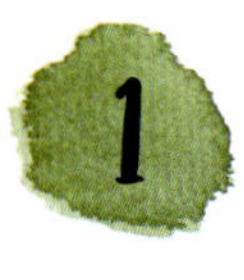

Dip your #8 round brush into some burnt umber or another shade of brown, and make a tapered stem by lightening your pressure on the brush as you move toward the tip of the stem.

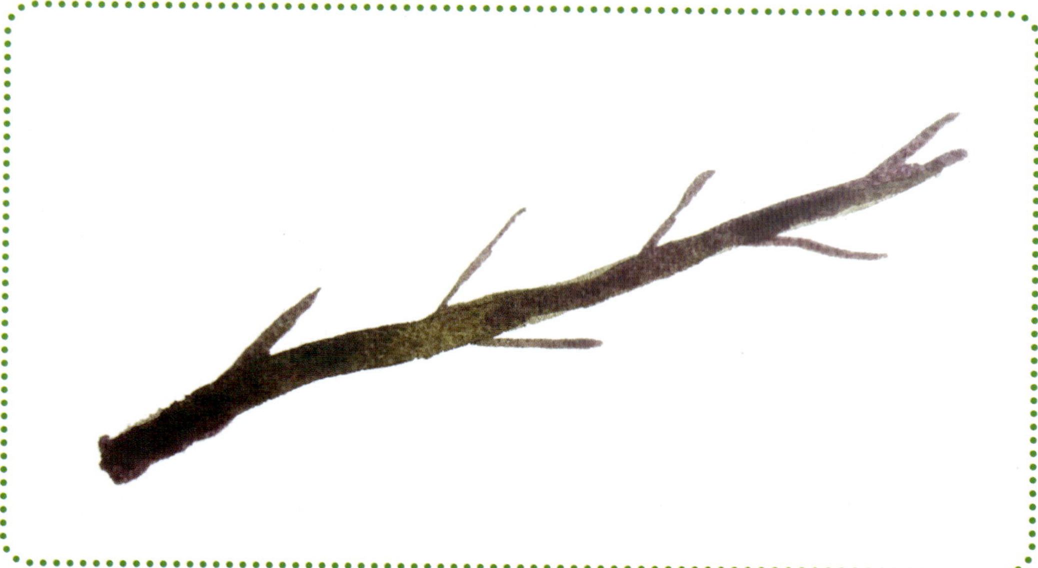

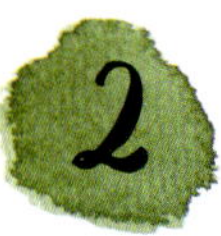

While the brown paint is wet, tap some violet paint into the tip of your brush and add smaller branches to the main stem. Tap a little violet paint into the main stem too, letting the two colors flow into each other.

If you look closely, almost nothing in nature is a solid, one-dimensional color.

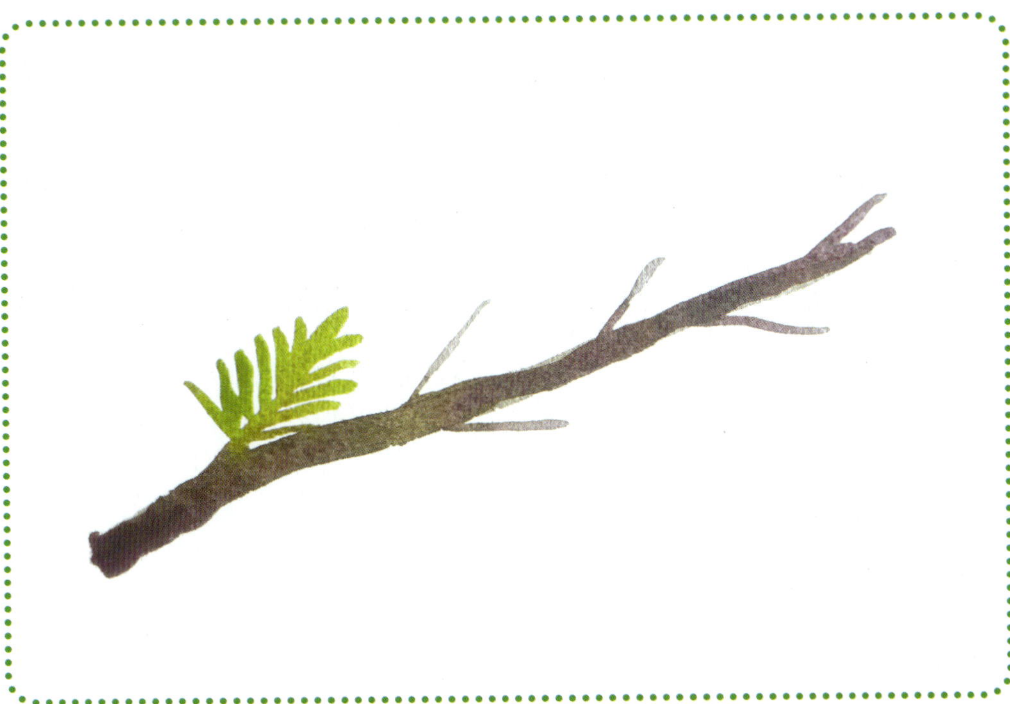

3

While the small branches you just created are still wet, use light yellow-green or green-gold to make the needles of the evergreen, ensuring that you follow the direction of their natural growth. I like to start on the outside edge and drag the brush toward the stem to create a nice effect of green coordinating with the other two colors.

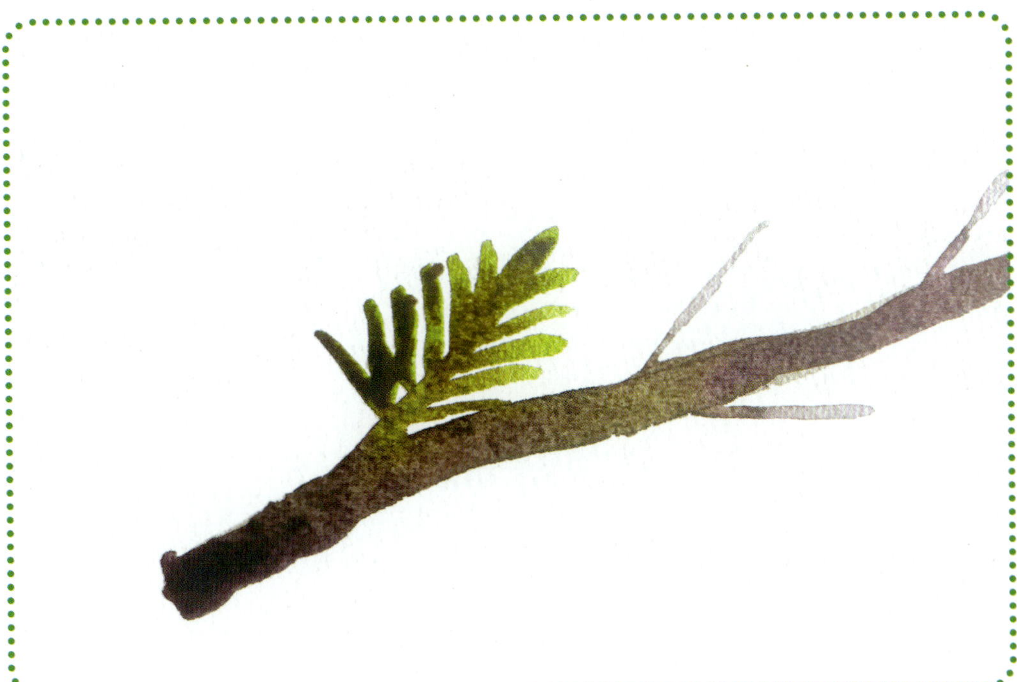

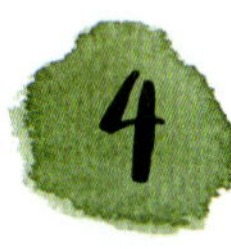

While the needle paint is wet, tap a more intense, earthy green into the outer edges of the needles.

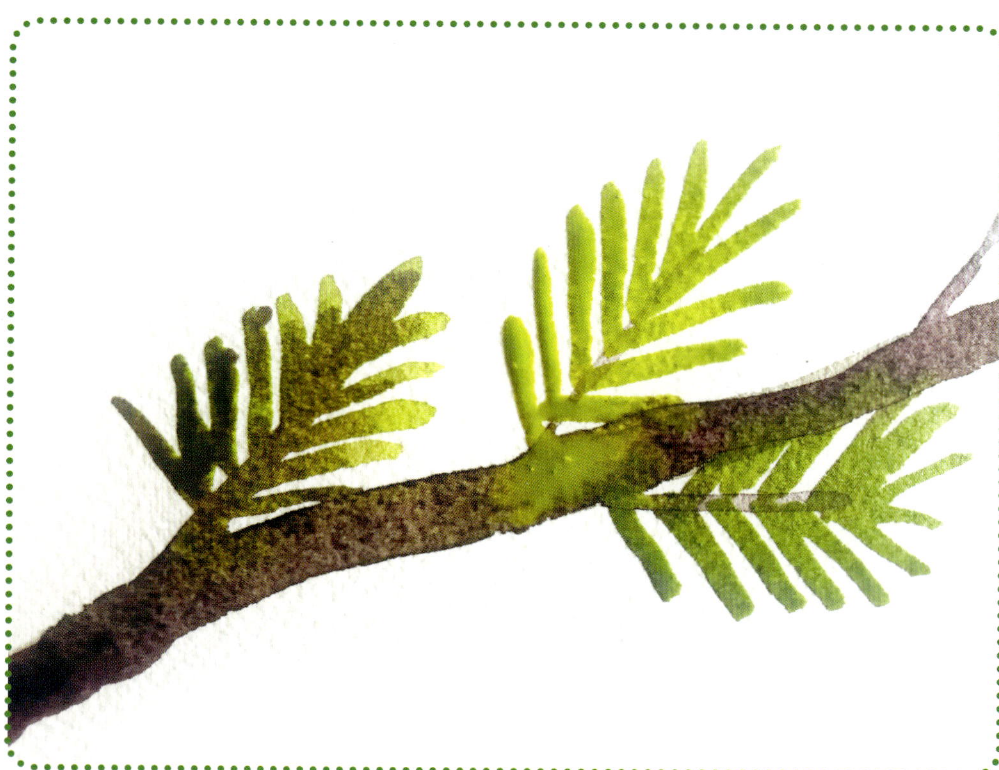

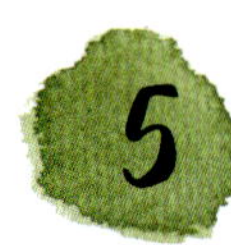

5 Follow the same steps on the smaller stems. I've used a heavy hand on one sprig, but I love how the green floods the area. "Happy accidents," as I say!

This is watercolor magic!

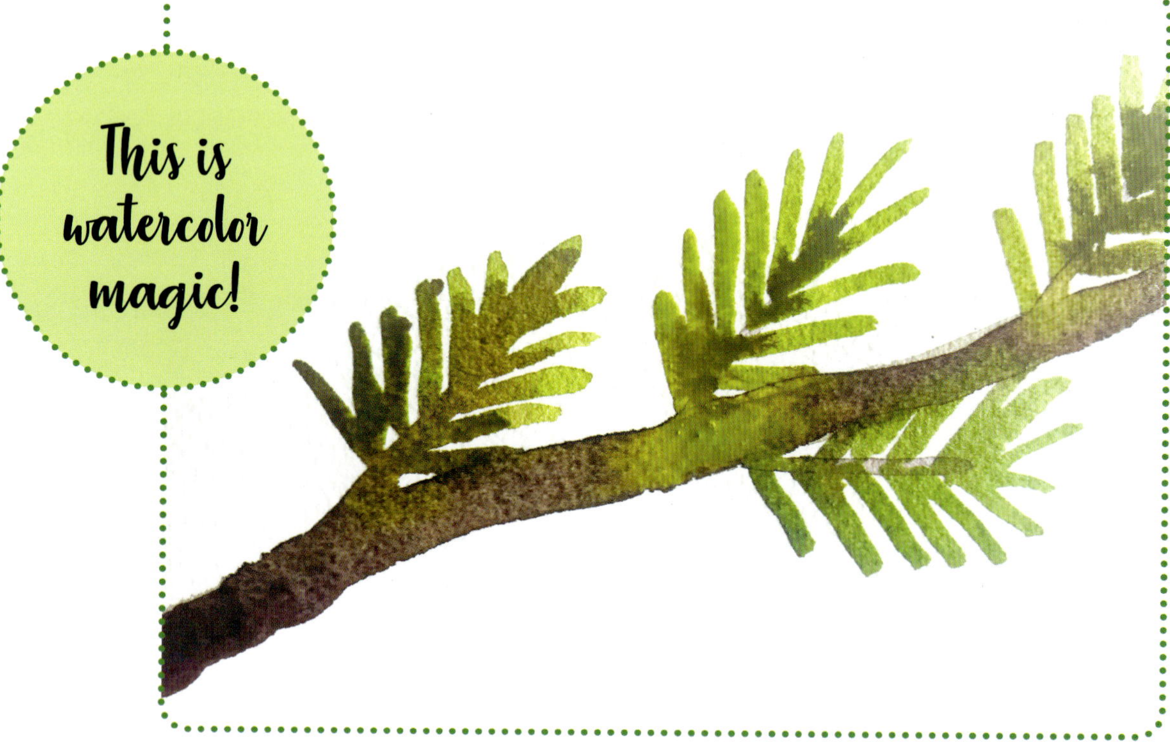

Notice the colors bleeding into each other in the last stem.

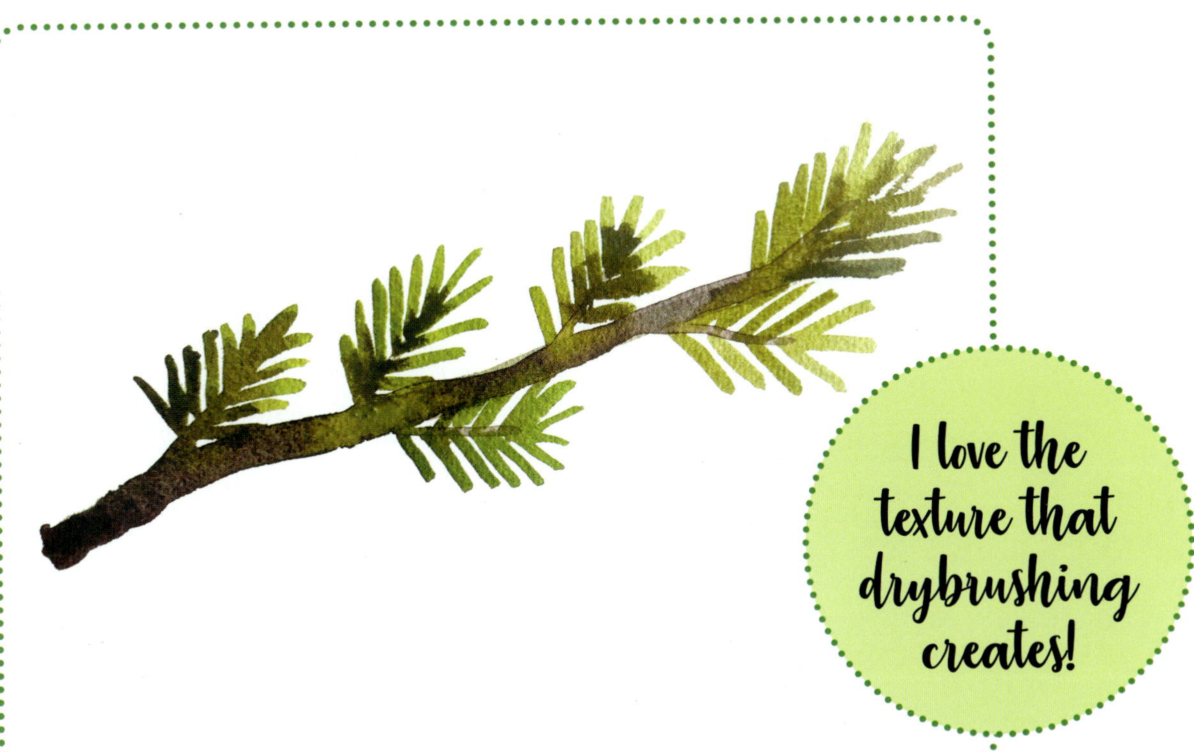

6 Finish the outer stems with needles. Alternate using a very wet brush with a dry brush for different outcomes.

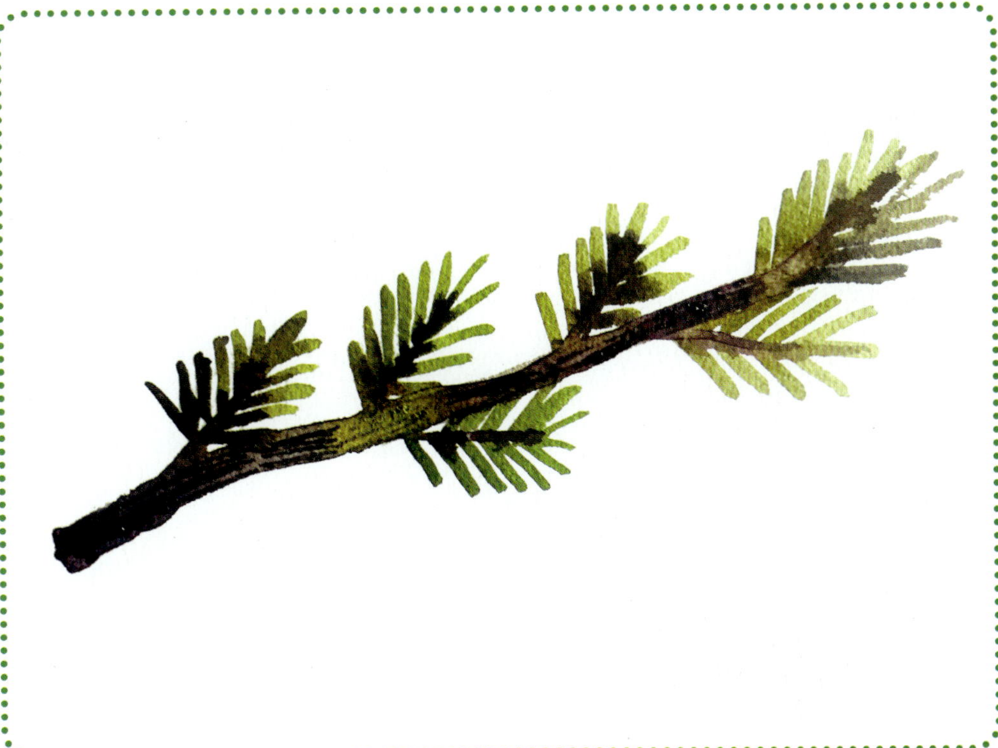

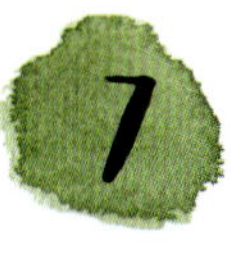

Now try scoring the stem with a toothpick to give it a little of that scratchy pine twig texture. If the paint on the stem is dry, you can add in another wash of burnt umber or violet. I've gone around that green washy area because I want to preserve it. But you will see, as you score, that the areas will deepen in color. This technique is useful for creating pine and several types of bark.

GINKGO LEAF

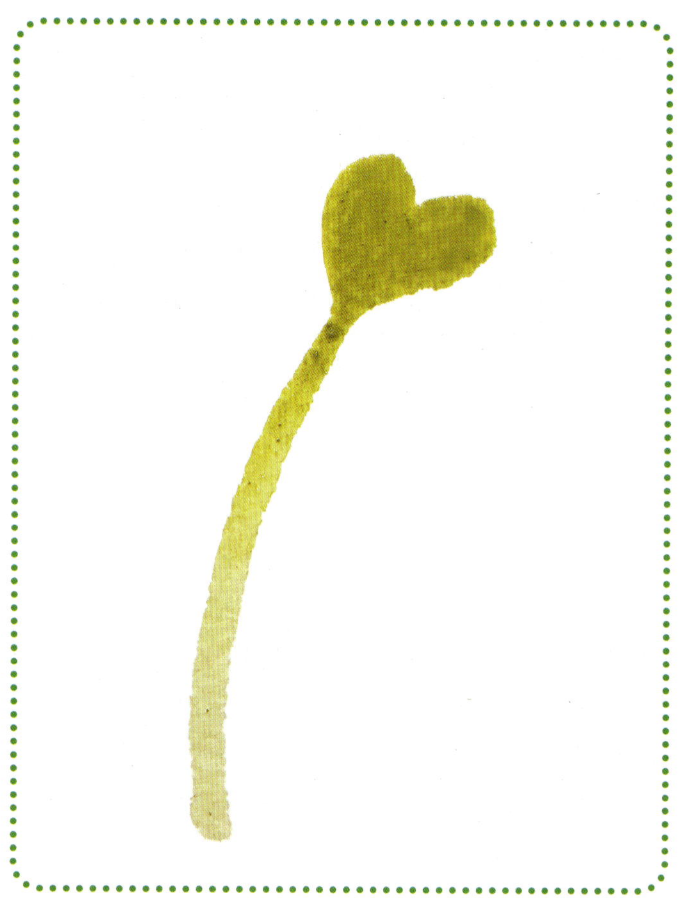

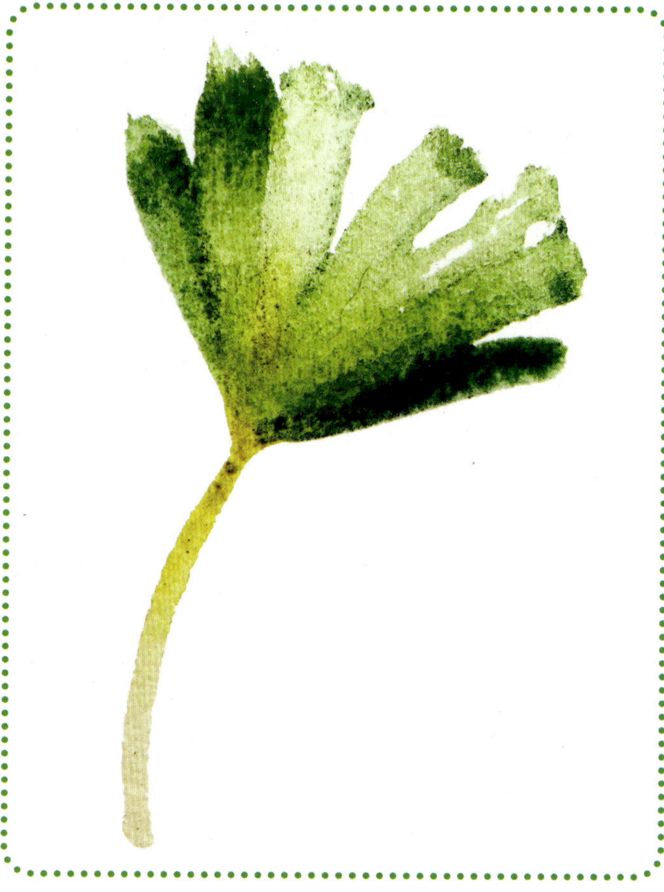

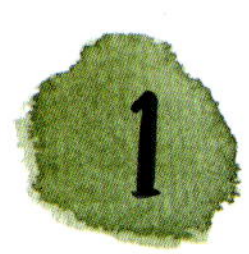

With a pale green, make a curved stem with your liner brush. Then make a tiny pointed heart at the top of it. This will form the curvy part where the stem connects with the base of the ginkgo leaf.

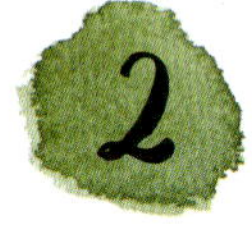

Now use your #4 round brush and a darker green to make broad strokes out from the heart.

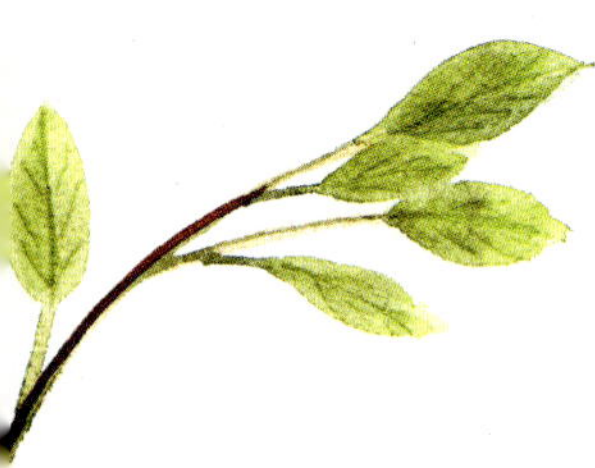

This is an easy one!

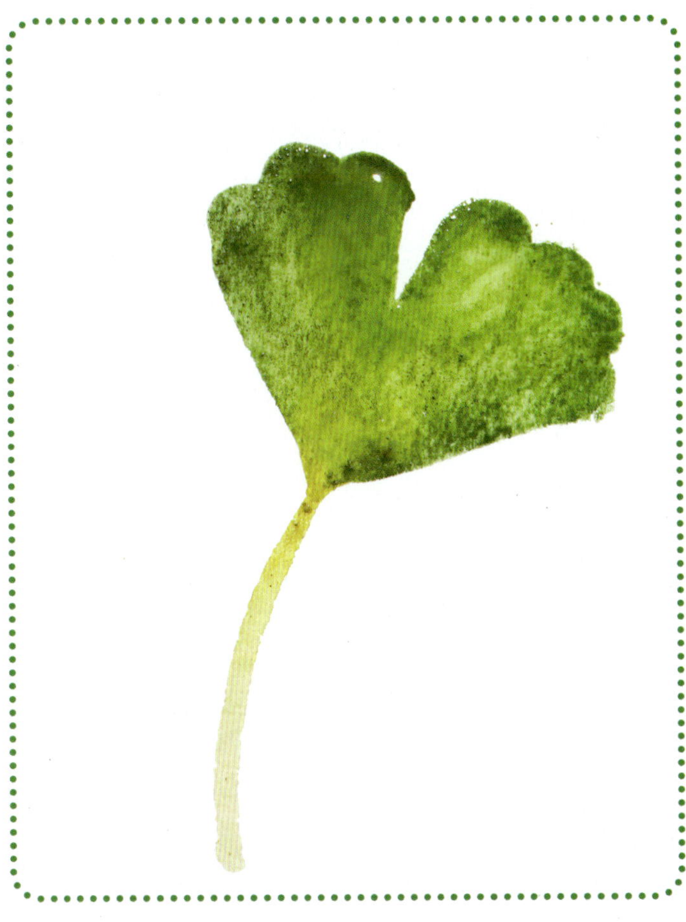

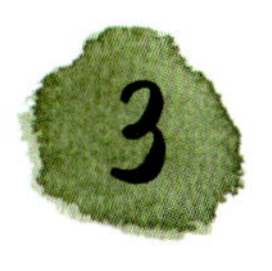

Round out the tops of these brush marks, keeping that distinguishing split in the leaf. Flood the entire area with water.

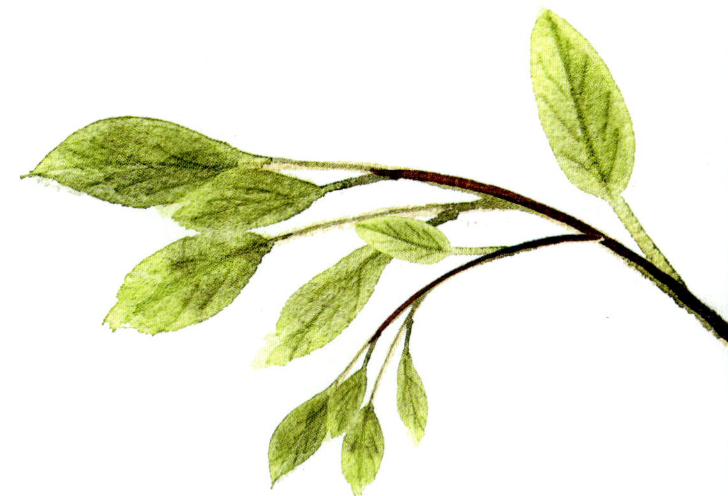

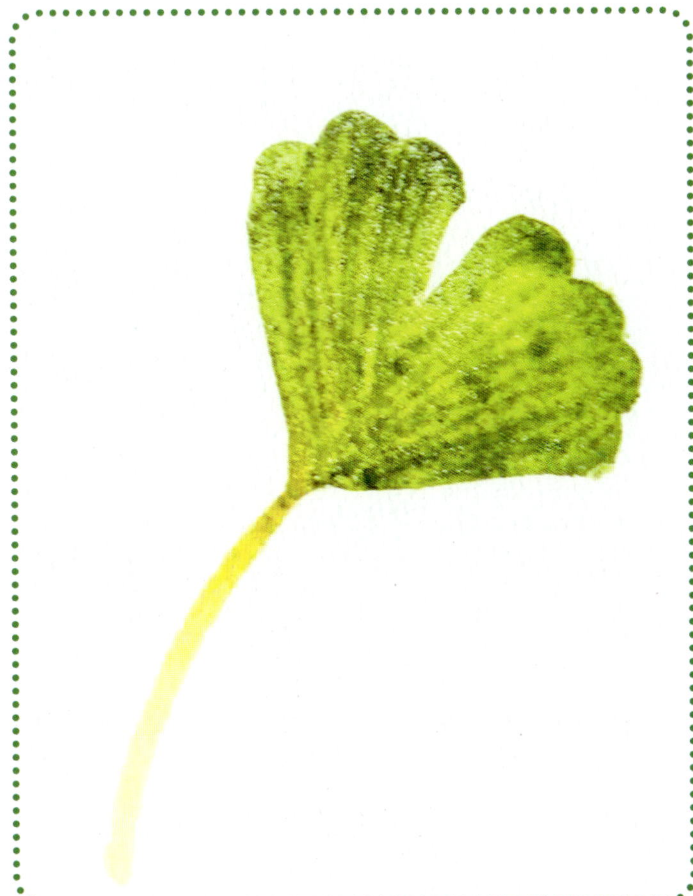

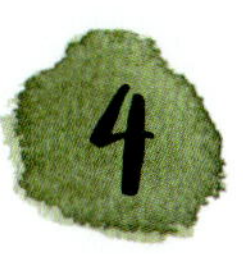

Use a toothpick to score the leaf and create the ginkgo's defining veins.

SASSAFRAS LEAF

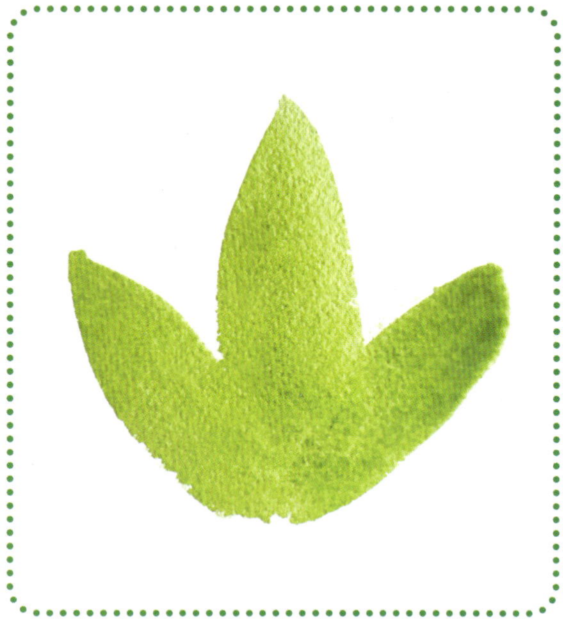

1 Using a #8 round brush, create three simple curved blades, starting with the tip of the brush and pressing down as you near the center. Use plenty of water here.

2 Add bowed shapes to the center of each blade to give it that unique sassafras appearance. Round out the base.

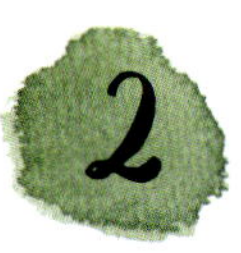

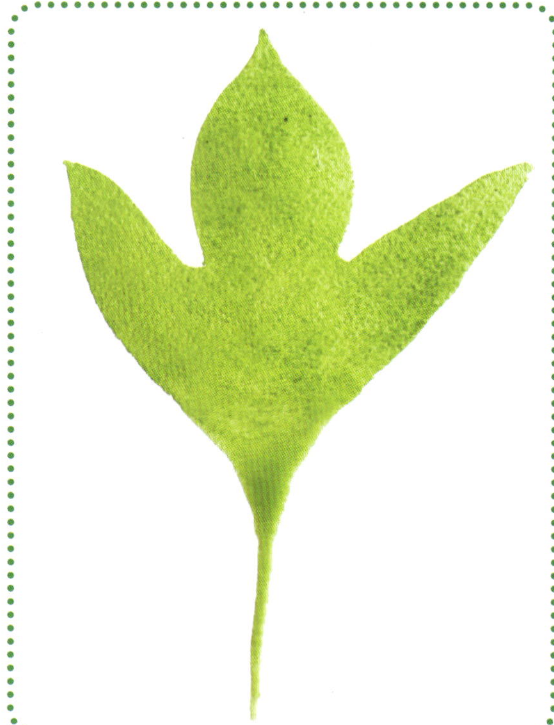

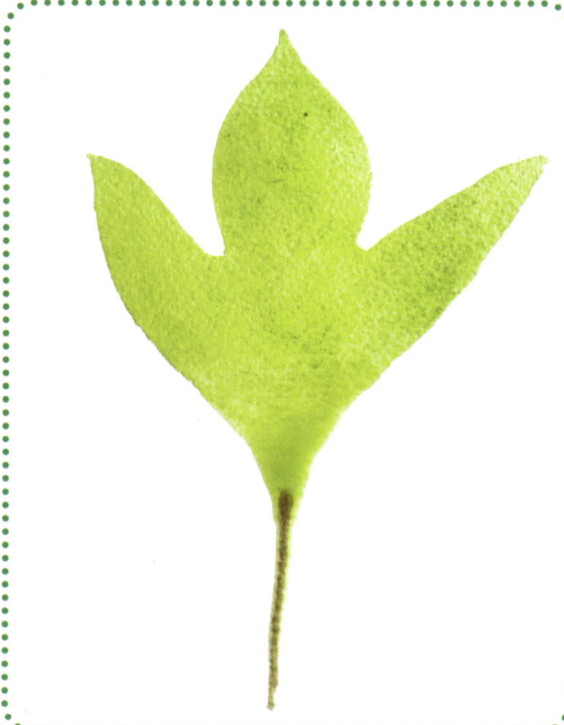

3 Time to add a stem! Using the pool of water at the bottom of the leaf, drag a smaller brush straight down to form the stem.

4 Tap in a bit of burnt umber or another brown and let it travel up the stem.

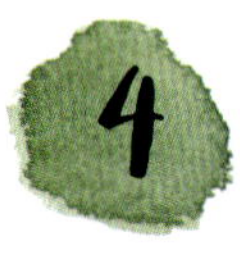

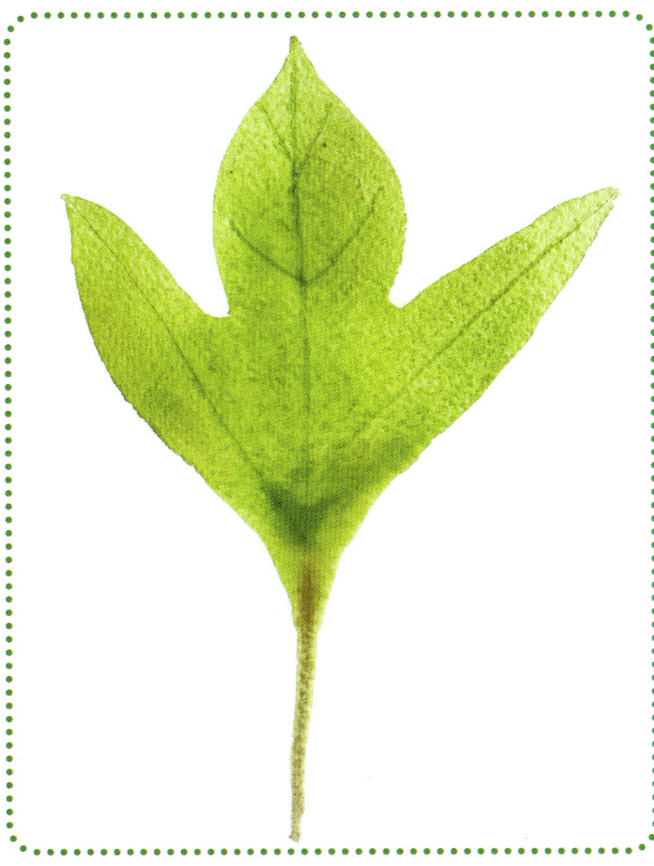

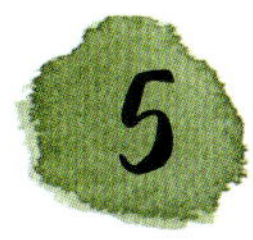

Use a toothpick to score veins into the leaf. Be sure to connect the points to the main veins in the blades.

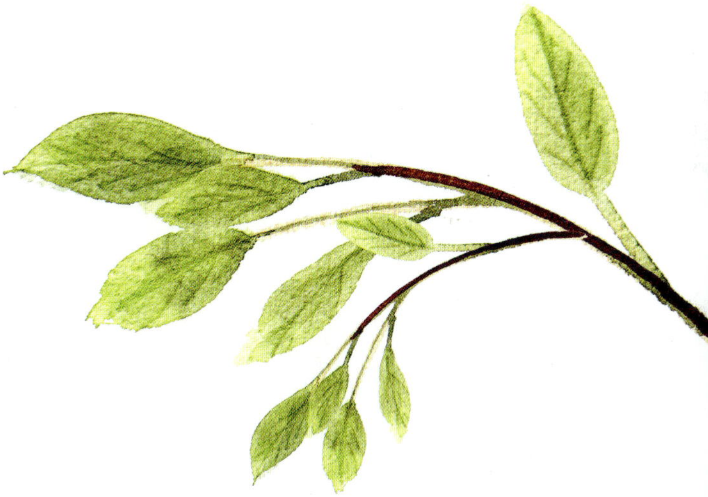

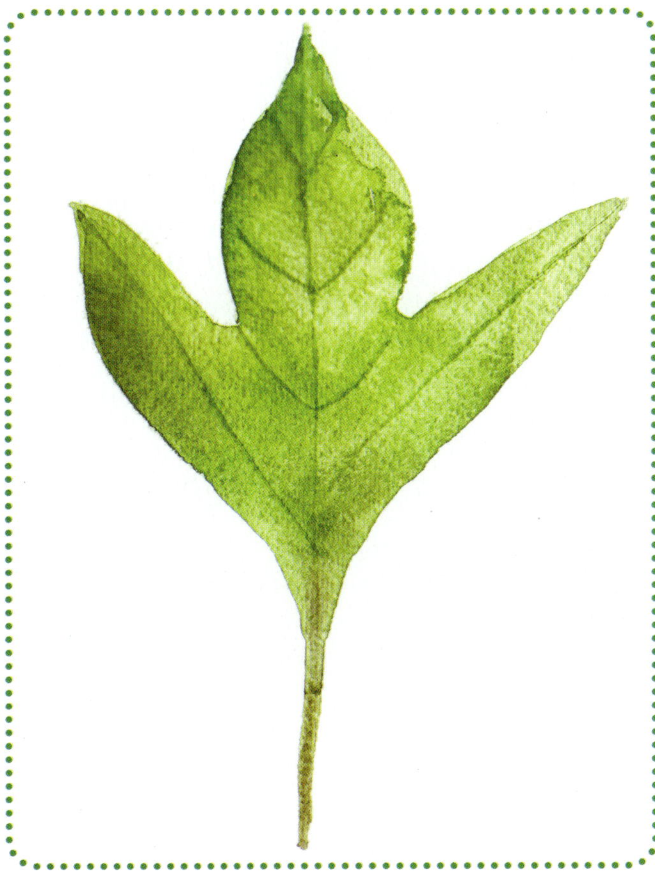

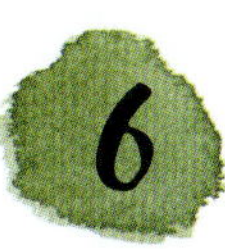

Finish scoring the blades and add touches of darker green to give the leaf more depth.

CALADIUM LEAF

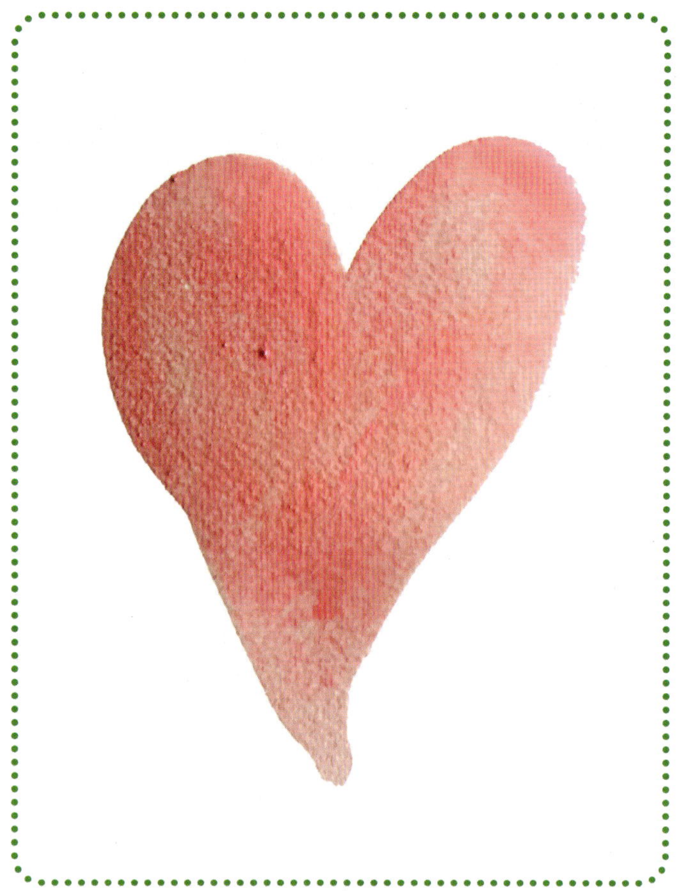

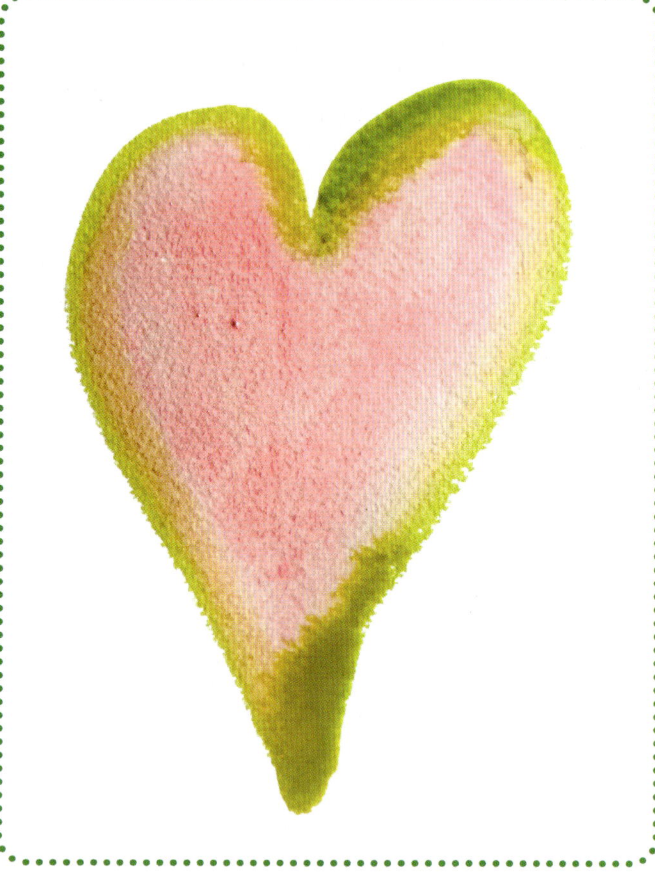

1 Using a #8 round brush and plenty of water, paint a simple pink heart.

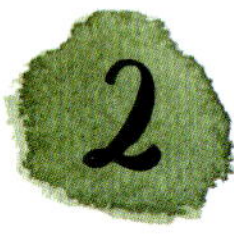

2 Dip the brush into a green-gold mixture and draw around the perimeter, allowing the green to blend into the pink.

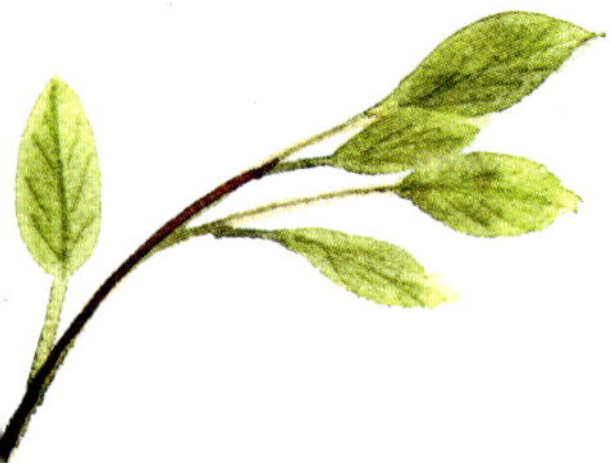

This is an easy one too!

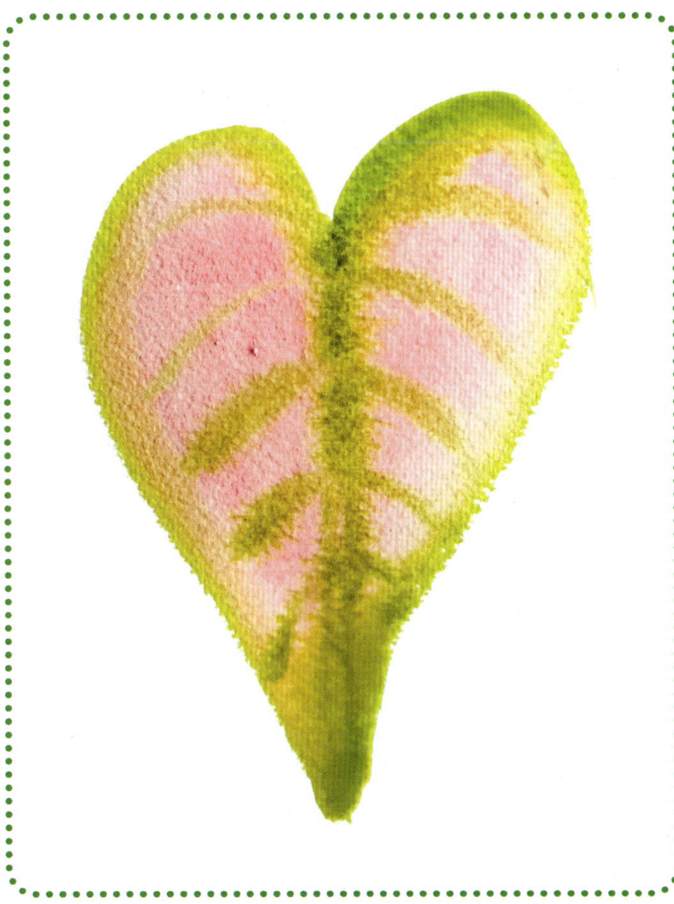

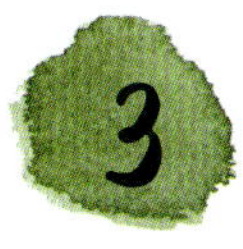

Use the tip of a smaller #4 round brush to create a vein down the middle of the leaf, and then add rounded veins that slope down and out to the edges of the leaf.

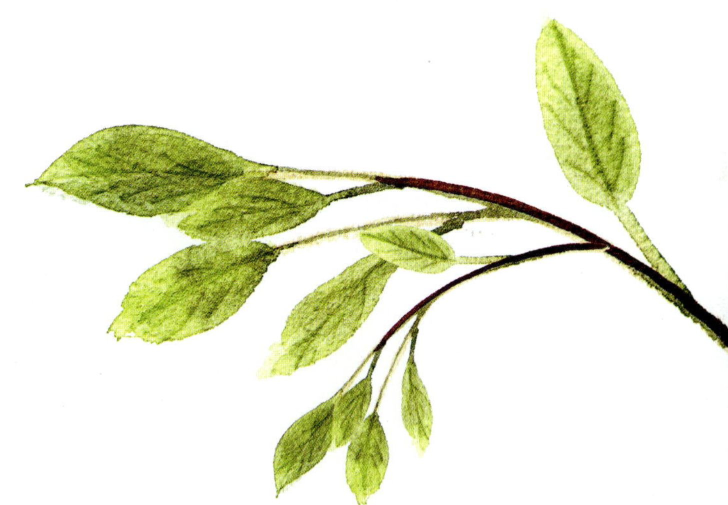

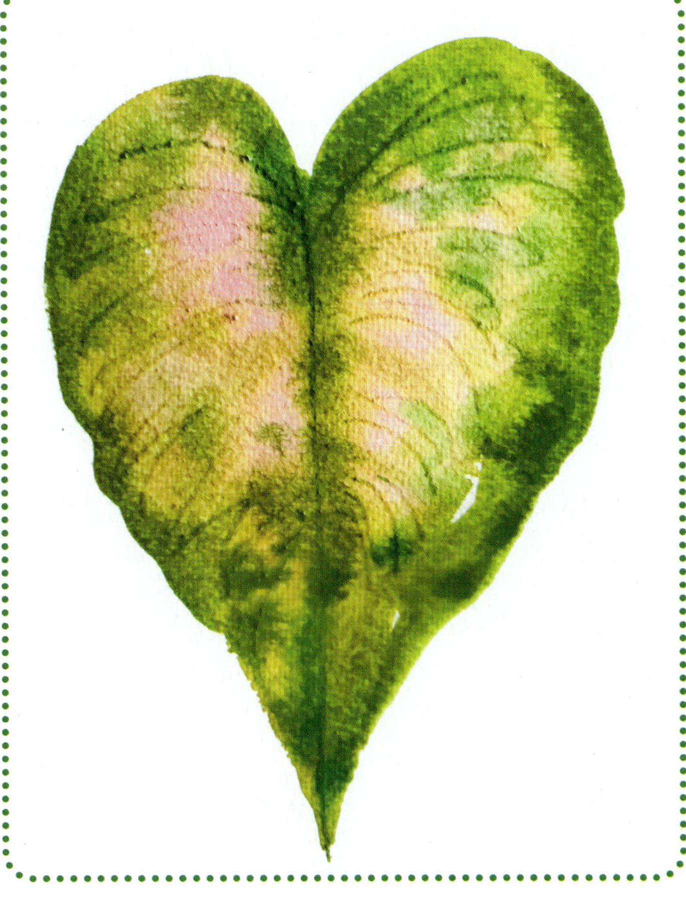

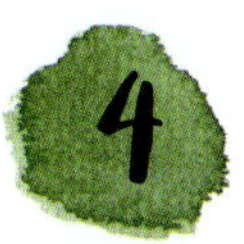

With a darker green, use the tip of a #8 round brush to tap randomly into the wet leaf shape and around its perimeter, allowing the colors to bleed into each other. Finally, with a toothpick, score tiny vein lines into the wet paint.

SYCAMORE SEED POD

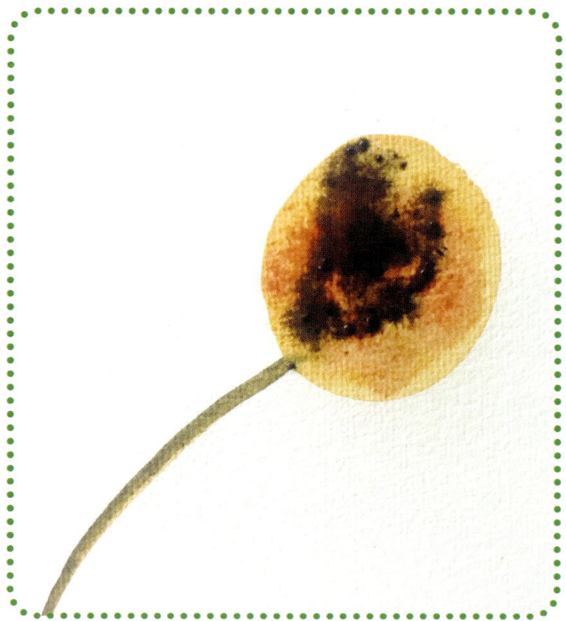

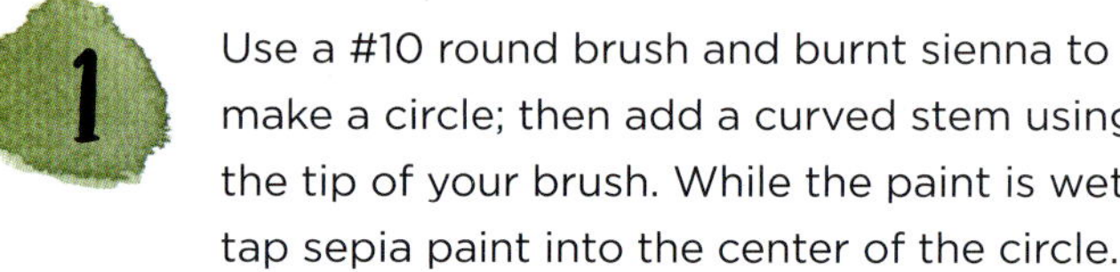

1 Use a #10 round brush and burnt sienna to make a circle; then add a curved stem using the tip of your brush. While the paint is wet, tap sepia paint into the center of the circle.

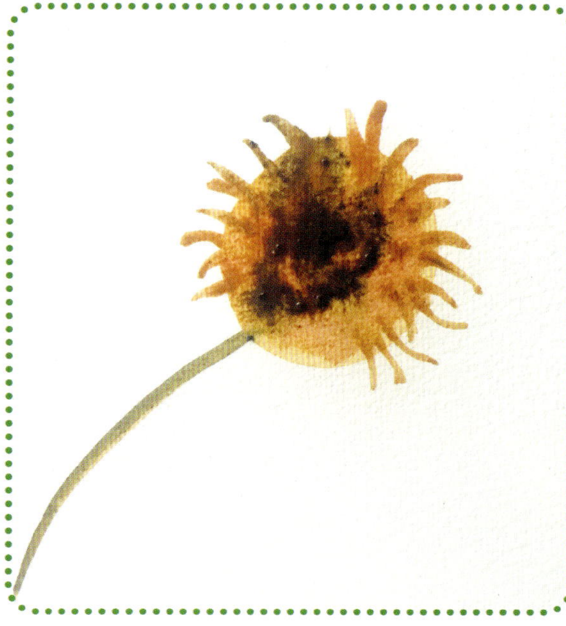

2 Using a smaller, wet brush, drag the tip from inside the circle to the outside, making little squiggly lines around the perimeter. Be sure to go in the direction of the curves.

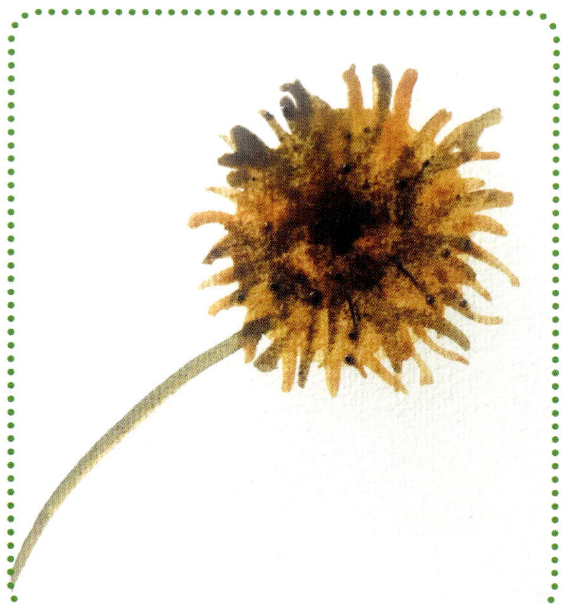

3 Give the circular seed some dimension by adding more sepia to the middle. You can gently tap paint into the squiggles from the last step and the color will move about.

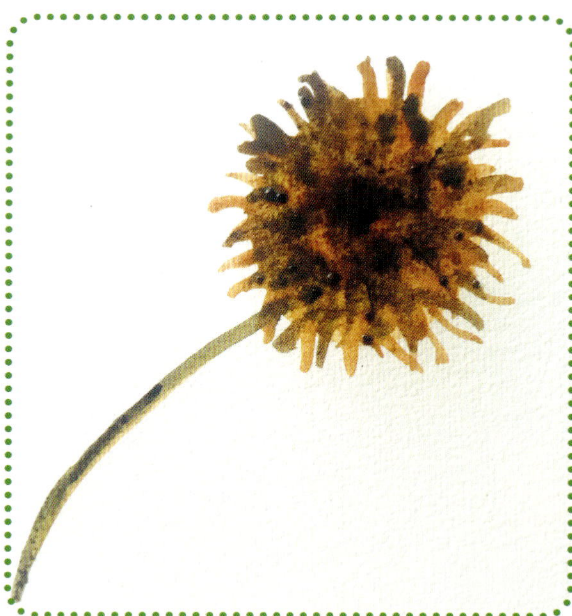

4 Now give the stem attention and add a little sepia in different spots. At this point, you can also let the paint dry, and then go back into the seed to add more squiggles in the center. Sycamore seed pods sort of look like spiky lollipops and are super easy to paint!

MAPLE 'COPTER/WHIRLYBIRD

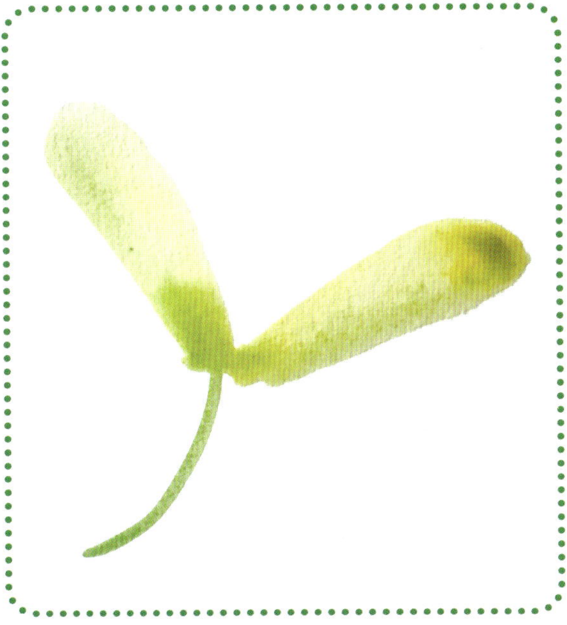

With watered-down green-gold, use a #8 round brush to create an elongated wing by pressing down on the tip and then applying pressure with the rest of brush. Repeat on the other side to form the two "wings" of the seed; then add a small curved stem.

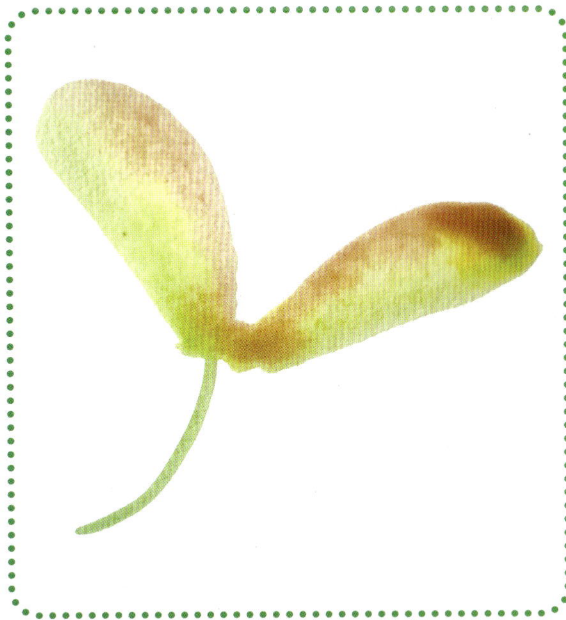

2

While the paint is still wet, tap burnt sienna into the tops of the wings, letting the color flood into the green. Be sure to tap where the two wings meet to create the impression that there are seeds tucked inside.

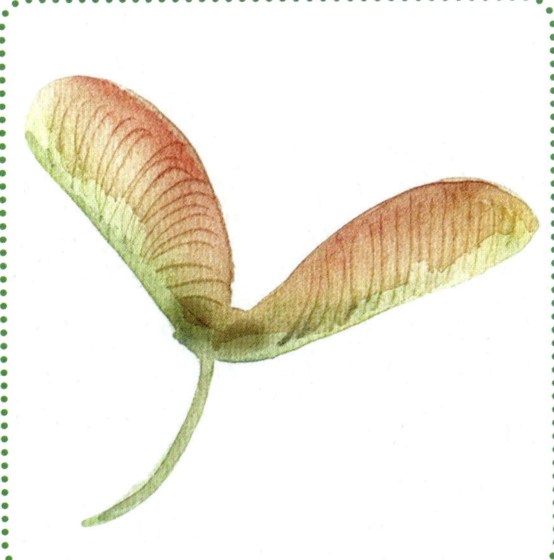

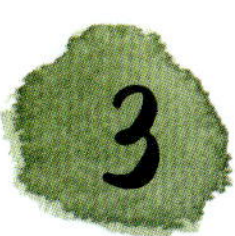

Add more green-gold at the base of the wings and stem. Now use a toothpick to score the wings and give them a thin, gossamer look. Be sure to score in the direction of the curves moving from the center of the wing outward.

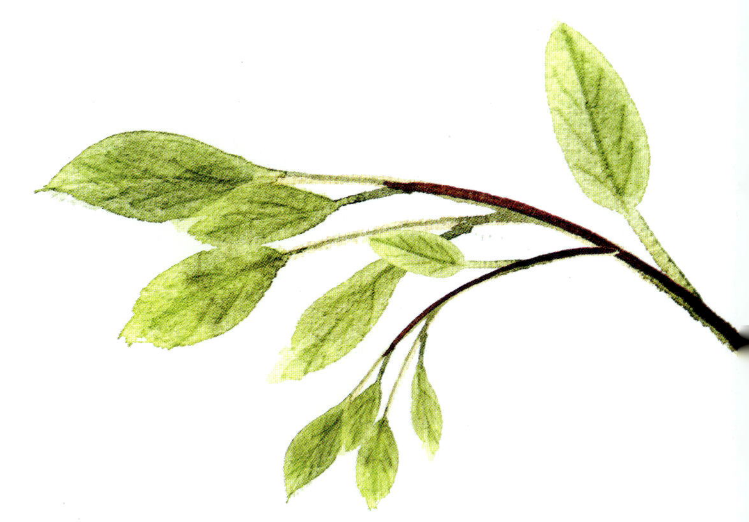

MILK THISTLE SEED

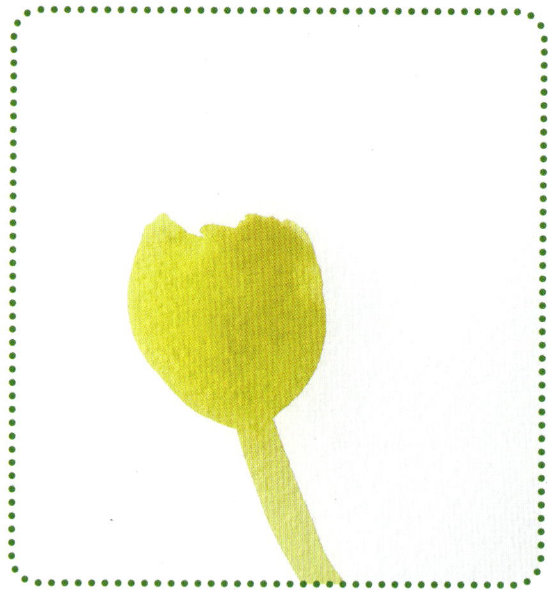

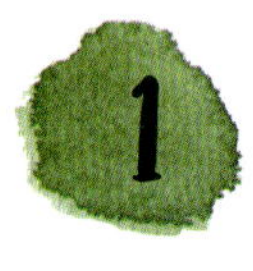

1 Use light-green paint and a #10 round brush to make a semi-thick curved stem. Add a cap at the top, making sure to keep the top edge somewhat irregular and not too straight. This cap will hold the flowery bloom and can feature a more freeform shape. Let the paint dry completely.

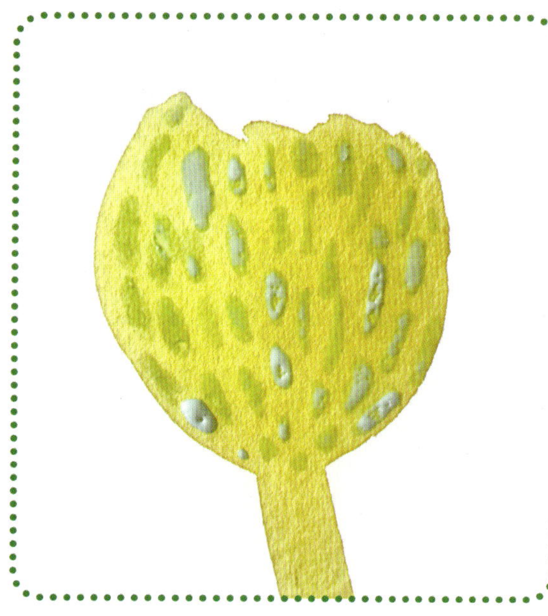

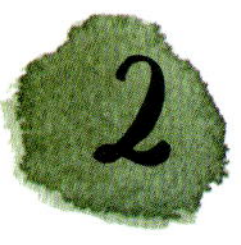

2 Use masking fluid and an inexpensive brush to create the marks of the ribbed cap. Be sure to follow the curve of the cap, especially on the outer edges.

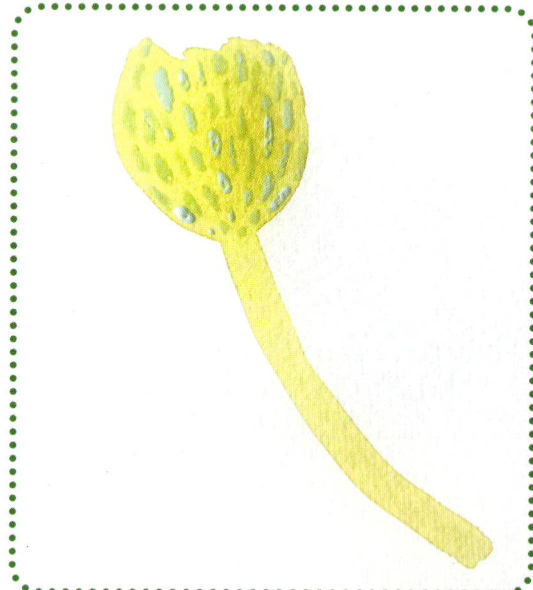

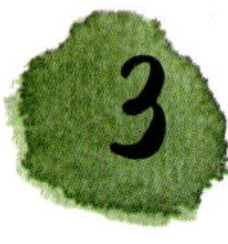

3 While the previous step dries, add a wash for the flower using violet or purple paint mixed with a bit of red. Create a simple shape almost like a mushroom cap. You can add more color as you go, but focus on the shape for now.

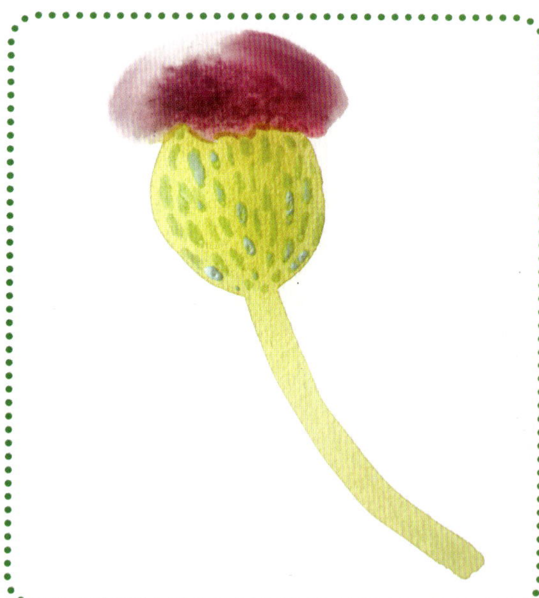

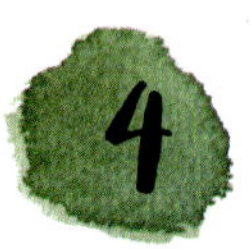

4 Using a toothpick, lightly score from the center out so that the flower gets a prickly edge all around. Have fun here—these flowers have lively edges!

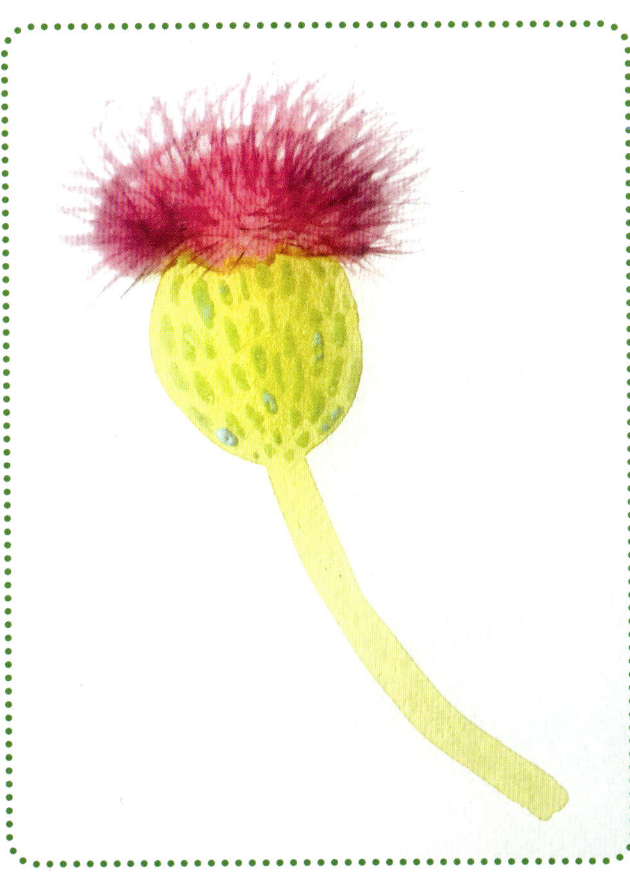

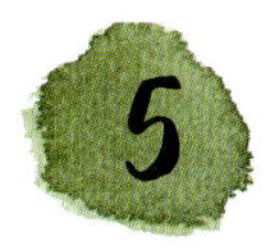

While the flower dries, return to the cap and add darker greens to create depth. Tap your finger on the masking fluid to make sure that it's dry. It should feel tacky but not wet. I've used a Filbert brush here and kept my wash primarily to one side and down the stem.

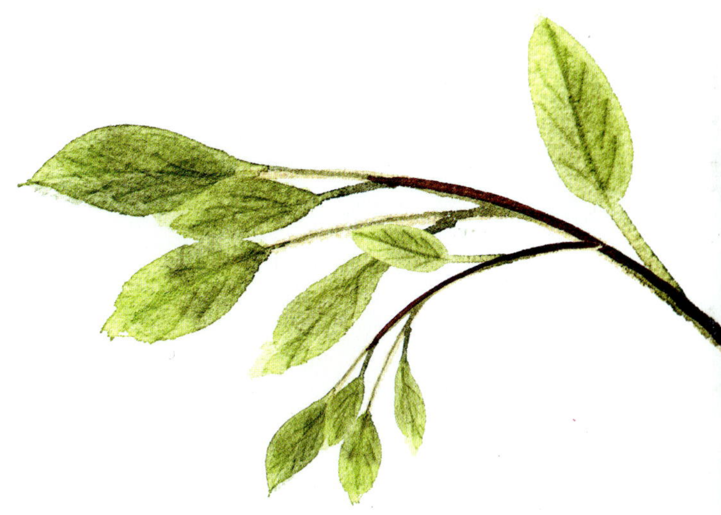

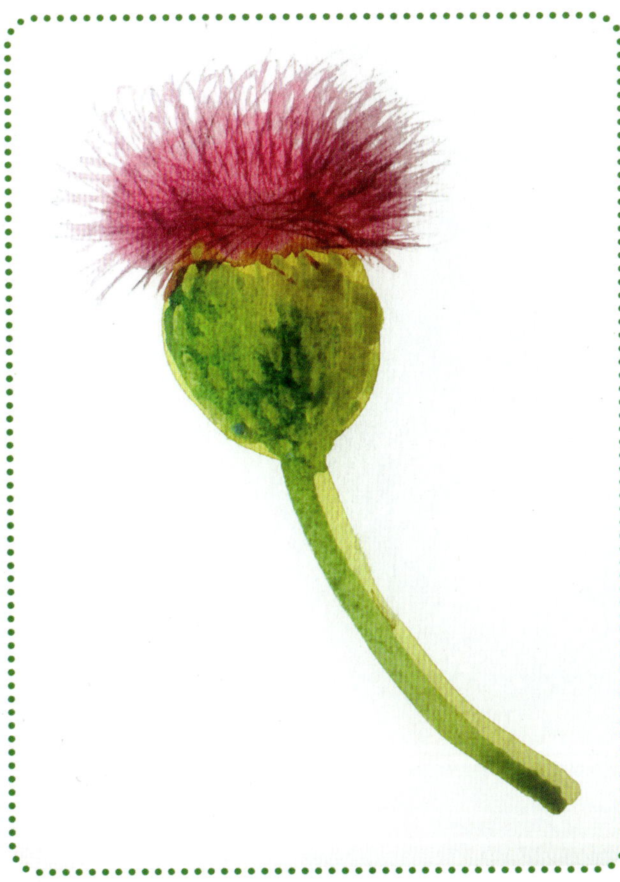

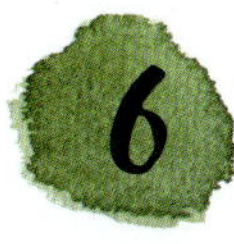

Once everything is dry, remove the masking fluid using a clean finger or a rubber square, and see how it looks. You will likely need to go back in and add some darker colors to give it more "pop." I've mixed a bit of blue into my violet color and tapped at the base of the flower. Then I've used a small liner brush to bring some of that color over the cap.

Trees: Barks, Branches & Roots

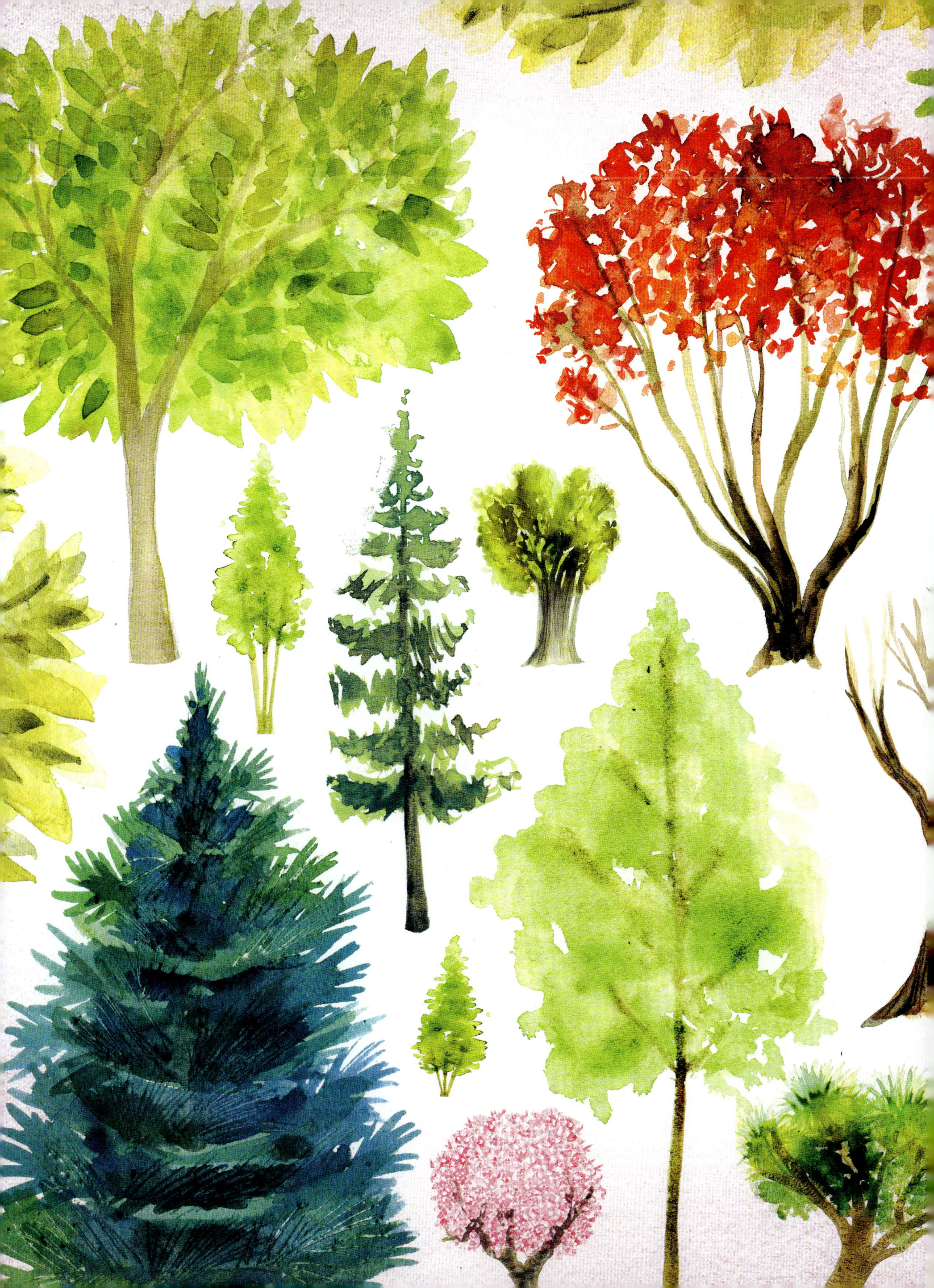

MONARCH BIRCH BARK

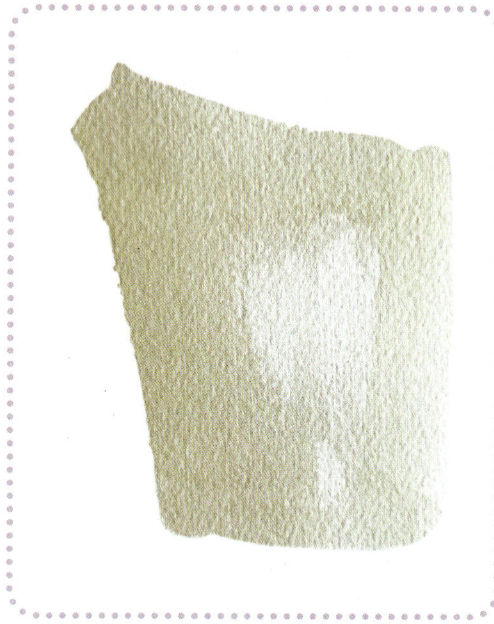

1 Begin with a light wash of a neutral color, such as soft yellow with a touch of burnt umber or gray mixed in. This shape will form a segment of a trunk with a bit of an offshoot of a branch.

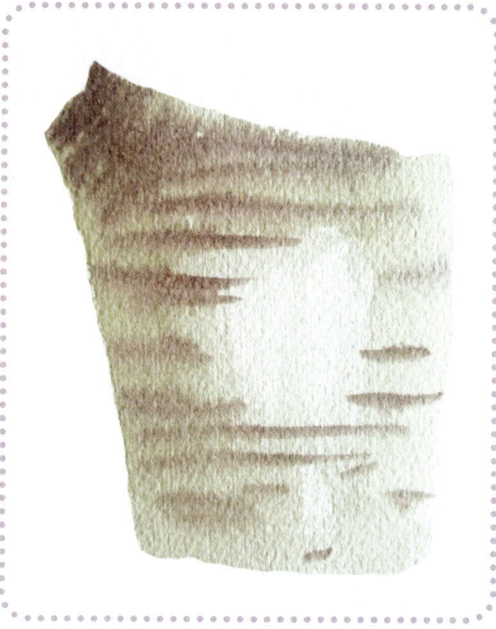

2 While the wash is still wet, swipe a brush with some additional neutral paint into the sides of the trunk and let the paint flow into the wash you created in step 1. This will give it dimension. Then take a #6 or #8 brush and quickly paint little lines using red-violet. Let these bleed together.

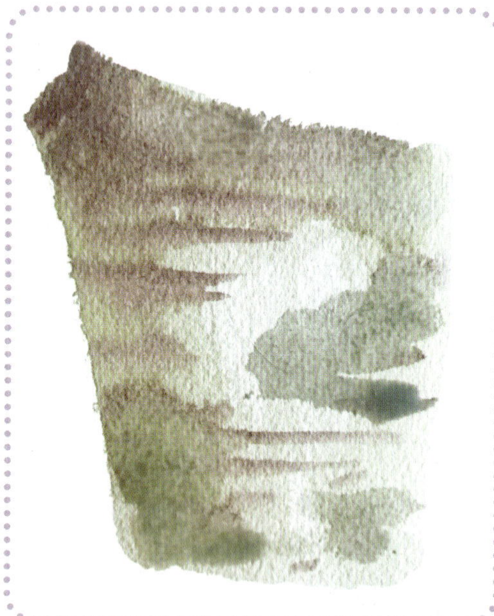

3 Working these washes while they're still wet, dip the same brush into a mixture of gray and brown and swipe some areas of the wash. Let the paint mixtures bleed. These will form the shadowed areas of the birch bark.

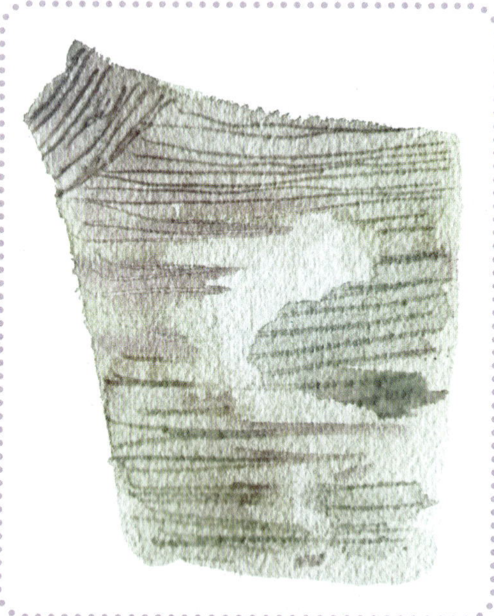

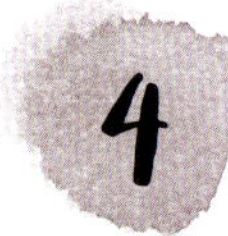

Use a toothpick to score the bark and give it a papery feel.

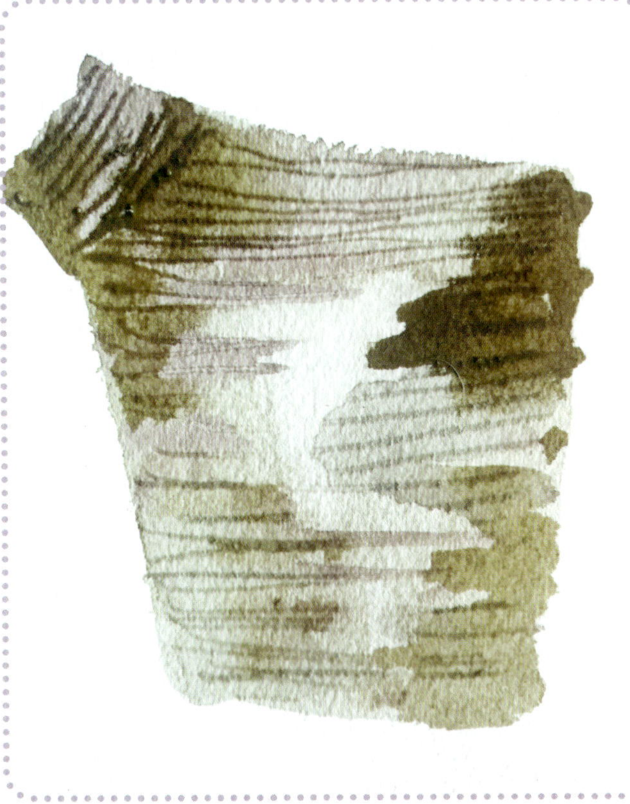

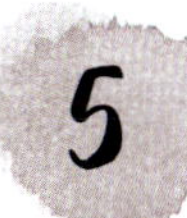

5

Remember to go in the direction of the curves. For example, use a left-to-right motion to demonstrate the roundness of the main bark, but use a bottom-to-top motion for the offshoot branch stump. This too will give it roundness and dimension.

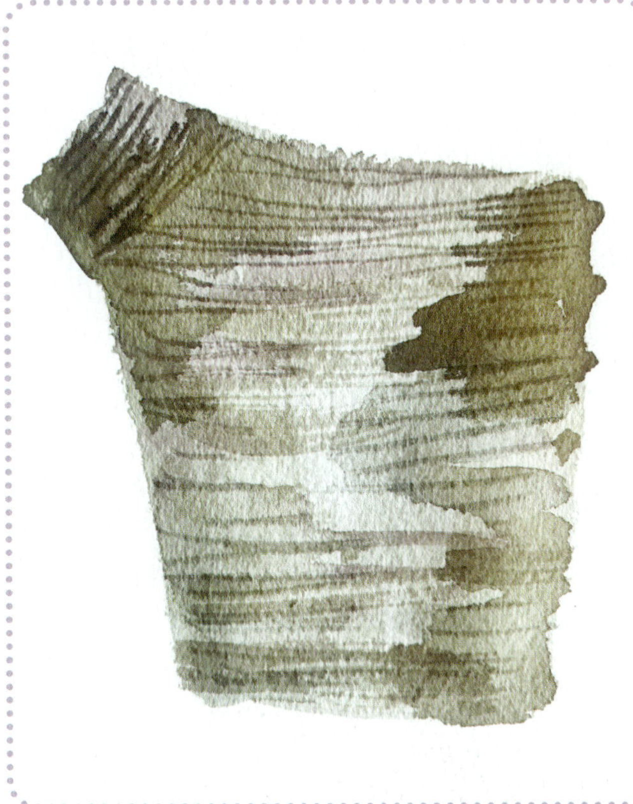

6

You may want to add contrast to the darker, mottled areas of the bark using more burnt umber or gray.

BARK STUDIES

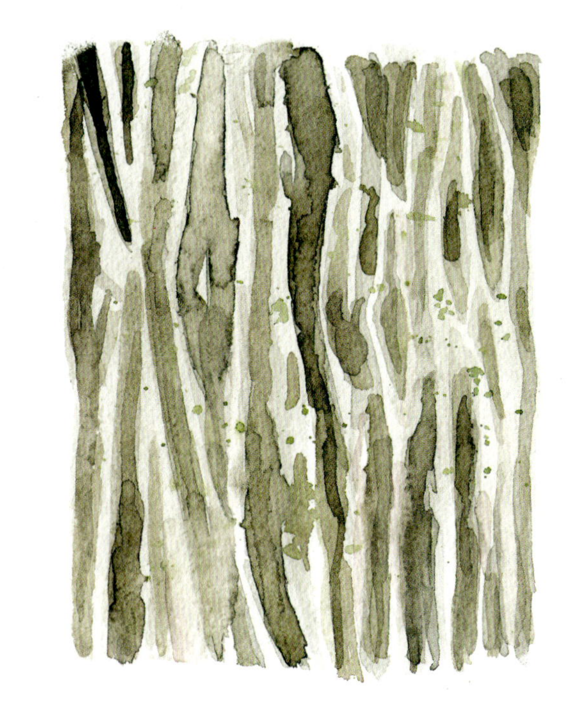

WHITE ASH

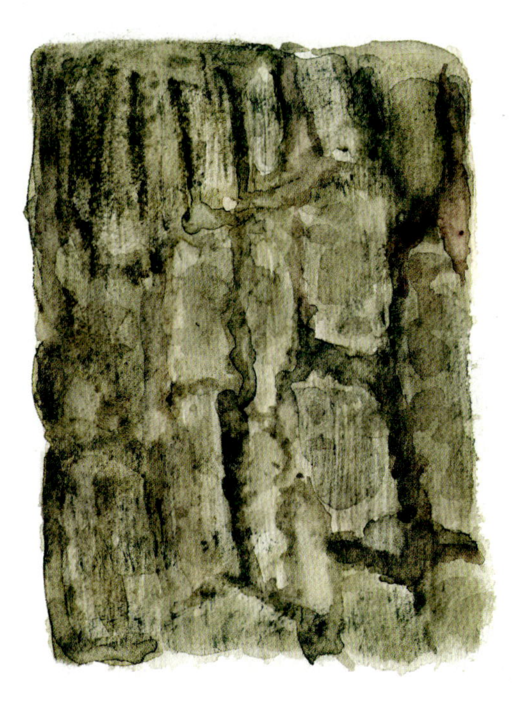

BLACK WALNUT

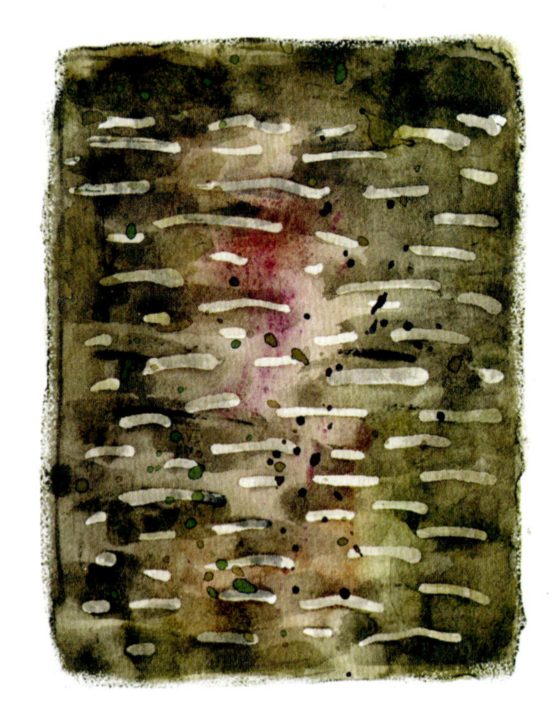

CHERRY

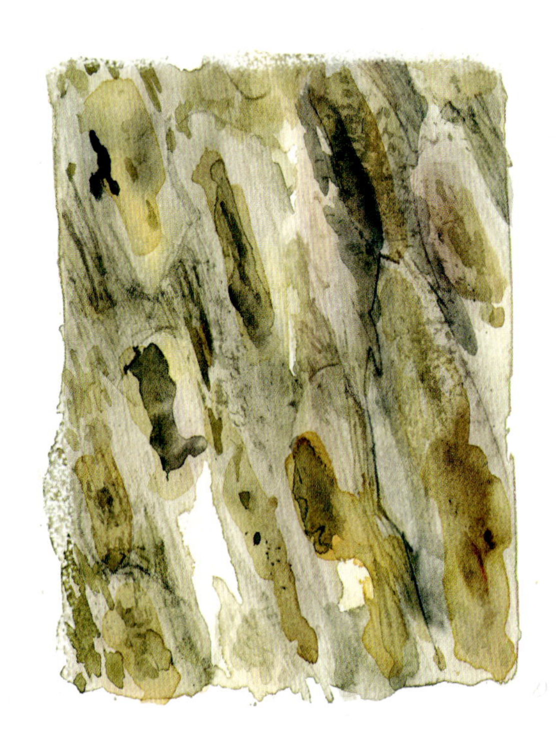

SYCAMORE

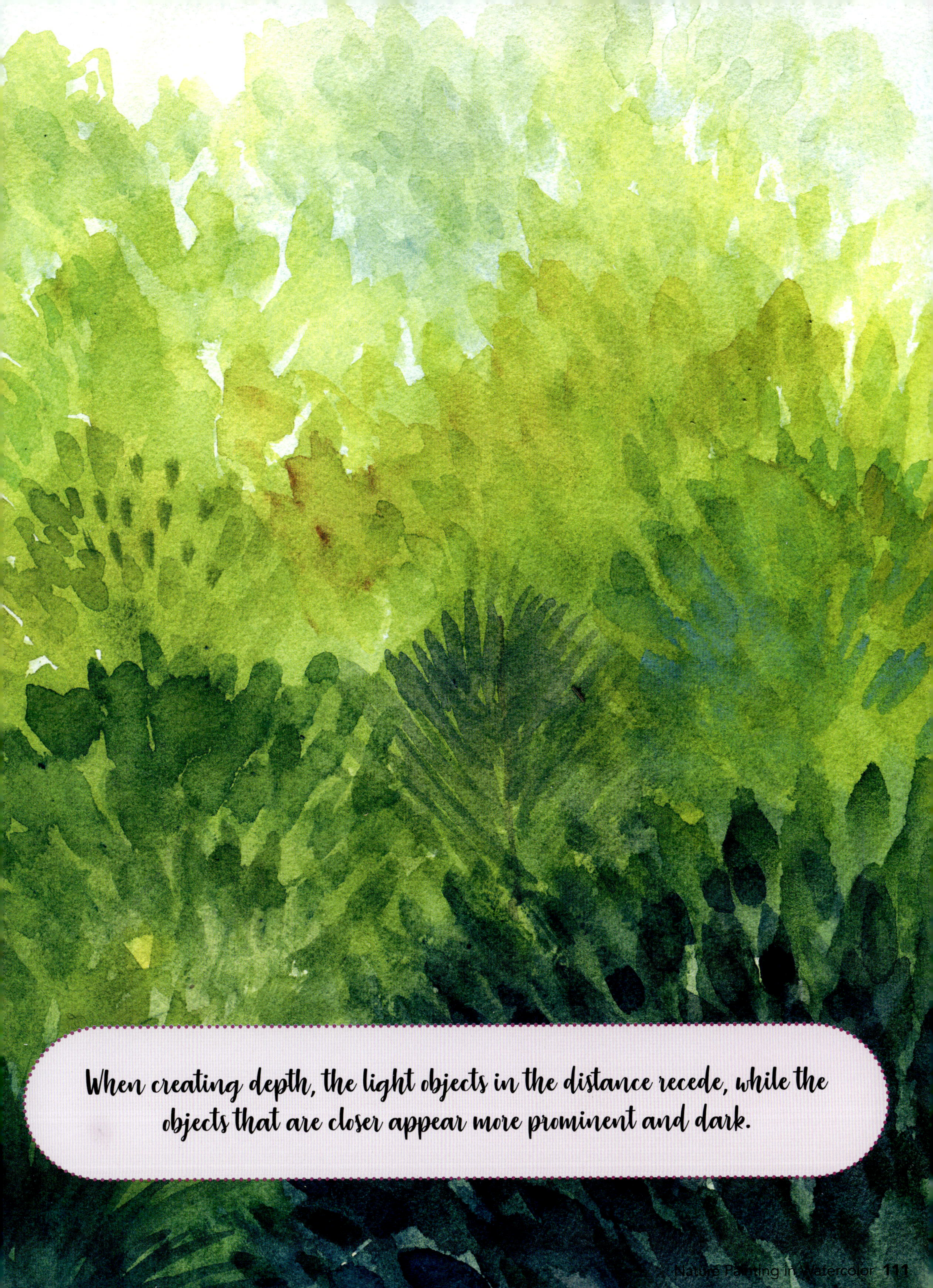

When creating depth, the light objects in the distance recede, while the objects that are closer appear more prominent and dark.

SIMPLE MAPLE TREE

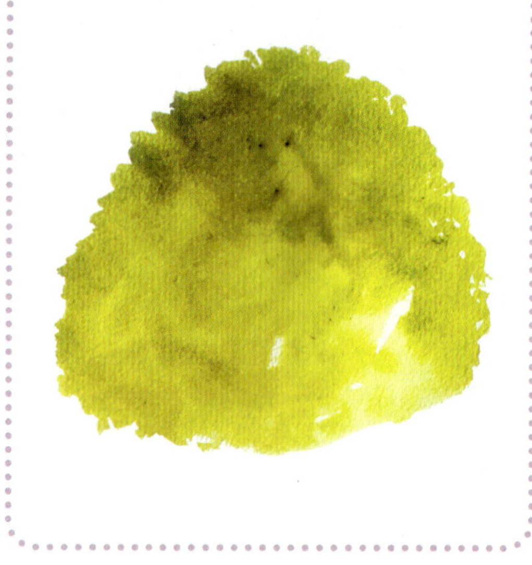

1 Make a rounded triangle with a #12 round brush. You can use a mop brush to fill the large area inside once you've created this shape. Take the tip of your brush and dot it around the perimeter of the triangle to give it a more organic edge.

2 Go back in with a darker hue, such as green-gold, and tap the brush into various areas to begin to create depth.

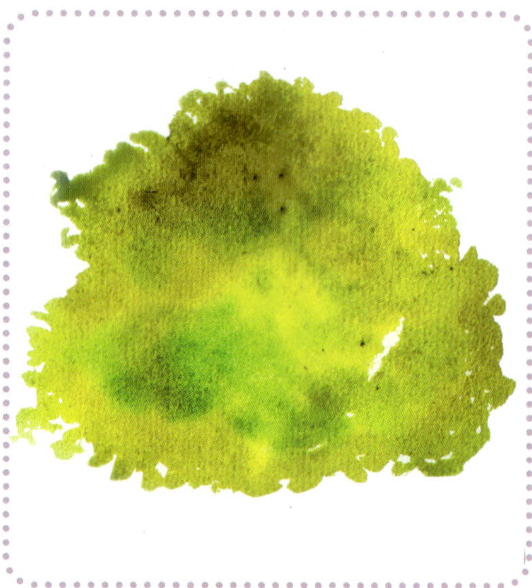

3 Tap another hue of green into the center of the tree. You've used only wet-into-wet techniques so far, so keep tapping the tip of your brush around the perimeter of the shape, experimenting with different values as you go. You want to give the edge some wild-card areas for realism. I've chosen to add more edges to the bottom and sides of the shape.

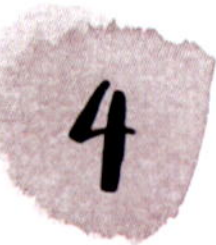

4 As you add pigment to the tree mass, you will see the tree come to life. Remember that dark areas recede, while light ones come to the front.

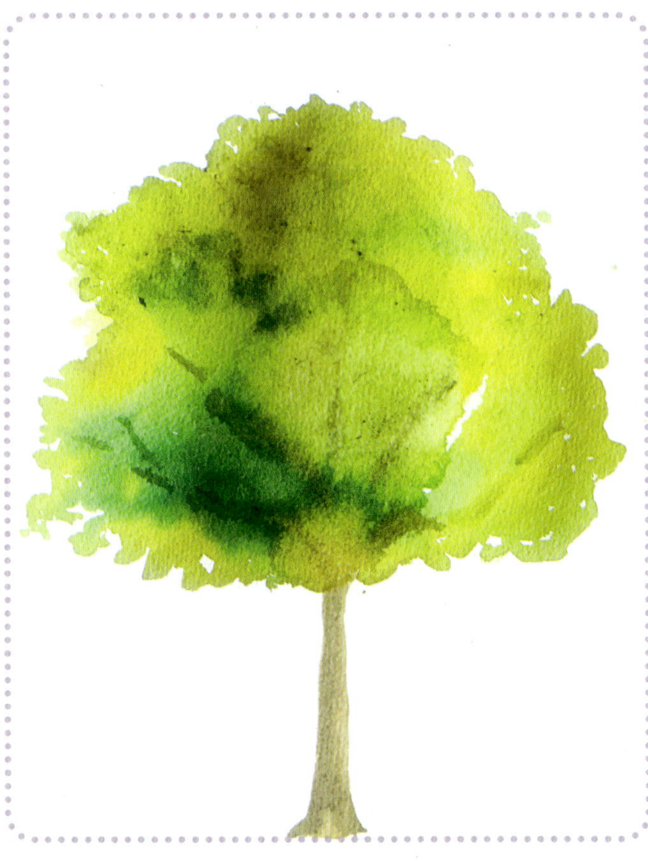

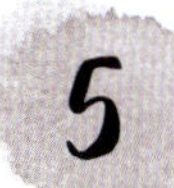

5

Time to add the tree trunk! This one is a simple, rather thin one without too much texture, so I've used my #8 round brush to draw a line from the green section down. It's OK if the brown bleeds into the green a bit here; it will look more natural. As you get to the base of the trunk, flare the sides out a bit.

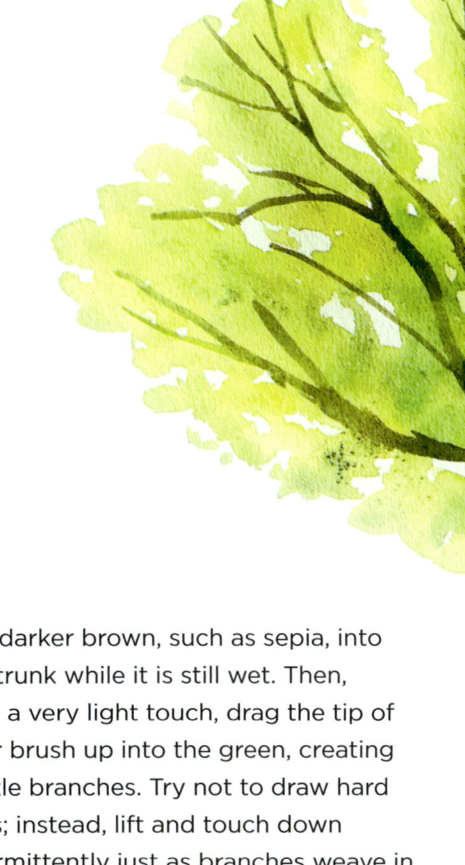

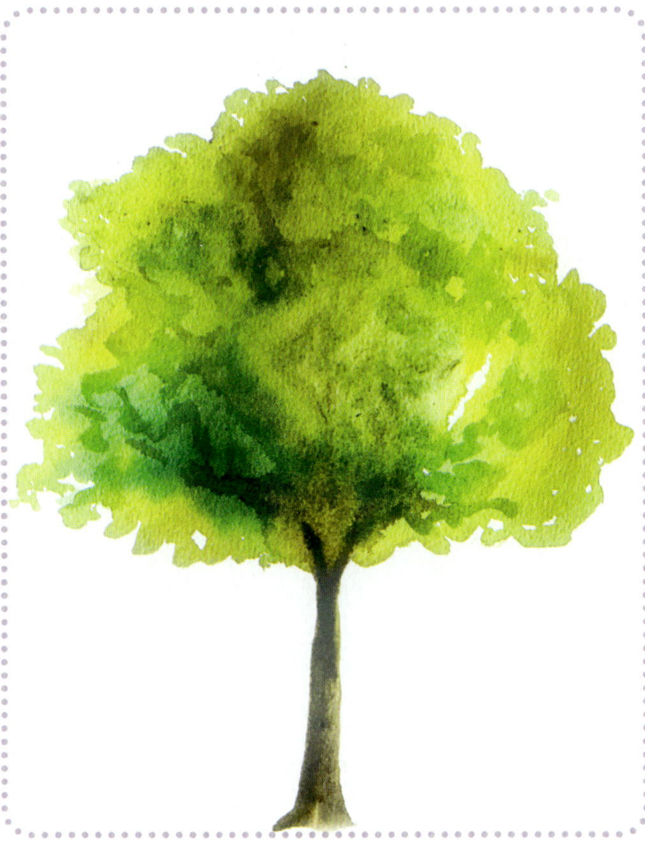

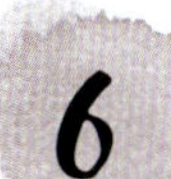

6

Tap darker brown, such as sepia, into the trunk while it is still wet. Then, with a very light touch, drag the tip of your brush up into the green, creating subtle branches. Try not to draw hard lines; instead, lift and touch down intermittently just as branches weave in and out of foliage. You can also lightly score the trunk with a toothpick.

BLACK WALNUT TREE

1 Start by making lyrical brushstrokes with a #12 round brush dipped in a light-green wash. Dance your brush about using both the broad side and the tip. Make about five repeating areas that all angle in toward the center of your paper. They will look a bit like romaine lettuce leaves.

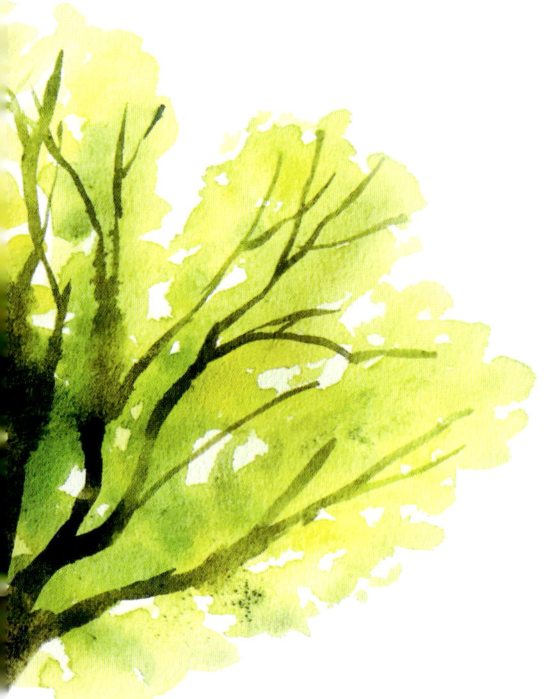

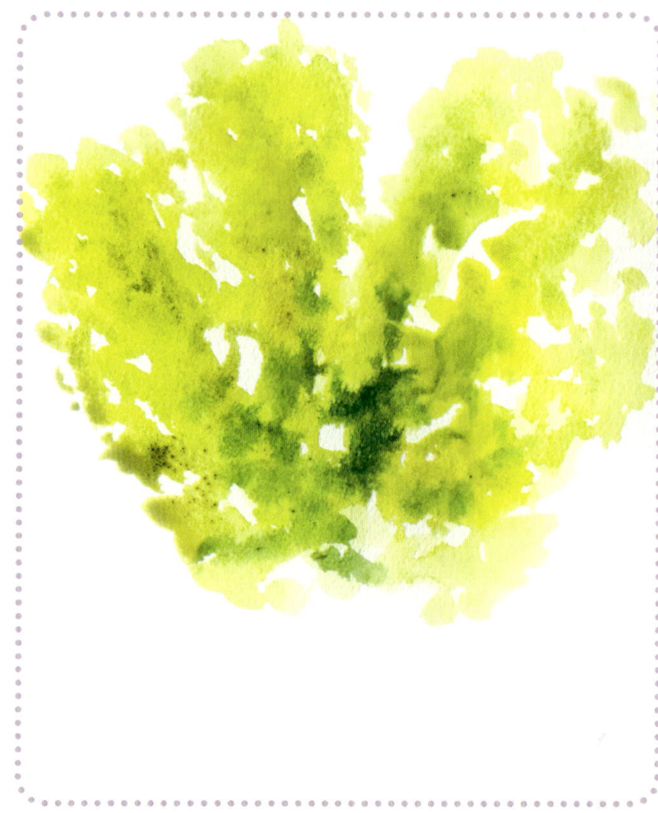

2 Apply darker-green paint to your brush and tap into the wet areas to allow the color to move around.

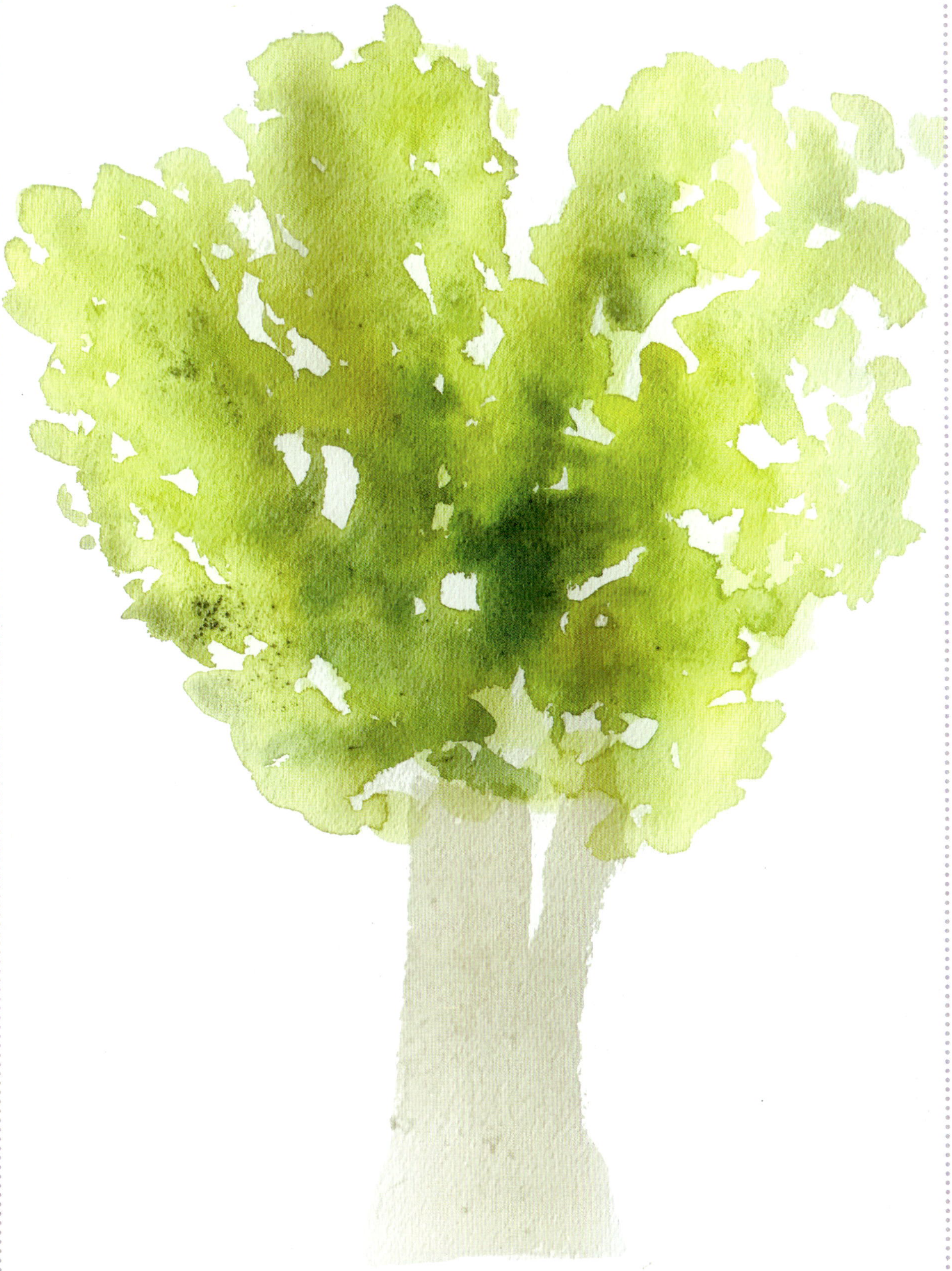

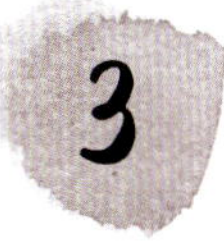

Dip a wet mop brush into pale-brown pigment to create a tree trunk. I've started lightly to get the shape I want; you can always add more pigment in the next step.

4

Once the treetop is dry, you are ready for the next, bolder step. Dip the tip of a #10 round brush into sepia paint and touch down in some areas to give a rounded dimension to the tree trunk. Using the tip of the brush, drag upward to create the branches of the tree. Remember to go from thick to thin as you move up and out. Don't be afraid to throw some curves in there too! Branches are a lot of fun as they twist and turn in all directions.

While the paint is wet, you may want to apply darker green to certain areas by and over the branches to create recessed areas. It's up to you!

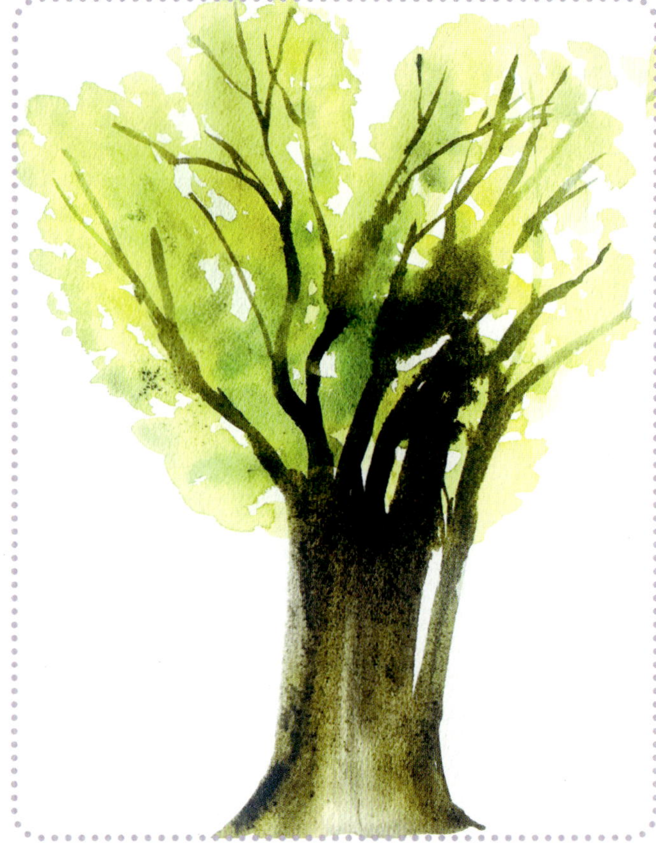

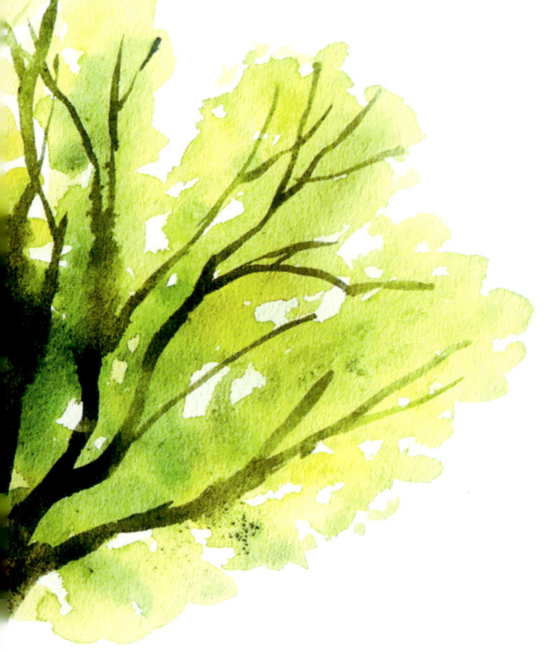

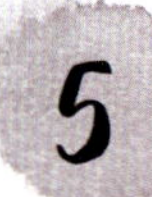

Focusing on the tree bark, use a toothpick to score vertically while the paint is still wet. You will see the pigment pool into the scored areas, instantly creating texture.

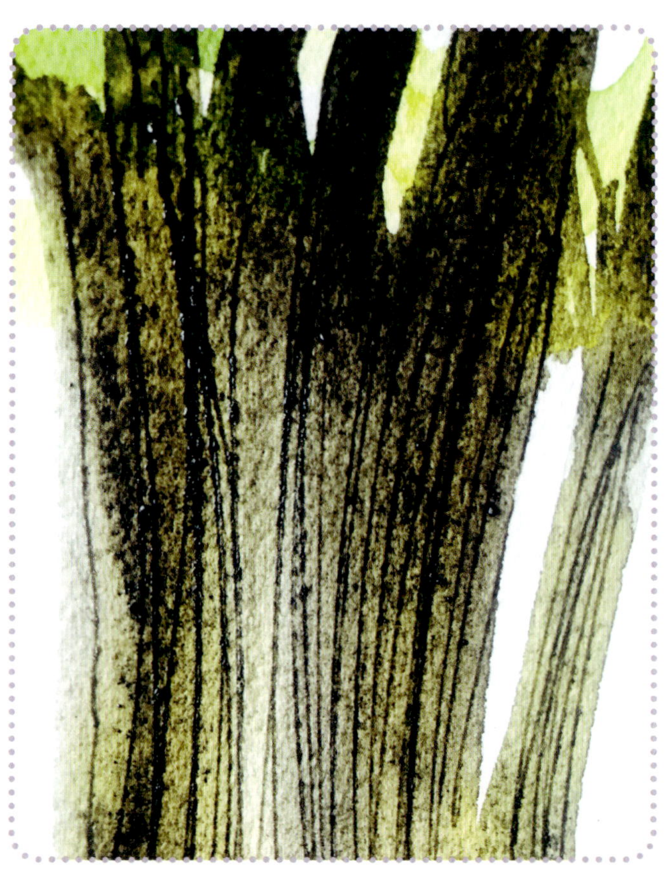

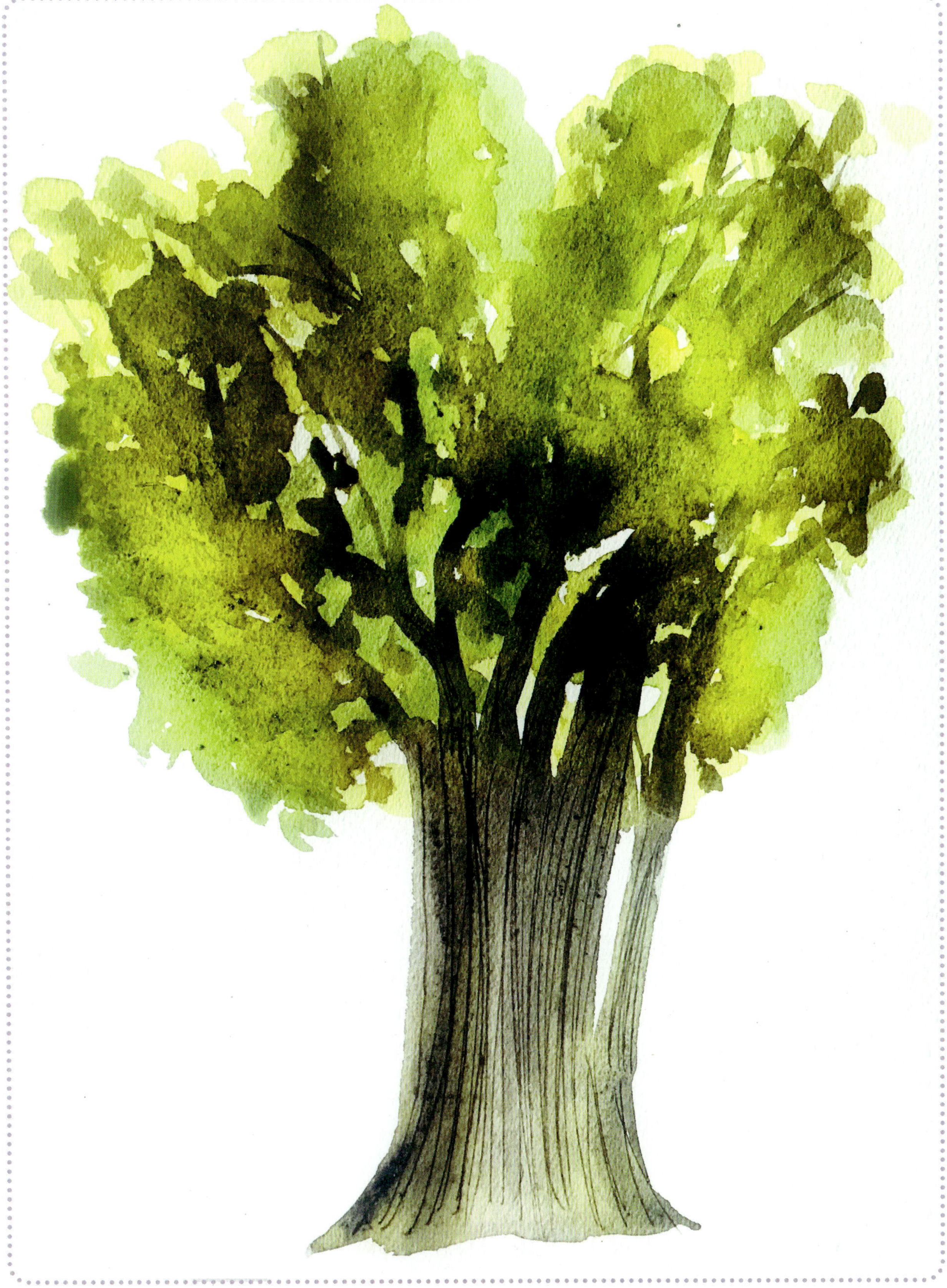

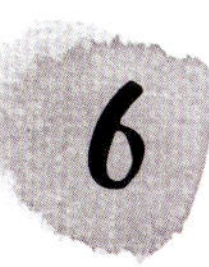

You're almost done! Now is the time to rework some of the leafy-green areas. Be bold here. Trees have a lot of recessed spots, and these darker areas bring the lighter shades forward, just like leaves. Be careful not to overwork this step, as it can get a bit muddy.

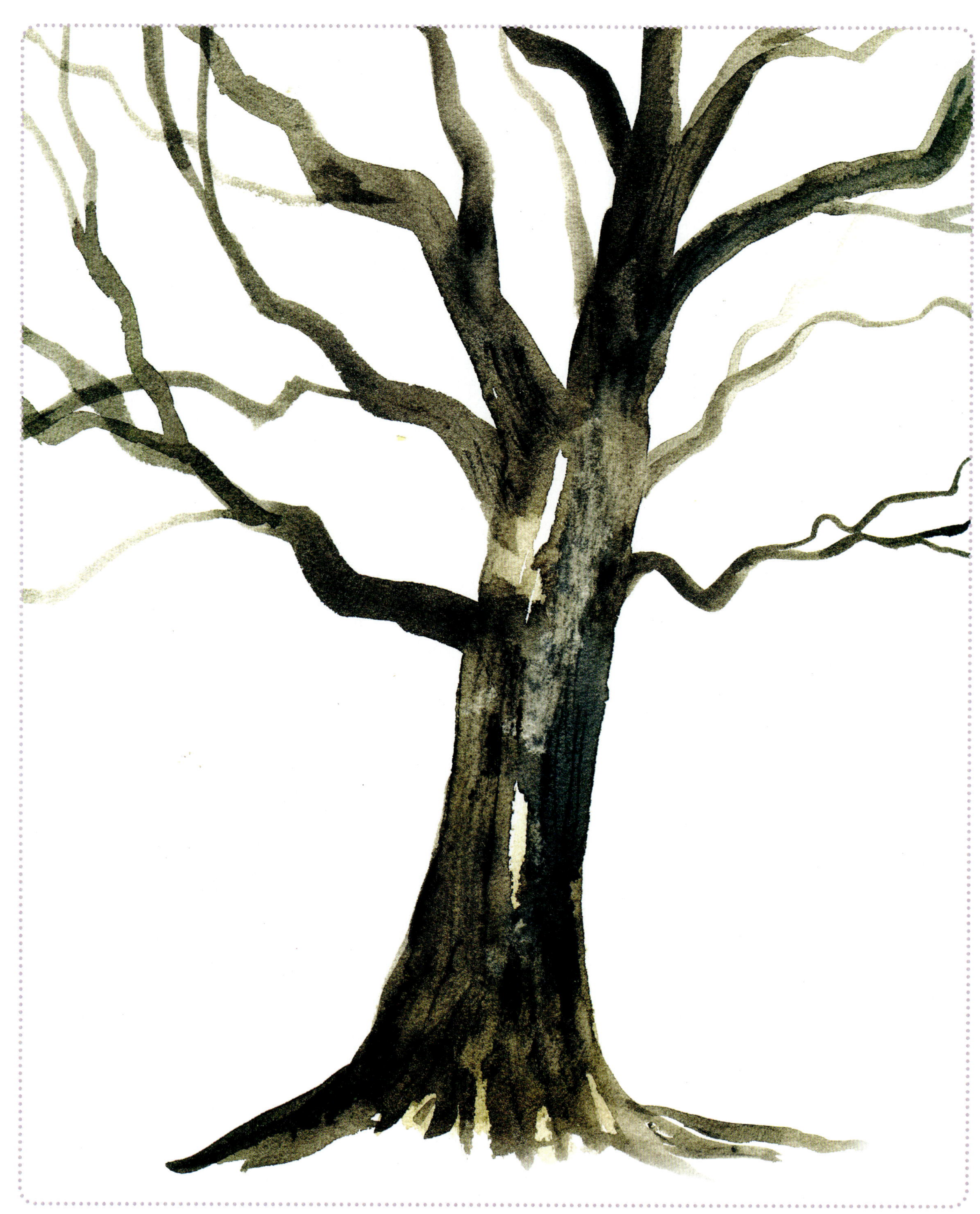

BARE WINTER TREE

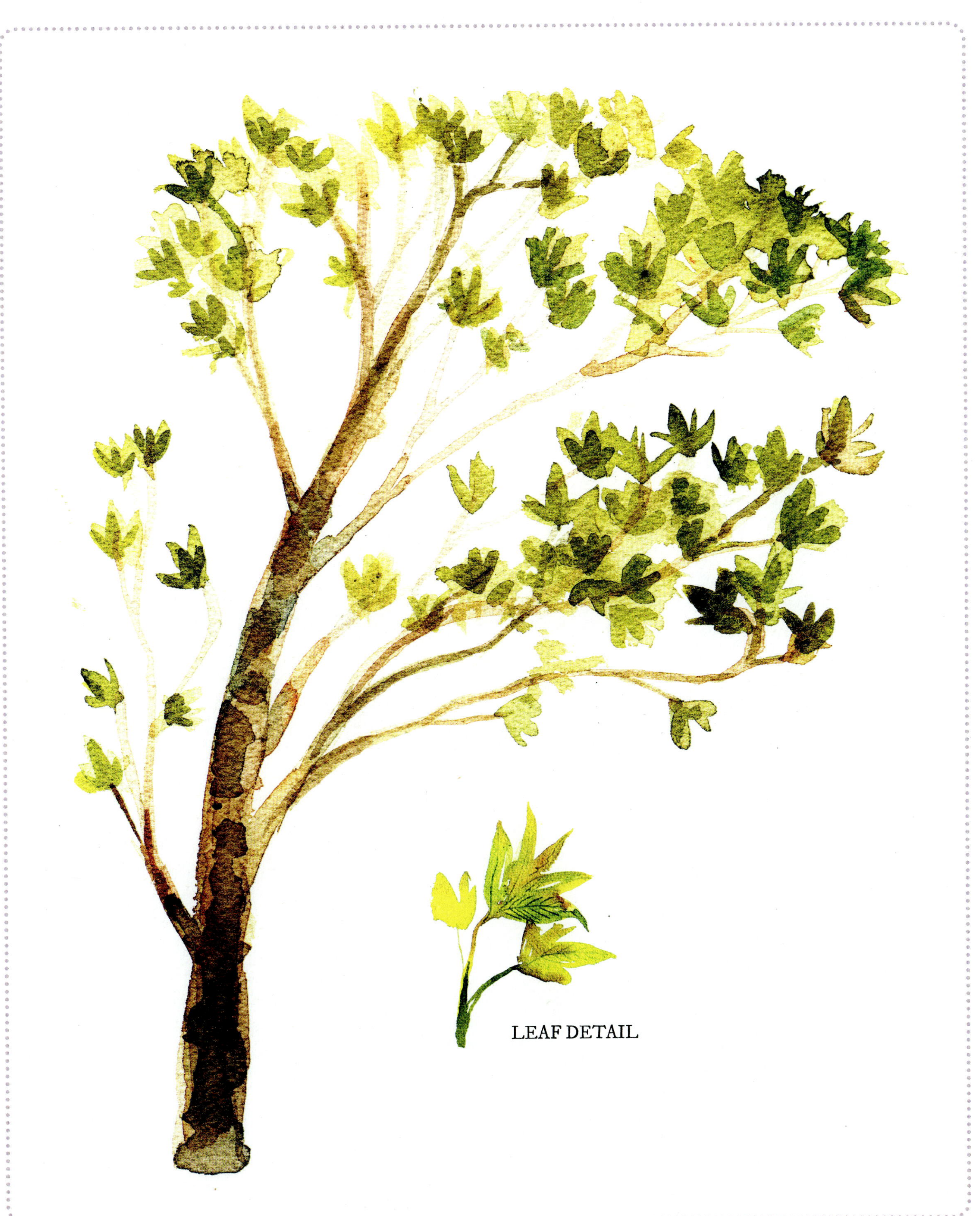

JAPANESE STEWARTIA

DRAGON TREE

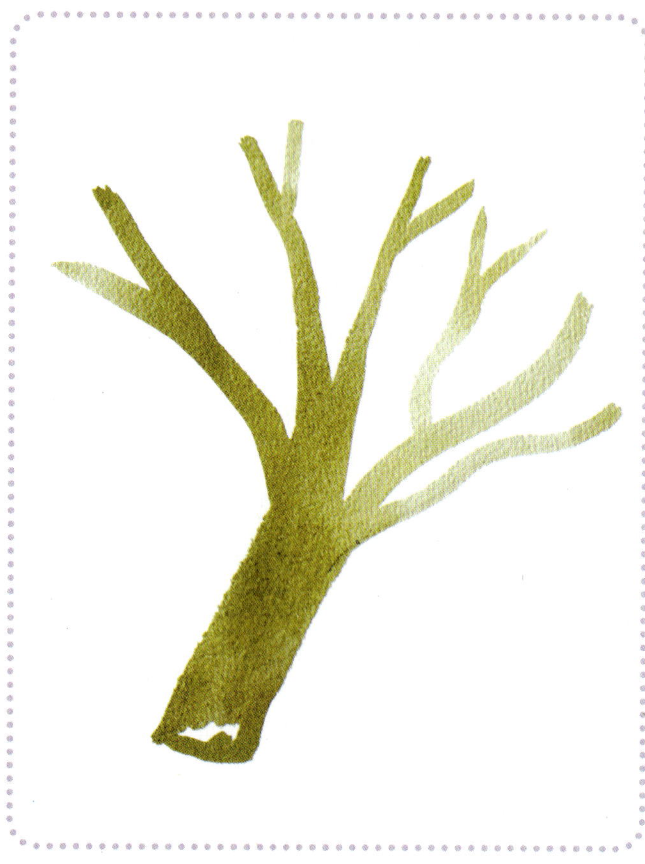

1 Using a #12 round brush and burnt sienna, make a slightly crooked trunk with thick branches that end in "V" shapes. You can add more paint in the next step; this is just to lay down some color.

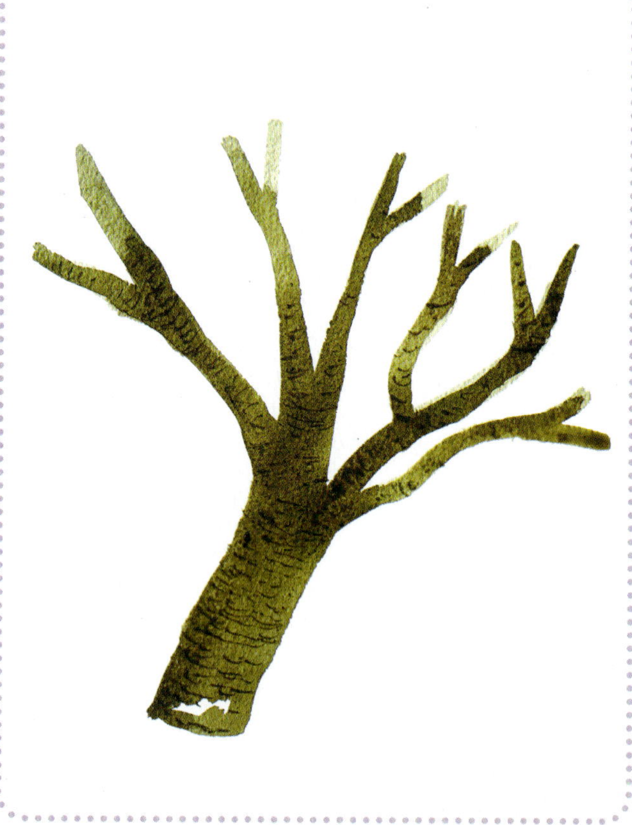

2 With sepia-colored paint, tap the brush into the wet wash, including on the outer edges of trunk, as well as the spots where two branches come together. This gives the skeleton visual interest and varying values. While the paint is still wet, use a toothpick to score tiny, curved, horizontal lines into the trunk and branches, following the natural curvature of the tree.

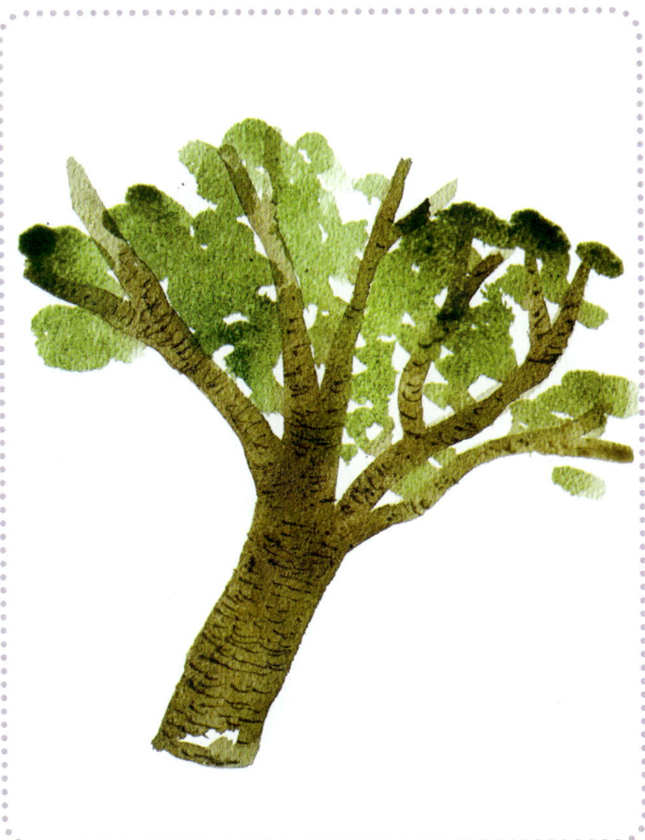

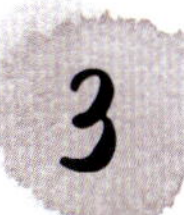

Using a large brush, such as a mop or #12 round, add bold areas of greenery in and around the branches. Leave the outer tips of the tree alone for now.

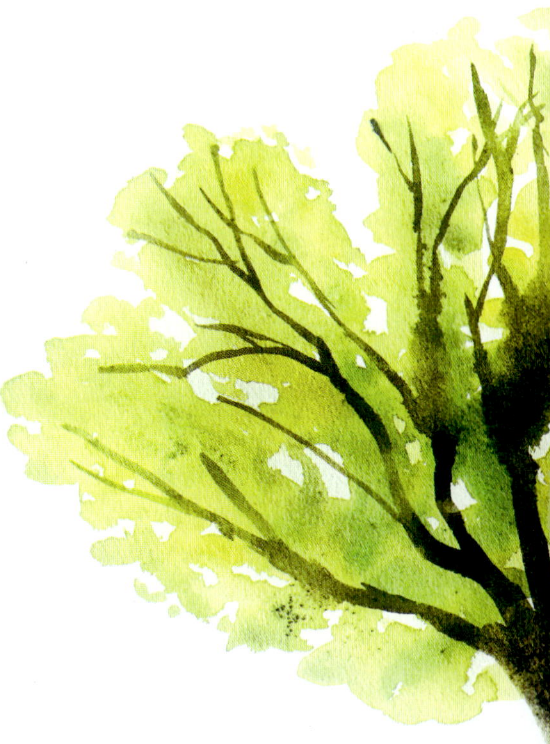

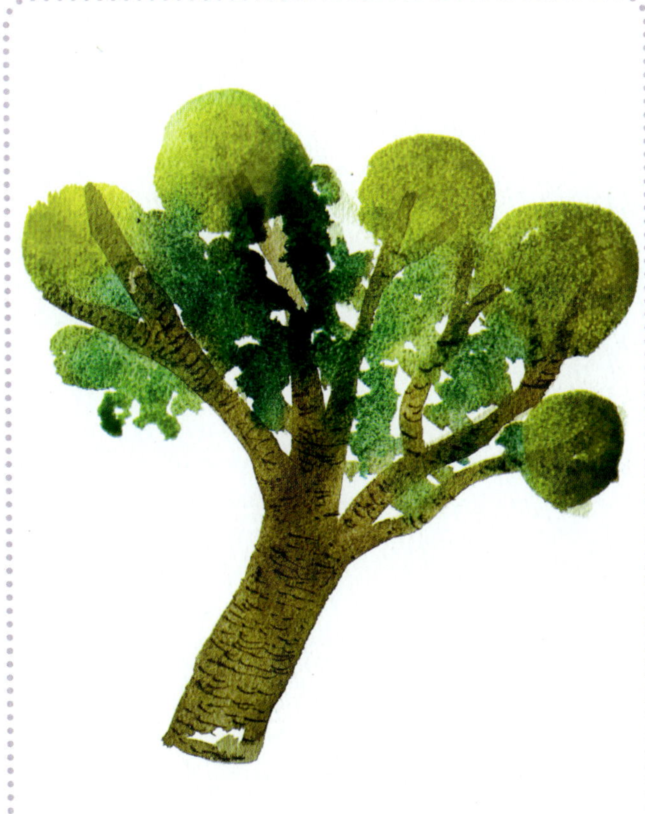

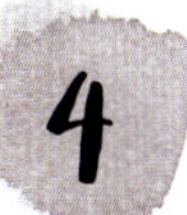

While the paint is still wet, dip a #12 round brush into green-gold paint and create large circles at the ends of the "V" shapes. Be sure to use lots of water in this step.

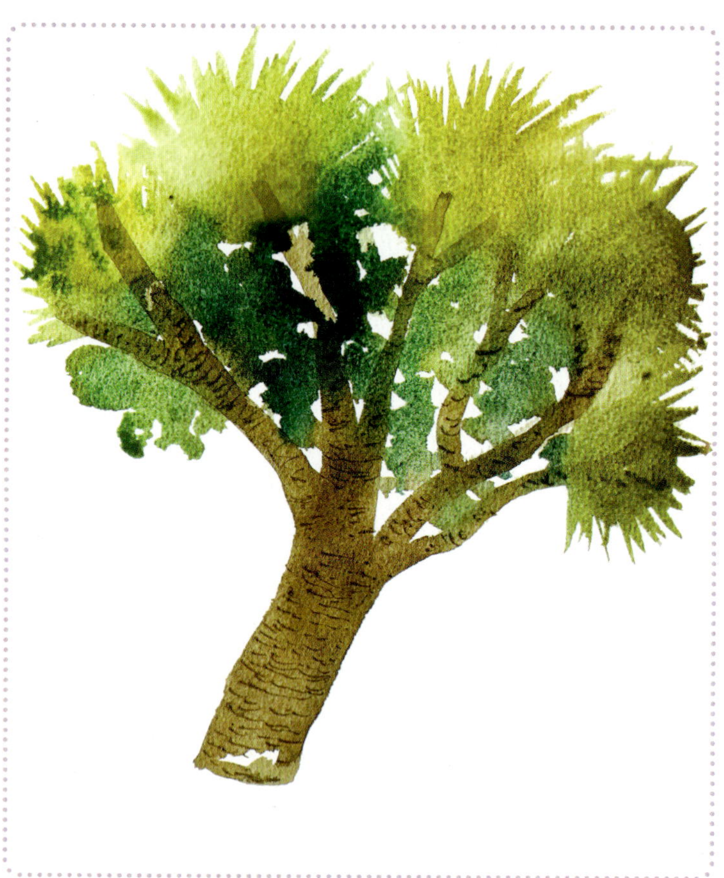

5

With a liner brush, drag the color from the center of each circle out past the edges, tapering and applying less pressure as you go. Think of these details as small, elongated triangles, with the skinniest tips outside the circle. Continue in the direction of each circle, working quickly to get through all of them. This is the fun part!

Let the paint dry completely.

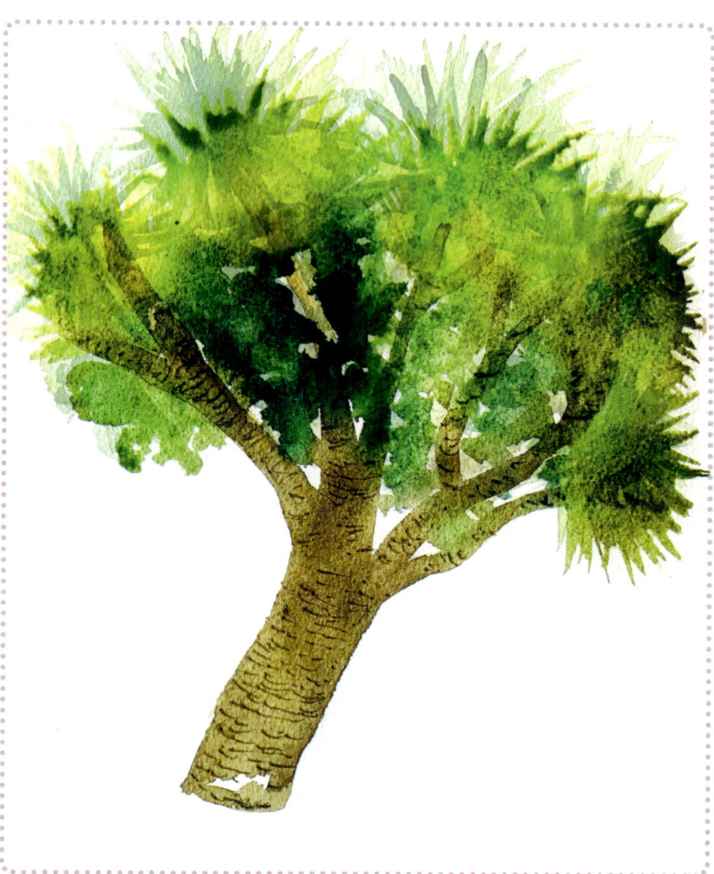

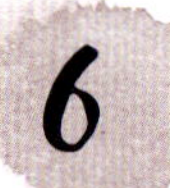

Use the liner brush again to repeat the same basic technique as in step 5, working in reverse this time. Using a darker shade of green, start at the outer edge of each circle, working inward and applying most pressure at the core of each circle. Repeat this again and again, using alternating opacities of the color by adding more water.

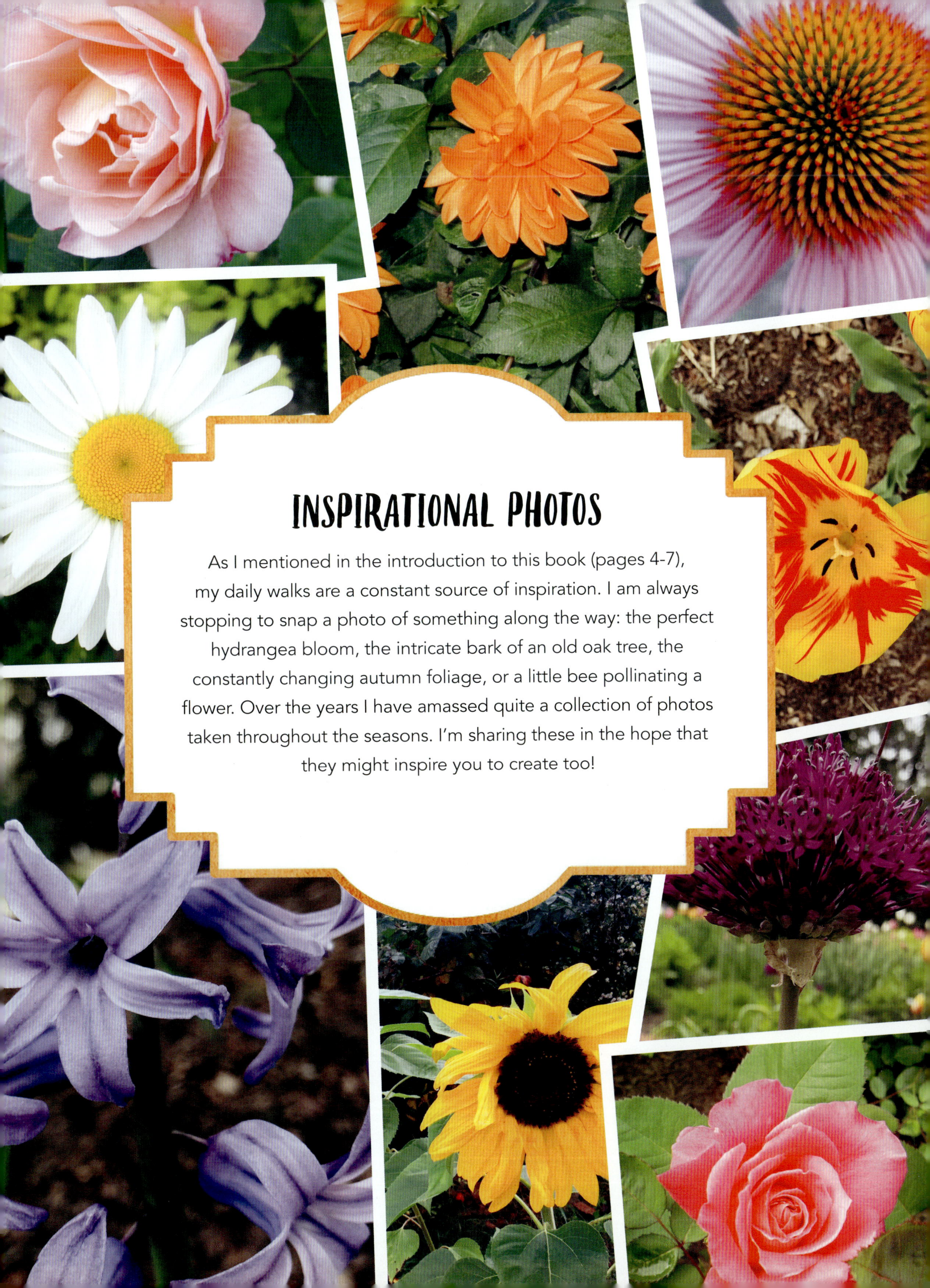

INSPIRATIONAL PHOTOS

As I mentioned in the introduction to this book (pages 4-7), my daily walks are a constant source of inspiration. I am always stopping to snap a photo of something along the way: the perfect hydrangea bloom, the intricate bark of an old oak tree, the constantly changing autumn foliage, or a little bee pollinating a flower. Over the years I have amassed quite a collection of photos taken throughout the seasons. I'm sharing these in the hope that they might inspire you to create too!

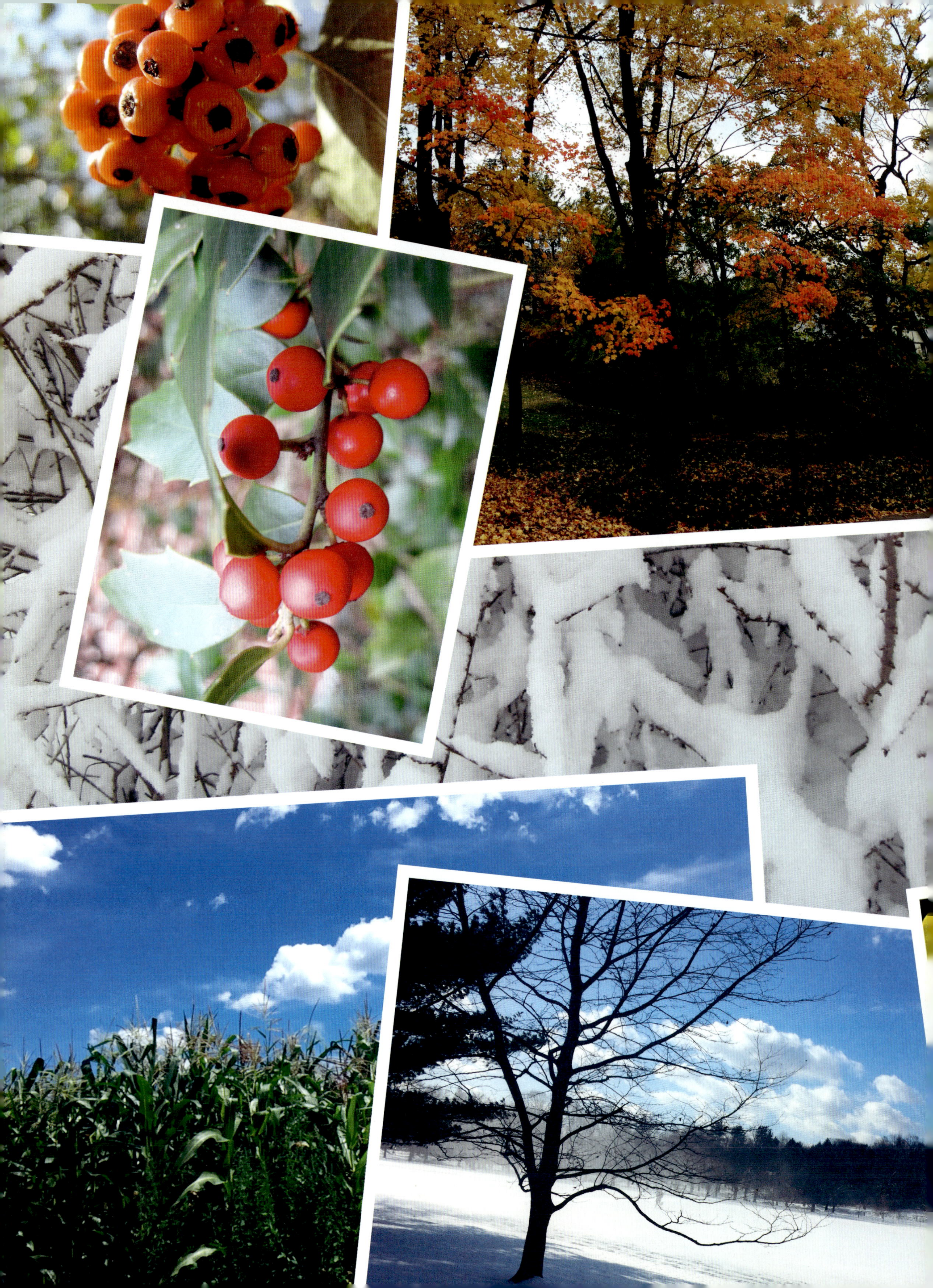

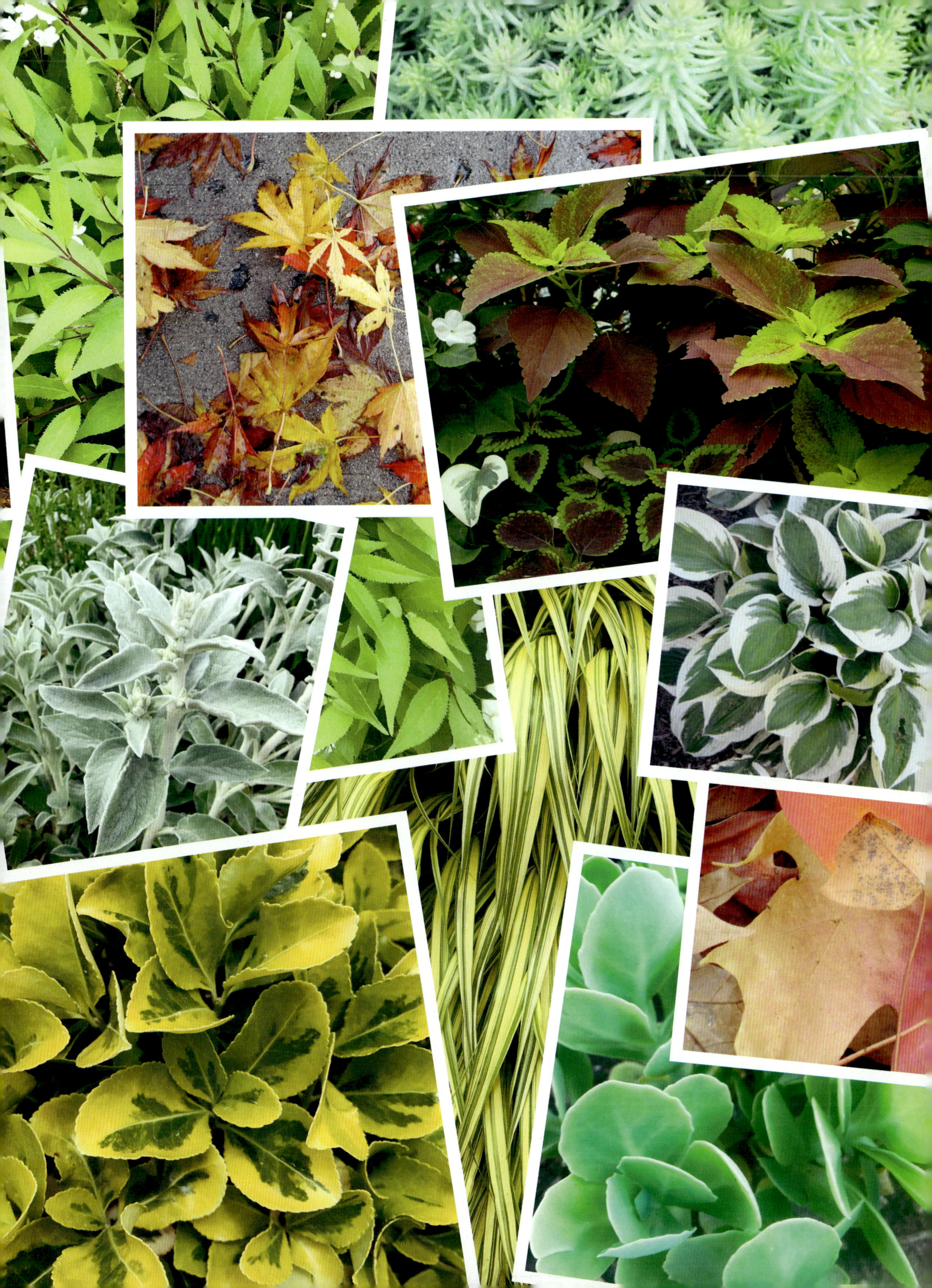

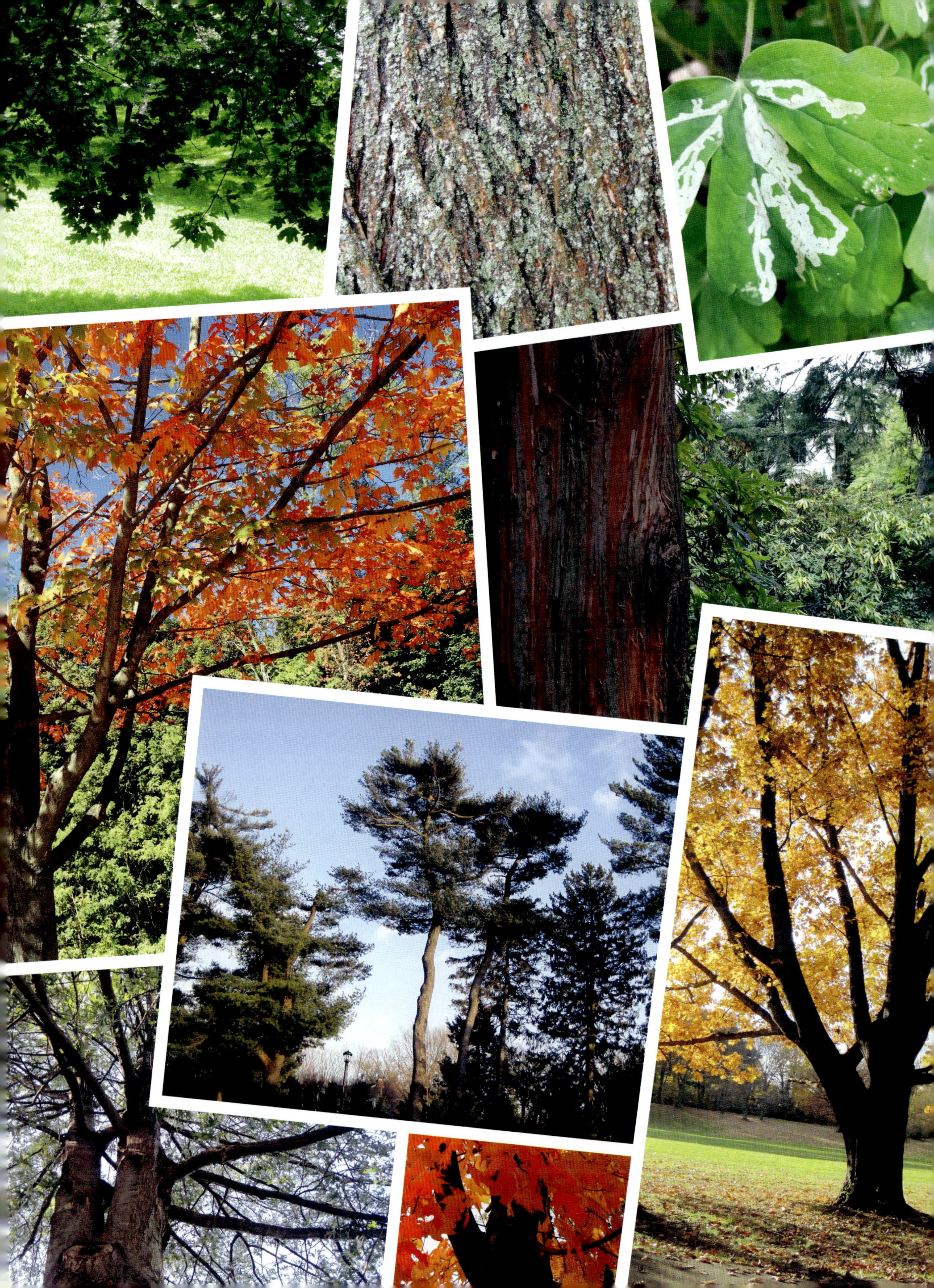

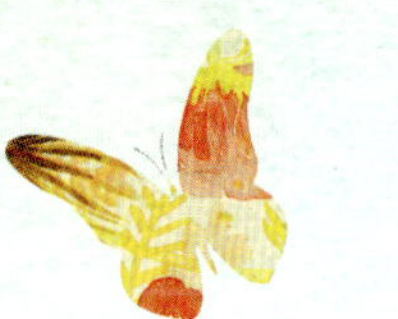

EPILOGUE

Well, you made it to the end of this book! I hope you have enjoyed it and are well on your way to painting more and more of nature's beautiful abundance. On these final pages, I've included some of my favorite bits of greenery, trees, and blooms for you to use as reference. I realize that many readers may not have the same climate or access to parks, botanical gardens, and so on, so consider these pages your own virtual field trip. As I've mentioned earlier in this book, I am constantly taking photos and chronicling what is around me. It's nice to be able to look back on these photos during the dead of winter or on those days when painting outside is not possible. I hope you will begin taking pictures of where you live as well. Our phones make it so easy now.

It is my sincere hope that each of you finds peace in the natural world. We are in such a turbulent time as I am writing this. Seeking solace in the beauty of your surroundings is a wonderful way to shake off your anxious thoughts and worries. Take a deep breath—maybe close your eyes and listen to the birds above or the scurrying of little squirrels in search of the perfect acorn. Nature has a way of calming and slowing us down. There is always something to appreciate if you make the effort to look and listen. I wish all of you the very best and hope that you continue to create.

ACKNOWLEDGEMENTS

I'd like to thank Annika and Rebecca at Quarto for believing in this book and making it possible; the Montclair Women's Club for their impeccable work at the Avis Campbell Gardens, where I've spent so many of my days "oohing and ahhing" over just about everything that blooms; the Van Vleck House & Gardens, whose formal gardens soothed my soul when I needed an oasis from urban life; and the librarians at the Montclair Public Library who are always so incredibly helpful, resourceful, and kind. I'd also like to mention my gratitude for all the beautiful parks in my area—most notably, Brookdale, Edgemont, and Verona. To Sharon—I can't express just how much I learned from you, and thank you for sparking my interest in watercolor during all those Friday afternoon classes at MAM. Thanks to my wonderful students and friends for all your support and encouragement. A special thanks to Ken for consistently challenging me to explore new paths. Our marathon late-night talks are legendary! And as always, thanks to my loving parents, who are always happy that I follow a creative life doing just what I love.

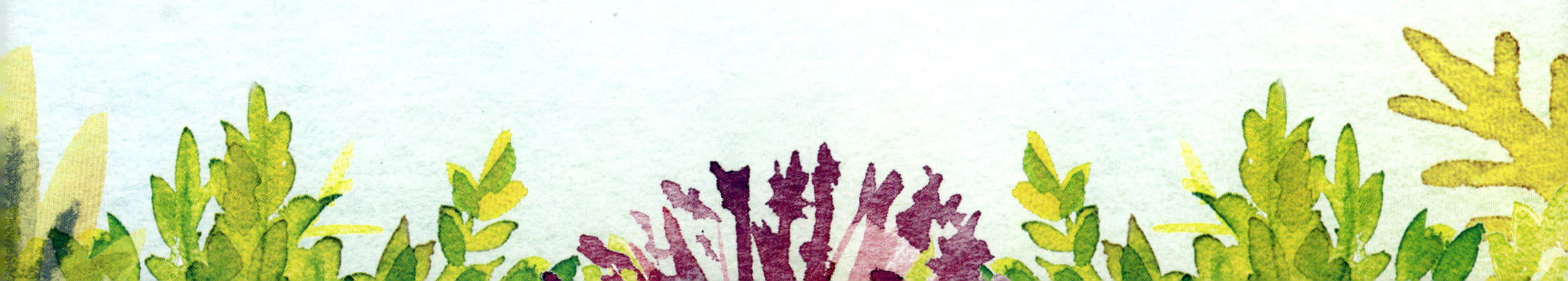

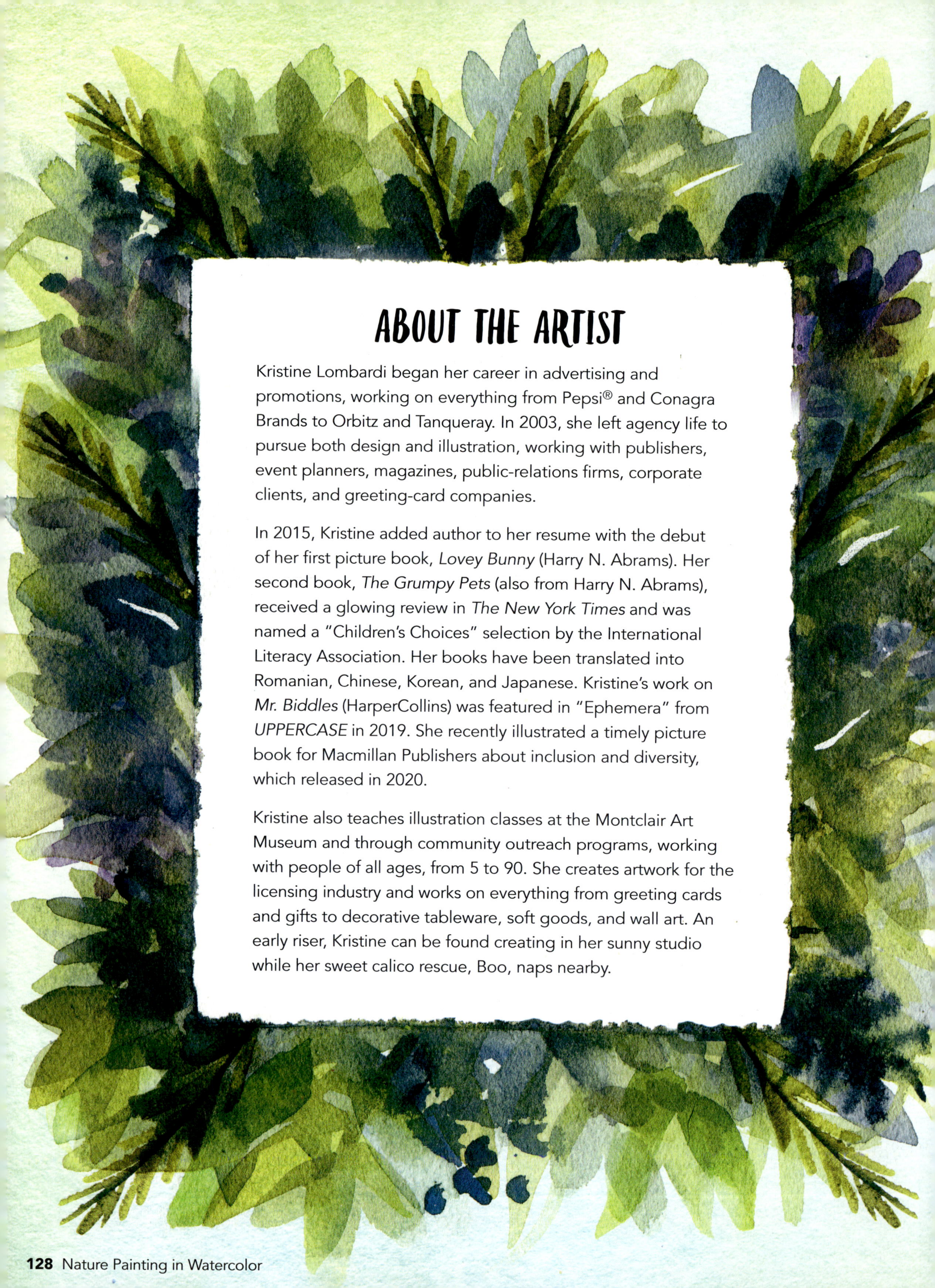

ABOUT THE ARTIST

Kristine Lombardi began her career in advertising and promotions, working on everything from Pepsi® and Conagra Brands to Orbitz and Tanqueray. In 2003, she left agency life to pursue both design and illustration, working with publishers, event planners, magazines, public-relations firms, corporate clients, and greeting-card companies.

In 2015, Kristine added author to her resume with the debut of her first picture book, *Lovey Bunny* (Harry N. Abrams). Her second book, *The Grumpy Pets* (also from Harry N. Abrams), received a glowing review in *The New York Times* and was named a "Children's Choices" selection by the International Literacy Association. Her books have been translated into Romanian, Chinese, Korean, and Japanese. Kristine's work on *Mr. Biddles* (HarperCollins) was featured in "Ephemera" from *UPPERCASE* in 2019. She recently illustrated a timely picture book for Macmillan Publishers about inclusion and diversity, which released in 2020.

Kristine also teaches illustration classes at the Montclair Art Museum and through community outreach programs, working with people of all ages, from 5 to 90. She creates artwork for the licensing industry and works on everything from greeting cards and gifts to decorative tableware, soft goods, and wall art. An early riser, Kristine can be found creating in her sunny studio while her sweet calico rescue, Boo, naps nearby.